THE SAVING REMNANT

Also by Herbert Agar

THE PRICE OF POWER
THE PRICE OF UNION
A TIME FOR GREATNESS

THE
Saving Remnant

AN ACCOUNT OF JEWISH SURVIVAL

By

Herbert Agar

NEW YORK . THE VIKING PRESS . 1960

LIBRARY OF CONGRESS CATALOG CARD NUMBER: 60-14088

PRINTED IN THE U.S.A. BY THE COLONIAL PRESS

*To the workers of the JDC
in recognition of their
selfless devotion*

MAPS

	PAGE
Jewish Pale of Settlement	23
Secret Routes of the Bricha from Europe to Israel	195
Israel	221
JDC-Assisted Emigration, 1949	225
Changes in Jewish Population, 1914-1960	255

Preface

This is not a horror story, although horrors abound, as they are likely to do in a book dealing with modern times. On the contrary, this is the story of a brave effort, financed by American Jews but helped by Jews everywhere, to save and enrich the lives of countless people. The effort goes back forty-six years and encompasses the globe. It has often failed: the Germans killed some six million Jews, while between two and three million have vanished into the mystery that is Russia. But it has often triumphed against prodigious odds.

The American Jewish Joint Distribution Committee is the hero of this long struggle to alleviate injustice. The men who founded the Committee call it "the JDC"; but abroad it is known as "the Joint." An affectionate good will, world-wide, accompanies that familiar phrase, "the Joint"—from Shanghai to Poland, Israel, France, Persia, and Morocco, not to mention the lands behind the Curtain. So for the most part I shall use the foreign rather than the home-grown name.

I can give only samples of the Joint's many-sided work—sufficient samples, I trust, to prove the scope of that work, the per-

Preface

sistence, the high intelligence, and the whirl of melodrama which has surrounded it from the start.

The early chapters contain bits of elementary Jewish history which will seem redundant to many people; but I am assuming that some readers may be as ignorant as I was when I began to study the subject.

My title is taken from the Biblical phrase, *Sheerith Hapletah.* A literal translation would be "the Surviving Remnant"; but in Europe after the Second War the words came to mean, as they had always meant to Chaim Weizmann, the Remnant which would save and accomplish the ancient dream of Israel.

The book could not have been written without help and encouragement from the staff of the Joint, at home and abroad. In America I am most indebted to Edward M. M. Warburg, Moses A. Leavitt, Morris C. Troper, Paul Baerwald, and Joseph Schwartz. Overseas I have been helped by numberless friends, among whom I give grateful thanks to Charles Jordan, Herbert Katzki, Charles Passman, and especially Samuel Haber, who conducted me through the doleful Jewish graveyard which is modern Poland.

In spite of this help, the Joint is in no way responsible for my book, which is not a definitive history, which mentions names and episodes at random because they fit the pattern I have woven, and which omits many names and deeds of equal or greater importance.

Harold Epstein has once more given me invaluable aid in finding material and in calling attention to errors, exaggerations, unproved statements, and other pitfalls for the historian. He has saved me from many mistakes, but he is not to be blamed for those in which I may have stubbornly persisted.

HERBERT AGAR

April 1960
Beechwood, Petworth, Sussex

If, before I die, there are a half-million Jews in Palestine I shall be content, because I know that this "Saving Remnant" will survive.

—CHAIM WEIZMANN, 1933

THE SAVING REMNANT

Introduction

In Warsaw, on October 16, 1940, a decree establishing the Ghetto was placarded across the city in German and in Yiddish. This had long been feared and predicted by a few; but most people are able to believe that the worst things in the world will not happen, at least to them.

Within a fortnight 150,000 Jews who lived outside the dilapidated area which was now proclaimed a ghetto had to move inside it, while 80,000 non-Jews had to leave. Then the famous Wall was built and the gates clanged shut. Imprisonment at first, and later death, was the fate of any Jew found outside the Ghetto without a permit. Next, the Jews from many small communities in Poland were pushed into this doorless and pestilent slum. More than four hundred and fifty thousand people were living in an area of a thousand acres: about fourteen people to a room.

The Ghetto had its own Jewish police: the unhappy few who

will always betray a neighbor for bread if they are hungry, or for a few weeks of disgraced life if they are afraid to die. And it had its own currency: paper marks printed in German but bearing the six-pointed star and the seven-branched candlestick. With such marks the Jews could buy and sell among one another the goods which they no longer possessed.

The Germans assumed that these people would starve with reasonable speed, or at least die of typhus. They died, of course, from both maladies, but not fast enough to suit their masters. Only 43,000 starved during the first year of the Ghetto. And the figures for typhus were also unsatisfactory: from February to June 1941, only 13,451 dead. Stubborn and clannish, as the "Aryans" had long complained, the Jews of Warsaw had a discouraging tendency to stay alive. At first they even took comfort from their predicament, feeling safe behind the Wall and planning schools and other cultural institutions.

This would not do, so on July 22, 1942, the deportations began —to Treblinka, which lies northwest of the city. Here the Germans had built a rough murder-camp, with small gas chambers using an inadequate gas and with only a single oven. Everything was primitive at Treblinka compared with the masterpiece of death-making at Auschwitz. The supply of Jews from Warsaw overburdened this frail machinery, so many thousand were beaten to death. Others were electrocuted. Children were thrown alive into bonfires.[1] And all were buried in such hurried graves that the starving Polish peasants were soon digging them up to make sure the Germans had not missed anything valuable, such as a glass eye or a metal plate in a skull which had been trepanned.

Inadequate as the tools must have seemed to the men in charge, Treblinka did its job. Within six months of the first deportations to that ghost-ridden plain, more than five-sixths of

---

[1] The word means "a fire of bones"—and thus, by the sixteenth century, "a fire of heretics."

the inhabitants of the Warsaw Ghetto had been consumed. Instead of living fourteen people to a room, the survivors found
themselves lonely.

We shall return to these lamentable days in Poland in the
proper sequence of our narrative. We mention them here only
to call attention, at the outset, to something beautiful in the spirit
of the Jews and to the omnipresence of the Joint.

In February 1942, at the height of the starvation period and
five months before the first experiments at Treblinka, a group
of doctors in the Ghetto noticed that they had a chance to make
a useful study, a study which has seldom been the subject of careful work because the raw materials have seldom been present in
a laboratory; namely, what happens, in physiological detail, to
people who have always been well fed and who suddenly starve
to death? The doctors knew that they themselves would soon be
gone. Whoever else might survive the Ghetto (and there were
still optimists who denied that they were all doomed), the doctors had no chance. The German had shown a special interest in
killing Jewish doctors, so that the "sub-race" should not be prolonged by aid from modern science.

So the doctors of the Warsaw Ghetto, aware of their fate, set
to work to examine their own diminishing bodies and the corpses
of their friends. They produced a work of abiding value, which
was published in 1946 under the auspices of the American Jewish
Joint Distribution Committee.[2] The officer of the JDC who
sponsored the publication was David Guzik, who survived the
Ghetto by a miracle and lived to preside over the revival of the
Joint amid the rubble of postwar Poland. He died in an airplane
accident in 1946.

The doctors, inevitably, were pushing themselves too fast, since
any morning they might be en route to Treblinka. They complained that the Germans were snatching their research material

[2] *Maladie de Famine: Recherches cliniques sur la famine exécutées dans
le ghetto de Varsovie en 1942.*

too quickly and hiding it in the grave. Yet the work went forward and was completed a fortnight after the chief of the team was killed. *Non omnis moriar* was the motto: always some Jews will survive somewhere, and some fragment of civilization will survive which those Jews must help to refresh. Though all friends, all relatives, all reasonable hope may perish, the Saving Remnant will not die. "The coalized kings threaten us," cried Danton in 1793; "we hurl at their feet, as gage of battle, the head of a king." The coalized tyrants of all the earth threatened these doctors, and they hurled at the tyrants' feet, as gage of their contempt, a contribution to knowledge.

Equally remarkable, as a sign of the Jewish passion for learning even in the midst of dissolution, was the OS, or *Oneg Sabbath* (the Sabbath celebrants). This was the name of a secret society created by the young historian Emmanuel Ringelblum, to preserve for posterity the record of the destruction of Polish Jewry. There was no need for Ringelblum even to be in Poland, let alone to take up this heavy task, which ended in March 1944, when he and his wife and sons were executed by the Germans. When the war began he was safely in Geneva as a delegate to a World Zionist Congress. But he felt impelled to return to his people and to his work in the office of the Joint, which had become more than ever the last hope of the helpless. As early as October 1939, when the dust from the German bombing and shelling had barely settled in Warsaw, he had begun to organize the OS. In a sense he had begun his work of rescue the day he got back from Geneva, when he saved the files of the Joint from a building which had been badly hit.

This is no desultory record which the OS compiled. It is detailed, many-sided, imaginative history, told with a calmness which is noteworthy under the circumstances. Perhaps Ringelblum hoped, at first, that his records of what the Germans were doing might reach the outside world and help to move its conscience; but by the time he knew that nothing could save the

The Saving Remnant

Jews of Eastern Europe the keeping of the records became an act of pure scholarship: posterity must have the facts.

During all this time Ringelblum was working for the Joint, at first begging money from America to bribe the Germans not to decree a ghetto; then, when that failed, setting up community kitchens, looking after homeless children and refugees, contriving shelter for the aged, and smuggling food and cash.[3] In April 1941 the Germans allowed the Joint to have an official office in the Ghetto; so for a few months contact with the neutral United States was relatively easy. But after Pearl Harbor relations with the outside world steadily faded. As the opportunities for relief diminished, the sense of duty toward the great historical record increased. The OS produced monograph after monograph, and Ringelblum summarized his own impressions in a journal, parts of which have been published as *Notes from the Warsaw Ghetto*.[4]

These *Notes* were not always favorable to his people. He writes of "the hoggishness of the rich Warsaw Jews," and his contempt for the Jewish police rivals his distaste for the Germans. This contempt is permissible to a man who left Switzerland for Warsaw knowing what that dolorous town must soon be like, and who chose a line of study which must one day cause the Germans to kill him. It is not permissible to those of us who have never been starved, or beaten, or alive with lice, and who have never had the best of German ingenuity lavished upon the degradation of our souls. "And lead us not into temptation" is the most that we can say.

In any case, no historian should be surprised to find people under deadly pressure behaving like hogs, or like cruel cowards;

---

[3] In addition to Ringelblum and David Guzik, the chief officers of the Joint in Poland when the war began were Isaac Giterman and Leo Neustadt. When the Germans killed Giterman and Neustadt, Guzik (who had been the accountant in the Warsaw office) became the nominal head of operations.

[4] New York: McGraw-Hill, 1958.

but what does attract attention is to find them behaving like scholars. Most of us, perhaps, would lose our equanimity at learning that we had been marked for slaughter. We might drop our cultural pursuits while waiting sullenly to die. But even after the deportations began, those Jews who expected daily to be chosen for Treblinka went forward with their task.

"The work was too holy for us," wrote Ringelblum; "it was too deep in our hearts; the OS was too important for the community —we could not stop." All he asked was time to finish the documentation. "With a little peace," he wrote, "we may succeed in making sure that not a single fact about Jewish life at this time and place will be kept from the world." "A little peace" was a lot to ask from Warsaw in those days. Yet in a sense it was granted; for although Ringelblum was executed three months after writing those words his precious archives had been hidden deep under the rubble. Some were recovered in 1946, and the rest in 1950.

2.

Perhaps "the work was too holy" for this young man to abandon because he knew he was witnessing the end of an era, the end of Judaism as a life-giving force in Eastern Europe. A thousand years of building and consolidating a civilization within a surrounding civilization, on the borderlands between Slavic and Central Europe, were now declared to be the hateful work of degenerate men. Unless he foresaw the rise of Israel, Ringelblum must have died believing that the last strictly Jewish center on earth had been undone and that all Jews in the future would live their lives submerged in non-Jewish communities.

Neither the Babylonians nor the Romans had believed in "the final solution." After both of the ancient dispersions many Jews had survived in exile to tell the story and re-create the tradition. This time, unless the Germans should be interrupted by Russian or Western armies, there would be no Jews at all in the homeland

The Saving Remnant

of the rich Yiddish culture, and no exiles, for they would all be dead. Nothing would remain except the precious documents of the OS.

Long after Pearl Harbor, Ringelblum was able to smuggle a letter to New York. It sounds almost cheerful, with its list of accomplishments, until the reader notices that the author has no hope for his people or for the way of life he loves and represents. He merely prays that his world will die not frightened, but fulfilling to the last its ancient purposes. "Through the active and generous aid of the American Joint Distribution Committee," he writes, "a large net of institutions for communal welfare was spread throughout Warsaw and in the country. . . . Tens of thousands of children and adults were able to survive for a longer period because of the help of these institutions and of the ramified network of house committees which cooperated with them. These organizations conducted their self-sacrificing work up to the last minute, as long as even the slightest spark of life still burned in the Jewish group. . . . The watchword of the Jewish community was 'To live with honor and die with honor.' We made every effort to carry out this watchword in the ghettos and concentration camps. An expression thereof was the wide scope of the cultural work which was undertaken notwithstanding the horrible terror, hunger, and poverty, which grew and spread until the martyred death of Polish Jewry." [5]

This letter was written a week before Ringelblum died. It shows that he was forever thinking of the larger picture of the whole Jewish community, not merely of Warsaw and its Ghetto. From all over Eastern and Central Europe, Jews were being

[5] Even after Pearl Harbor the Joint got almost a million dollars into Poland, by parachute and by couriers from neutral Switzerland. This relatively small sum produced the large results mentioned by Ringelblum because for more than twenty years, as we shall see, the Joint had worked in Poland by strengthening and subsidizing existing Jewish institutions rather than by pushing itself forward. A wise man once said, "There is no limit to what you can do if you don't care who gets the credit."

assembled at Auschwitz. Add Treblinka and Maidenek, and in Poland alone was the machinery to kill all the Jews of Eastern Europe. As a historian, Ringelblum knew this might be a mortal wound to civilization—not just the plentiful corpses, but the goodness and the richness of spirit which would perish. Had Hitler been a mere Tamerlane, an indiscriminate killer, he might have boasted, like his predecessor:

> Millions of souls sit on the banks of Styx
> Waiting the back return of Charon's boat;
> Hell and Elysium swarm with ghosts of men . . .
> To spread my fame through hell and up to Heaven,

and the world might have shuddered, without feeling unduly deprived. But Hitler was a most careful killer. He went straight for what was best, for what must die if the old Nordic barbarism was to triumph.

For many centuries the Jew in the small town of Eastern Europe had been a unique type of man: compassionate, holy, inward-looking, and essentially provincial. His culture borrowed little from the world around him, and cared little for that world. His poverty was a reproach; his living conditions were horrid; he was often attacked physically by his non-Jewish neighbors. Yet he was happy, in a strange, sad way, with his store of Biblical scholarship, his books, his family, and his deep love of God. In the shadow of the pogroms he was proud of being a Jew. His whole life was a symbolic act. Every gesture, every prayer, was so charged with meaning that his heart overflowed with the beauty and the tragedy of creation. In the muddy, narrow streets of his *shtetl* (town), or in his little wooden synagogue, which looked as if it had been designed expressly to give Christians the pleasure of burning it down, he still rejoiced that he was the Lord's chosen, although ever conscious of the burden of that election, and ever capable of making wry and bitter fun of his predicament.

The Saving Remnant

Many Jews, of course, lived in Warsaw, Vitebsk, Vilna, Lodz, and Minsk. They were not provincial or submissive, and for the most part their lives were not centered upon religion. Among them the Bundist movement grew strong after the Russian Revolution of 1905, preaching that socialism would put an end to the oppressions which had so long burdened Jew and Gentile in the empire of the Czars. Among them, also, Zionist nationalism and the Yiddish literary flowering led to a rejection of the clericalism and humility of the ancient shtetl. These movements spread from the metropolitan centers into the shtetls themselves, where youth by the time of the First World War was often in revolt. Nevertheless the time-honored piety and scholarship persisted, giving a continuity to Jewish life which neither modern politics nor modern literature could contribute.

Two streams of immigration had met to form this Eastern European Jewry. After the second destruction of the Temple (under the Emperor Titus in 70 A.D.), and the final dispersion of the Jews, many refugees went to Babylonia, where they joined a large Jewish colony descended from the captives taken into exile six centuries earlier. There they constructed the monumental Babylonian Talmud. There also they evolved the pattern of Jewish community life—of a cultural minority living apart, carefully apart—which was later to prevail in Eastern Europe.

Under the Sassanian Kings of Babylon the Jews were treated with no more than customary harshness. But, ever hopeful that someday, somewhere, they might be accorded a decent respect, they welcomed the Moslem conquerers when the Sassanid Empire fell before Islam in the second quarter of the seventh century. The new rulers proved a grave disappointment, so before long many Jews made their way to almost uninhabited parts of Europe across the Black Sea. They had founded a community on the north coast of that sea by the eighth century. Gradually they settled in what we now call the Ukraine, Bessarabia, Poland, and White Russia.

The Saving Remnant

Some centuries later, these Jews from Mesopotamia were joined by a larger group of Jews fleeing from the persecutions of Italy, France, and Germany, and from the crusaders, who were practicing how to kill "infidels" on their way to the Holy Land. (About twelve thousand Jews were killed in Germany alone by the warriors of the First Crusade.) After the Lateran Councils of 1179 and 1215 the Jews of Western Europe were segregated by law and surrounded by a rising tide of hatred. So they too learned to live a strictly Jewish life, ritual-bound and deeply religious, in the midst of an all-powerful alien community.

Ashkenaz is the Hebrew word for Germany, where Jews had arrived with the Roman armies and had settled at Trier at least as early as 290 A.D. Thus the Jews who fled eastward during the Middle Ages, toward Poland and White Russia, called themselves *Ashkenazim*. Their name was adopted by their co-religionists from Babylon—and so was their language, which was written in Hebrew and based on medieval German. They named it "Yiddish," which means "Jewish." In two thousand years of wandering, the Jews have learned all the tongues of the earth; but this, except for Hebrew, is the one which was most intimately their own.

At first the Jews were welcome in Eastern Europe, a relatively backward region which was happy to have immigrants experienced in commerce and the industrial arts. Poland, especially, offered them religious freedom and the right to run their own communities. So thankfully they settled down, with their religion, their language, their customs, and their exalted sense that all life is holy. During the subsequent eight hundred years they built an unworldly, unregarded way of life which we shall miss now that the Germans and the Russians have killed it: the life of the shtetl. These men and women, or at least the Orthodox among them, were not Lithuanians or Slovakians or Poles or White Russians who happened to have the Jewish religion. They were Jews, with their own autonomous life—nine million strong

12

in 1914. With help from the Joint, they survived the First World War and the Russian Revolution; but only those who fled before the storm survived Hitler. Unlike Tamerlane raging through the Near and Middle East and killing indiscriminately for the fun of conquest, Hitler had declared a war of total hatred against one group, one religion, one pattern of life. Some people cherish the cultures of the world as they cherish the works of art; others do not like anybody to be different.

At the other end of Europe, meanwhile, the Sephardim, or Spanish Jews, had long been cosmopolitan world-scholars, world-teachers, ambassadors between the Moorish and Christian civilizations. They had drifted westward with the expansion of Islam and were treated by their Moslem rulers with more respect and dignity than the Christian world offered. They built a sophisticated form of Judaism wherein the Bible and the Talmud mingled with the work of Plato and Aristotle.[6] These Jews, if permitted, could feel at home in any part of the world where they found educated men. They were, to some extent at least, Spaniards or Englishmen or citizens of Holland who happened to be Jewish by religion. But the Ashkenazim of Eastern Europe never aspired to be cosmopolitan (until dispersed by their enemies); they were not international scholars; they were Jews with their

[6] Their private language was Ladino, based on medieval Castilian, with many Hebrew words, and written in Hebrew characters. After the expulsion of the Jews from Spain in 1492, the Ladino-speaking center was Salonika until the Germans in 1943 killed the Jews of Salonika. The language still lingers in North Africa, and of course in Israel, which is the Society of the Ends of the Earth. For example, in 1959 the winner of the Miss Israel beauty competition at Tel Aviv—to compete for Miss Universe in America and raise money for the Bond Drive—was Rina Issacov, a soldier, a *sabra* (i.e., native-born), a student of sociology and economics, the daughter of a Sephardic father from the Aegean Sea and an Ashkenazi mother from Lithuania. A severe background from which to invade the Californian beaches, but anyone who has visited Israel will know that Miss Issacov must be beautiful. A new and lively people—exhilarating as the earliest, youngest Greeks—has been reborn into our tired world.

13

own intensely spiritual culture. They did not wish to roam the world and prove they could take root anywhere. They wanted to grow strong inwardly, in their own communities, which were small but in constant touch with one another. They thought they had found a home in Eastern Europe—an uneasy home, perhaps, subject to earthquakes in the form of repressive laws, and to volcanic eruptions in the form of pogroms. But, like the people who have lived for millennia at the foot of Vesuvius, after each eruption they crept back and rebuilt from the precious ashes.

The very names of their little towns, which to the outsider became the names of beastly slaughters, were to them holy names, lit with a divine mystery. Pogroms came and went; but these shtetls, these towns, were not to be sullied by the names of pogroms. These were the homes where for centuries Jews had learned to follow the precepts of Micah, where they had learned that the greatest sin on earth is callousness to suffering, and that charity is not an option but a command, and where they had built a life around the advice of Joshua to study the Torah "day and night."

"In this period," writes a philosopher, "our people attained the highest degree of inwardness. I feel justified in saying that it was the golden period in Jewish history, in the history of the Jewish soul." [7]

Clearly, there was no room for the people like this in the thousand-year Reich which the Germans were planning. The old stone gods from the northern forests, against whom Heine warned us long ago, had returned to grieve Europe. And they did not seem to be interested in the study of the Torah. Nevertheless, the despised scholars from the ghettos and the shtetl bred the doctors who compiled *Maladie de Famine,* and also the historians

[7] *The Earth Is the Lord's* by Abraham Joshua Heschel (New York: Abelard-Schuman, 1949). And compare Chaim Weizmann's description of Rabbi David Friedman (Reb Dovidl) of Pinsk: *Trial and Error* (New York: Harper, 1954), p. 38.

who found the records of the OS "too holy" to abandon until the day death claimed them.

Luckily for mankind, the Eastern European Jews did not all stay at home to be slaughtered. Some got out in the eighteenth century during the early days of the Enlightenment, irresistibly tempted to match their wisdom and their trained minds in competition with the gentile world. Others, to the good fortune of the United States, left under the pressure of repeated pogroms during the late nineteenth and early twentieth centuries. Some were dispersed by the First World War, and some by the renascent dream of Zionism from the time of Herzl onward. But most of them stayed where they were, because they cherished their own way of life in spite of marauding armies and marauding governments and the persistent contempt of their neighbors.

3.

So much for this gentle culture, wih its hidden light, which the Germans vowed to extinguish. What of the American Jews who have tried since 1914 to keep it alive?

When the First World War began, the American Ambassador to Turkey was Henry Morgenthau. Foreseeing that the Turks would join the war on the side of Germany, Morgenthau sent a cable to the American Jewish Committee[8] pointing out what would happen to the Jews of Palestine, of whom there were almost a hundred thousand. Many of these were old people who had gone to die in the Holy Land and who depended on remittances from abroad. Most of these remittances would stop when the Turks became enemies of the Western Allies. Others were young, romantic Zionists, who had gone to Palestine to found a new agricultural life, and who depended on selling their fruit and

[8] Founded in 1906 to seek to protect the civil and religious rights of Jews in all parts of the world.

vegetables to the West; but this commerce also must stop when the French and British fleets closed the Mediterranean.

Had the Turks been friendly, and concerned over the fate of Palestinian Jews, they might have found a way to help. But the Turks had never been notable for loving-kindness and did not want the Jews in any case. The Jews were only 14 per cent of the population of the Holy Land, and the Turks regarded them as a bother. If the exigencies of war decreed that they must starve to death, the Turks would not feel incommoded. Four centuries of Ottoman rule had turned the country into a desert, and it would not break Turkish hearts to see the desert become a Jewish cemetery.

Louis Marshall was the president of the committee that received the ambassador's cable. Fifty thousand dollars were raised in a hurry and telegraphed to Morgenthau with the help of the Standard Oil Company's office in Constantinople. Maurice Wertheim, who was visiting the ambassador, took the cash to Palestine.

This was, of course, a mere token payment; but it called attention to the need for uniting all American efforts to save the Jewish victims of the World War. The handful of Jews in the Turkish Empire, who were finally cut off from their friends when Turkey joined the war on October 14, were again only a token group of sufferers. Most of the Jews in the world lived in the lands where the vast Russian and German and Austrian armies were assailing each other. And nobody in the three countries cared very much what happened to them. They were not treated in modern German fashion; but they were underfoot, and in spite of their patriotism to their respective countries they were distrusted. And their own cultural and charitable organizations were disrupted by the war. Thus no one lifted a hand to save them, except the Jews of the West.

Early in October the Orthodox American Jews formed a Central Relief Committee to help their suffering friends abroad. Late in November this group joined with the American Jewish Relief Committee, headed by Louis Marshall, to form the Joint Distribution Committee under the chairmanship of Felix Warburg. And the following year the labor organization, the People's Relief Committee, joined in the common effort. At first each group raised its own funds, turning the proceeds over to the JDC.

Everything about this casual coming to birth of an organization destined to have world-wide influence is interesting and is a sign of the political intelligence of the founders. Anyone who has worked for a citizens' committee knows the jealousies which arise and which are directed toward all similar committees. If there are three in the same field, they often take more pleasure in frustrating one another than in forwarding their respective aims. In this case the groups that came together not only were rivals in the sense that they had all been formed to serve the same cause, and that each might therefore be expected to think that it alone could do the job properly, but they had stood for diverse interests long before the war. Louis Marshall's group represented what might be called the rich Jews of uptown New York, mostly the descendants of German mercantile families who had emigrated from 1848 onward. These were the Ashkenazim who had not fled eastward before the persecutions, but who had stayed in Germany and grown rich, and whose ancestors and relatives, in the course of the nineteenth century, had become—as they thought—an important part of the cultural life of Germany. They were still proud of their German heritage, just as their cousins and aunts and grandparents were proud of their German citizenship.

The Orthodox group, on the other hand, were for the most part less rich, less assimilated to American life, and much less German. They were then—and are today, in the Williamsburg and other districts of Brooklyn—the pure descendants of the religious aspects of the shtetl. And the labor group, the third element in this remarkable coming together, could scarcely make up its mind who were the more out of date—the rich or the religious. It was composed mostly of socialists of Eastern European descent, and with the perennial hopefulness of the Left these people thought that the World War must result in the triumph of socialism.

And there was still another group, very small but noisy, which cut across all three of the groups we have mentioned: the Zionists. They thought the war was but a prelude to the "true" solution to the Jewish problem: a world-wide movement of Jews back to Palestine. Ever since Theodor Herzl (as Paris correspondent of a Vienna newspaper) had watched with astonished eyes the Dreyfus case, he and his followers had preached that no matter how wise, how useful, or how patriotic the Jews might be, they would never be left in peace, anywhere on earth, until they had their own country.

In 1914 the Zionists were a tiny minority in American Jewry. The powerful and largely assimilated Jews believed that anti-Semitism was an aberration which could be overcome by wisdom and patriotism on their part, and by the good will of the non-Jewish American public. The socialist Jews believed that the whole Western way of life was an aberration which would be overcome by the Revolution, and that the Revolution would put down anti-Semitism forever. Even the Orthodox Jews, who were Zionists in religion, tended to look askance at Zionism as a political agitation.

In spite of all these discordances, however, the three main committees and the rebellious Zionists had one thing in common, their Jewishness, which meant an age-long heritage of helping their neighbors who were in trouble. And strange as it may seem in our disaster-ridden time, the Jews of Eastern Europe when the First World War began were in the greatest trouble they had yet known.

Hence the Joint, which was formed to give emergency relief in what was thought to be a unique crisis, which found itself in a world of perpetual and mounting crises, which has always hoped it could soon go out of business but which has lasted for forty-six years and which has spent about seven hundred million dollars contributed by American Jewry.

If one man can be given the chief credit for building a strong and lasting machine out of such unlikely material, it is Felix M. Warburg of New York. He was born in Germany, emigrated to America as a young man, married the daughter of the renowned banker Jacob Schiff, and himself entered the banking house of Kuhn, Loeb and Company. He represented on the one hand that long-dead Germany where the cultivated Jew—the connoisseur of art and the master of languages—felt thoroughly at home. And on the other hand he stood for a sense of *noblesse oblige* toward everything in America which served the cause of a high civilization, a civilization into which a cultured European, Jew or gentile, could be assimilated with ease. His Germany was a dream which has perished; his America was a dream he helped to make come alive.[9]

Among his many gifts, of kindness and tact and charm, Felix Warburg had supremely the gift of persuading people to work together. He made his neighbors ashamed to be quarrelsome, ashamed to be jealous while there was great work to be done. Perhaps no one else could have welded harmoniously the Joint Distribution Committee. He served as chairman until 1932, and then as honorary chairman until his death in 1937.

---

[9] Compare Heine, who divined all the tragedy of the German Jew:
 Ich hatte einst ein schönes Vaterland . . .
 Das küsste mich auf deutsch, und sprach auf deutsch
 (Man glaubt es kaum
 Wie gut es klang) das Wort: "Ich liebe dich!"
 Es war ein Traum.

Chapter One

The Joint describes itself as a nonpolitical agency. Yet, as it confesses, it "makes the basic assumption that Jews have a right to live in countries of their birth or in countries of their adoption; they have a right, as human beings, to reside there; they have the right to emigrate if they so wish." Since many sovereign states today make the opposite assumption—that Jews have no right to reside where they wish or to emigrate when they wish—it would seem that the Joint is engaged, willy-nilly, in a political struggle. An attempt to make the life of Jews agreeable, or even possible, is regarded by certain governments as subversion.

It was not always thus. During the First World War a humanitarian task such as that of the Joint was treated with respect and was sometimes even welcomed. For example, the first act of the new organization was to plan a shipment of food and medicine to the sufferers in Palestine. Turkey had entered the war, and her coast was blockaded by the Allies. Nevertheless, the Joint got guarantees from Britain, Turkey, and Germany for the safe-conduct of a Palestine relief ship.

The safe-conduct was a blessing; but where find the tonnage at a time when the Great Powers were busily destroying one another's ships and buying as many as they could from neutrals? The Joint approached the American Secretary of the Navy, who felt that Congressional approval might be needed to infringe a blockade. This would have meant long debate. Luckily, President Wilson intervened, promising that the next American ship leaving for the Near East would carry the supplies. So on March 15, 1915, the collier *Vulcan* sailed with nine hundred tons of food and medicine and with two agents of the Joint to supervise the distribution in Palestine. The long work had begun.

An even more startling sign of the respect for humane ideas in those vanished days is a meeting between Bernhard Kahn and General Ludendorff at Kovno in February of 1916. Kahn was born in Sweden, and in the course of a life devoted to the welfare of his fellow Jews he became a German citizen, and then a Frenchman, and then an American, ending as a vice-chairman of the Joint in New York City. He was called before Ludendorff as the representative of a German agency for helping Jews in Eastern Europe. Officers of neutral steamship lines were also summoned.

Ludendorff was worried about feeding the Jews in the immense areas of Russia which his armies had taken. And he did not want them cluttering the ground while the fighting took place. He proposed getting rid of them, or as many as possible, by sending them in a fleet of ships to America. The immigration laws of the United States still made such a project thinkable, and compared with any plans put forward in the Second War this was the acme of kindness. But Bernhard Kahn did not approve. The youngest of the Jewish representatives present, he took the floor and attacked Ludendorff's plan as an inhuman measure. These Jews had done no harm, he said. They were living in their own homes, within their own towns, where their ancestors had lived since long before the names of some of these turbulent nations had been invented. Ludendorff had not accused them of being spies or traitors. He had not accused them of anything except being alive. Were they to be dumped abroad like redundant cattle when the price of meat falls?

The general said nothing and closed the meeting; but he asked to see Kahn at 7:30 the following morning. We have no record of what was said. We know only that the Ludendorff plan was abandoned and that the German deportations from Poland and Latvia stopped.

Presumably Bernhard Kahn had not been in the war zone, or he might have thought that any fate, even being dumped abroad like cattle, was better than what awaited the Eastern European Jews at home. The world contained some fifteen million Jews in August 1914. Ten million lived along the Eastern Front: six hundred thousand in Germany, two and a half million in Austria-Hungary (including Galicia, where the Russian armies advanced and retreated six times in less than three years), and seven million in the Russian Pale of Settlement. This was two-thirds of all the Jews on earth, and, except for the group in Germany and Austria, they had long been subject to brutal laws, to pogroms, and to the hatred of their neighbors. They had also been helped, most generously, by the assimilated and well-to-do Jews of Western Europe; but such help, their only benefice, ceased when the war began.

The Pale of Settlement, which was decreed by Catherine II in 1791, looks comfortably large on the map; but in fact the Jews were increasingly compressed, by local and imperial edicts, into smaller and smaller quarters. They were excluded from the land, except in some of the Polish provinces, where they were given farms in the hope that they would therefore be grateful to Russia and oppose Polish nationalism. This merely made the Poles hate them a little more. In 1882 Russian Jews were forbidden to live

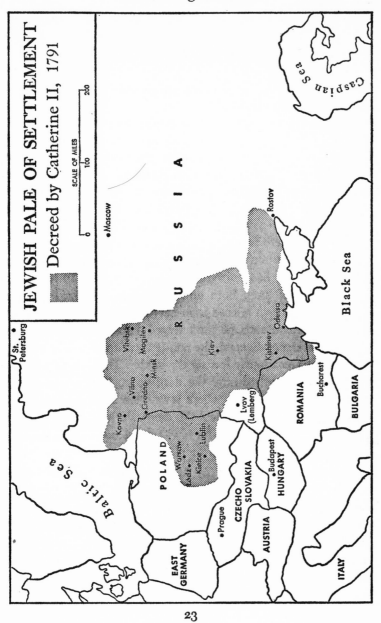

JEWISH PALE OF SETTLEMENT
Decreed by Catherine II, 1791

SCALE OF MILES
0   100   200

in villages—and the difference between a "village" and a "town" was decided by the local authorities. In 1887 they were forbidden to move residence from one "town" to another. (What happened if overnight their "town" became a "village"?) By 1914 the Jews made 4 per cent of the population of the Russian Empire; but they were—if the edicts were obeyed to the letter—allowed to live only in one two-thousandth of the area of the Empire.[1]

In the autumn of 1914, when the Russians occupied Lemberg (later Lvov) in Galicia, a journalist described the plight of the Jews. "I saw dens of naked starving people," he wrote "—people driven insane by what they had experienced." Doubtless the gentiles were none too comfortable when the Russian armies stormed in, or even when the home troops drove the Russians out. But there were two differences. First, even to the enemy the non-Jews had certain faint rights pertaining to them as human beings. The Jews had no rights, once war had let slip the beast that inhabits all men. Both armies robbed and murdered the Jews, seemingly as a release from nervous tension. The fact that hundreds of thousands of Jews served bravely in both armies made no difference. Second, the non-Jews, at the start of the war, were not so precariously low on the ladder. They had more economic fat to absorb during the dark years. Many of them, of course, lived on the land, where Jews were not permitted. And armies, though they may steal the crops, do less damage to the land than to the cities—and for obvious reasons they kill farmers more sparingly than they kill shopkeepers.

---

[1] When he was twenty-three Chaim Weizmann wanted to visit Moscow to sell the first of his many discoveries in chemistry. "I had no right to travel outside the Pale without a special permit, which I could not get," he explained in his autobiography. "In Moscow I would not be able to register in a hotel; and anyone who put me up privately without reporting me to the police would himself be liable to arrest."

The Saving Remnant

As the unhappy truth seeped through to the United States, American Jewry admitted—reluctantly but conscientiously—that here was a moral debt to be discharged. In 1916 the Joint sent two representatives into Germany, one of whom was allowed to visit the Russian lands occupied by the German and Austrian armies. The Germans had conquered more than half the Pale of Settlement—the half where lived four million out of Russia's seven million Jews. "If the war continues for a couple of years," the reporters for the Joint wrote home, "the Jewish population of Poland and Lithuania is doomed to destruction." [2]

The Germans were trying to be helpful. They encouraged the Jews within their zone of occupation to settle on the land. And they admitted a hundred thousand into Germany, where they found work in the war industries. They were not slaves, imported as in the Second War for the purpose of being consumed. They were immigrants who were treated almost humanely.

Nevertheless, as soon as Germany occupied a piece of Russia that parcel of land became subject to the allied blockade. Food, medicine, and clothes became scarce, no matter how much money might be available. And, according to the ancient habit of Eastern Europe, what was scarce for everybody must become even more scarce for the Jews.

While the United States was neutral, the Joint could get help to the German-occupied Jews via a relief committee in Berlin,

[2] Poland and Lithuania, of course, were merely geographical expressions. Poland had absorbed Lithuania in 1560, and had herself been absorbed by her three powerful neighbors by 1795—the whole of the Lithuanian part of Poland going to Russia. Until the Revolutions of 1917, the Allies had tacitly agreed that Russia after the war would take all the Poles of Europe under her wing: German Poles, Austrian and Hungarian and Baltic and Russian. This would have given her most of the Jews in the world, as well as almost all the Poles.

and to the Austrian-occupied Jews via a committee in Vienna. But the help consisted merely of money. The money could be distributed; but in the midst of war no one could promise what, if anything, the money could buy. Rumors reached New York that the funds were being mismanaged; but in fact the local committees, subsidized by the Joint, were doing a heroic job of lifesaving. All that could be hoped was that Jews might be spared starvation or massacre (luckily, anti-Semites are as easily bribed as anybody else) during the next few days, weeks, months.[3]

Then America joined the war, a few weeks after the first Russian Revolution. The Revolution cut the Joint off from Russia, while the war cut it off from Germany. The Revolution was the more formidable obstacle. Month by month Russia receded into her ancient isolation, but with the approval of the American Department of State the Joint formed a committee in neutral Holland (prominent Dutchmen plus two Americans) to take funds to the Jews in German hands. From Holland the money went to the Dutch ambassador in Berlin, and thence to the Dutch consul in Warsaw, who distributed it to the local Jewish communities.

Southward from the German zone, however, on the border of the Russian and the Austro-Hungarian Empires, the troubles of the Jews were still more acute and could scarcely be alleviated. Six times the Russians invaded Galicia and Bukovina, and six times they retreated. The repetitious horrors did not end until the October Revolution.[4] Some Jews fled into Austria; some were

[3] In January 1917, more than 70 per cent of the Jews of Warsaw were dependent on outside relief, and the death rate had doubled in the course of a year.

[4] According to the Western European calendar, to which the Soviets adhere, the second, or Bolshevik, Revolution took place on November 7, 1917. According to the Greek Orthodox calendar, which was still in use at the time, the date was October 25. Hence the sacred name, "October Revolution."

The Saving Remnant

deported into Russia; some stayed at home to be abused by friend and enemy. Each fate was as unpleasant as the others.

Descending the ladder of horrors, we find that the worst doom of all was that of the Jews in unoccupied Russia—in the part of the Pale which the Germans never reached. The Pale itself was abolished, to all practical purposes, by 1916, so that the Jews could be got out of the way. Half a million were deported by the Russian Army at the beginning of the war, under conditions which recall the German death trains of 1942 to 1945. They were not, however, sent to be murdered, but merely to starve inconspicuously in some place where they were no trouble to the soldiers.

Luckily, not all the Jews of Russia had been confined to the Pale. A few university graduates and merchants could live where they chose. And after five years of residence in the Pale, rich or professionally useful Jews could buy themselves out at an enormous price, thus gaining permission to live in Moscow or St. Petersburg—subject, of course, to all forms of supervision, interference, and blackmail by the police. These "privileged" Jews formed an efficient committee for the relief of the refugees from the Pale and of their other war sufferers, providing food and primitive housing, and even daring to put pressure on the Russian government to treat the Jews less like cattle. They established feeding stations along the chief deportation routes, and medical squads to accompany the trains. In some cities they provided textile plants so that the refugees could help to clothe themselves.

Here was an ideal chance for the Joint. From 1914 until the first Revolution, the machinery for relief existed. Men and women who knew the needs, the language, the local problem were eager to help. Money was the chief need, and money was the one commodity the Joint could supply to faraway Russia in the midst of a life-and-death war. Also, the Joint could use the Russian relief organization to get money to the refugees from Galicia and Bukovina, who were treated as enemy subjects by the Russian government. No Russians were allowed to supply them with money; but American money might be accepted.[5]

Then came the two Revolutions. After a period of high hope these proved to be the greatest calamities ever to have befallen the Jews of Eastern Europe. An inevitable result of the October Revolution was the disappearance of the Russian Jewish Committee for Relief. Private charities are not encouraged in a Communist state. Yet the provisional government in the spring of 1917 had declared the equality of all creeds and peoples and had abolished anti-Jewish restrictions. This was not as helpful as it sounded. And the second Revolution had ruined the Jews who held property, so they could no longer help their unfortunate neighbors. And their neighbors at that moment were highly unfortunate, because the Revolution was unfriendly to peddlers, moneylenders, small shopkeepers, and most one-man enterprises. Yet these were almost the only careers which Czarist Russia had permitted the Jews within the Pale. Meanwhile the whole Russian economy, shattered by war and turned inside out by revolutions, was coming to a halt. And famine was gathering.

The American leaders of the Joint knew painfully well that if a nation is in bad trouble the Jews get most of the blame and as much of the trouble as can be shuffled off upon them. In this case the outside world said the Jews had fomented the Revolution, while the revolutionists (including the Jewish ones) said the Jews were either implacable capitalists or religious maniacs —both distasteful to a Bolshevik. Desperately the Joint struggled to get money to these helpless and reviled people. The Department of State in Washington was sympathetic but could suggest no means for distributing aid through the dark, enormous hinterland of Russia. Suddenly the Zionist organization in Petrograd

[5] The official Russian view seemed to be that Jews who fought for the enemy were the most dangerous enemy of all, whereas Jews who fought on your own side were presumably traitors. And as for civilian Jews who didn't fight at all . . .

sent word that it had some funds which it could not use until "normal" times returned. It would try to put the money where it was most needed, if the Joint would promise to repay later. Thus a trickle of money (less than half a million dollars) was distributed. The recipients knew, at least, that although Chaos and old Night had returned to rule their world they had not been forgotten.

In 1919 the curtain fell. The Jews of Russia—unoccupied Russia—could not be reached by anyone until 1921. They must have thought it the darkest hour in history, but their children now know better.

3.

During the First World War the JDC received $16,583,996 from American Jewry. This was small change in the light of subsequent history; for example, in the twelve months of 1948 the Joint received just under $72,000,000. But it did not feel like small change to those who first took up this burden and who gave their money in addition to paying wartime taxes and contributing to war-bond "drives" at home. Aside from Felix Warburg himself, two men stand out especially during those early years when the American communities were awakening to the fact that the responsibility for most of the Jews in the world had fallen upon their shoulders: one for his power to exhort, the other for his willingness to give.

The first was Rabbi Judah Magnes, who settled in Palestine after the war and became the first president of the Hebrew University at Jerusalem. In 1915 he spoke at a concert hall in New York, telling the grim facts and asking for the most possible help. In cash and in pledges he was given a million dollars. The next year he went to Europe to see how the money was being used. He could visit only the German-occupied parts of the ancient Pale. Horrified at the suffering, he returned to tell his friends that they must raise at least ten million dollars in 1917. At a mass meeting he told what he had seen abroad, and for the second time his eloquence produced a million in a single evening.[6]

The second hero of the early money-raising days was Julius Rosenwald of Chicago, one of the most enthusiastic spenders on charity in modern times; he gave away about seventy million dollars during his life and left another thirty millions to be dispensed within twenty-five years of his death.

Rosenwald was born across the street from Abraham Lincoln's house in Springfield, Illinois, three years before Lincoln was murdered. This may have influenced him in his huge gifts to the cause of Negro education. He was a religious Jew; his generosity and his social vision stemmed from the synagogue. He was unsympathetic toward Zionism, believing that Judaism is a religion and not a nationality; yet he gave lavishly to Palestine relief and to the Hebrew University. During the money-raising campaign which followed Judah Magnes's trip to Europe in 1916, he contributed $1,000,000. And a few years later, as we shall see, he gave $5,000,000 to help another project of the Joint.[7]

4.

A week after the armistice of November 1918, the Jews of Lemberg were overwhelmed by a pogrom. This was the capital of Galicia, where all had suffered grievously for four years. Yet

[6] When America entered the war, Magnes confessed himself a pacifist, thus losing much of his influence. The same distaste for killing his neighbors led him in postwar days to oppose political Zionism in Palestine, on the ground that it must lead to an Arab-Jewish war. He wanted an Arab-Jewish commonwealth, genuinely bi-national, even to the detriment of Jewish interests. *"Berit shalom"* was his plea—"peace covenant." He was born into an unhappy time for the preaching of this gospel.

[7] He was a chief architect of the vast prosperity of Sears, Roebuck and Company; so his purse kept refilling, no matter how diligently he emptied it.

as soon as the shooting stopped, the Jewish quarter was almost completely destroyed by its surviving neighbors. In 1919 came the pogroms of Simon Petlyura, the Ukrainian nationalist, and of the White armies. Meanwhile the Lithuanians were not idle: they destroyed most of the pitiful few at Vilna who had survived the armies of occupation.

At the same time authentic news of the famine spreading throughout the Pale began to reach New York. This was not hunger which threatened; it was starvation. "Hunger can stand up," wrote Boris Bogen, who headed the first work of the Joint in Poland; "but starvation lies prone or sits hopeless against walls."

Clearly the work of the Joint had scarcely begun. Peace, or what passed for peace in Eastern Europe, bid fair to be more terrible than war. So Felix Warburg went to Washington to ask permission for the Joint to send men as well as money to succor the ruined Jews of Poland; but in Washington he ran into trouble. The American Relief Administration, under Herbert Hoover, had been charged with bringing food and clothing to the destitute of Europe, and the government saw no reason for private agencies to roam the unhappy and disease-ridden lands where the German and Russian armies had fought to the death—and least of all to enter Poland, which was getting ready for a new war all its own. Furthermore, Mr. Hoover was unenthusiastic about the Joint. He had asked it for $1,000,000 for nonsectarian distribution in Poland, and the Joint had said, "No, our money was given by Jews for the aid of Jews, and not to feed our enemies who began slaughtering our kin the moment the German armies withdrew."

This was the type of misunderstanding which Felix Warburg was adept at assuaging. "In Warburg," wrote Boris Bogen, "was the spiritual elevation becoming to the Jew. The small Jewish politics of the period raged about him, but he walked with his head high above it. For angry and envious men he set an example of sweetness." The seemingly implacable hatreds which competing groups of philanthropists feel for one another never impressed Felix Warburg, and never depressed him either. So before long the Joint gave Herbert Hoover's Relief Administration $3,300,000—half on its own and the rest as an advance in the name of a Polish Relief Committee. And the Joint received permission to send Bogen into Poland to survey the problems and to prepare the way for a first unit of workers.

The unit sailed in January 1920: specialists in medicine, public health, child care, religion. The inclusion of an Orthodox rabbi stresses an interesting point; namely, that the religious Jews of Eastern Europe were scarcely concerned with being kept alive unless their schools for the study of the Torah and the Talmud were kept alive also. Those schools are called the Yeshivoth (singular, Yeshiva). In Poland, Lithuania, and Hungary they were a center not only of Jewish learning but of Jewish life. To the devout, nothing was more desirable than to spend all one's days at a Yeshiva. If a man was acknowledged as a true scholar he brought the highest credit to his family and more than compensated for the trouble of paying his keep. The non-devout regarded life in a Yeshiva as parasitical and anti-social.

So here was another problem which faced the Joint and called forth the tact of its chairman. A very large number of the rich American Jews who gave money were not Orthodox, and the same was true of most of the members of the labor group which subsidized the Joint. The latter, in fact, were largely socialists who regarded a life spent poring over prayer books as an insult to the cause. Nevertheless, their sense of solidarity was such (the mysterious sense of Jewishness which is easier to observe than to define) that in the end all the contributing groups agreed that the Yeshivoth must receive some of their money. This was just as well, for in many instances it was found that money sent into wholly destitute regions for food and clothing was being used to repair or maintain a Yeshiva. ·

The Saving Remnant

Chaim Weizmann gives an example of the difficulties of assuaging such austere scholars and of persuading them to take a reasonable interest in staying alive. We have seen that before the beginning of the First War a group of Jews, mostly elderly, had settled in Palestine to spend their remaining years in prayer and study. Wholly unproductive, they lived on contributions from the Orthodox in other countries. "They lived in a strange world of their own," wrote Weizmann, "fantastically remote from present-day realities, and the majority of them were hardly conscious of the crisis through which the world was passing. . . . All they knew definitely about the war was that it had dried up the source of most of their income, since no money could now reach them from their European benefactors." Weizmann came upon this "strange world" early in 1918, when the British government sent a Zionist commission to Palestine to prepare plans for putting the Balfour Declaration into action. The Joint, knowing the plight of the aged in that distressful land, had given the commission money to distribute among Jews who were cut off from their previous pensions.

The commission discovered that most of the young men in Palestine had joined the Jewish battalions and were fighting, leaving the agricultural settlements understaffed. But the future of the Balfour Declaration depended on these settlements. They were the Palestine from which the national home was to grow. So the commission tried to persuade the recipients of the Joint's charity—for the good of the community as well as for the sake of their own food—to stop reading from time to time and do a little work on the land. The response was unfriendly. The purpose of life, according to those venerable men, was prayer and study, not "worldly" occupations such as digging holes in the ground and fretting about water. Also, they were not interested in wages. "One of them," wrote Chaim Weizmann, "very seriously explained to me that physical exertion entailed the consumption of more food, as well as greater wear and tear of clothes, so that he preferred less money and a sedentary and pious life."

5.

As early as the Babylonian exile, which ended about 538 B.C., the Jews had begun to develop self-governing communities within the framework of whatever state or empire they inhabited. Centuries later, in the Hellenistic world, these communities became a chief feature of Jewish life and were granted special rights by kings and emperors. In 201 B.C. Antiochus III proclaimed that they might "use their ancestral laws," and during the following century the Jews of Alexandria were allowed to elect a council of their own, to conduct their affairs according to the Jewish law, to build synagogues, and to maintain their own records office. Five hundred years later, in the West, amid the chaos of the dissolution of the Roman Empire, these communities became the main strength of Jewry. And later still they were welcomed by the newly emerging rulers of medieval Europe as a source of royal revenue: a united and orderly community offered the easiest possible plunder. After the so-called emancipation, following the French Revolution, these communities tended to grow weaker in the West, where Jews were increasingly assimilated, but they remained very strong in Eastern Europe. So here were the organizations (or in most cases, by 1920, the shattered remains of the organizations) which the Joint could attempt to succor.

To suggest the extent of the ruin: In many parts of Lithuania, whence the Russians had deported the Jews in 1915-1916, whole streets of Jewish houses had disappeared totally, leaving no trace behind. The invading Germans had begun by taking the contents for the use of their armies; then the neighbors, as their own needs grew, dismantled the houses bit by bit—for windows, for firewood, for chimney-bricks, or just for malice. Jews who survived the war and returned "home" sometimes found that the land on which their houses once stood had been plowed and transformed into somebody's vegetable patch.

Such was the state of general breakdown—always augmented by famine—under which Poland chose to launch a new war. In May 1920, just as the First Unit of the Joint was settling down to work, the Poles invaded the Ukraine. The Russians beat them and pushed them back to the gates of Warsaw, meanwhile beginning to attack from the northeast across the ruined land from which the Germans had recently been removed. Finally, with the help of French General Maxime Weygand's advice, the Russians were outflanked and driven back once more into the old battle-fields. In March 1921 an uneasy peace was agreed.

The whole of this useless war—in Poland, the Ukraine, and the edges of Lithuania—was fought through, and over, the centers of Jewish population. Hated ferociously by both sides, the Orthodox life of the shtetl might have been exterminated on the spot, without having to wait for Hitler, had it not been for the agents of the Joint. They had been allowed to wear American uniforms, so the Poles felt it was inexpedient to kill them, or even to kill their protégés too overtly. They followed the Polish armies into the Ukraine, bringing medicine and food and cash for bribery. When the tide of war turned they found themselves in the fighting zones, taking part in evacuations, finding transport for the wounded and the terrified, and above all using the prestige of their uniforms to diminish pillaging and to ward off pogroms. The Polish Army in retreat was not a kindly affair.

When the Russians advanced on Warsaw in the summer of 1920 the Joint found itself with about fifteen thousand Jewish wards whom it had housed, fed, clothed, and doctored, and most of whom had been promised visas for the United States. Yet the paperwork was not completed and might never be completed if the city fell to the Bolsheviks. In the midst of a panicky evacuation the Joint "liberated" sufficient freight trains to move fifteen thousand Jews to Danzig. Meanwhile the American consul at Warsaw had escaped to Poznań, where he had nothing to do. So the Joint brought him and his staff to Danzig and urged them to start issuing visas. A thousand Jewish emigrants were cleared in a single day.

Only two of the Joint's brave men were killed: Rabbi Bernard Cantor and the scholarly Israel Friedlander. Cantor was a member of the First Unit; Friedlander had been sent to discover, if possible, what was happening in the Ukraine, and what, if anything, the Joint could do in that lost land into which no American Jew had been permitted since 1914. The Russians would not let him near the Ukraine, so Friedlander went to Warsaw for permission to follow the Polish armies during their first gay advance. This was granted by the confident high command; thus Friedlander and Cantor met by accident in July 1920, deep in the Ukraine. By this time the good days were over for the Poles and the great retreat had begun. The Jews, as usual, were blamed by both sides for every misfortune and were robbed and killed by either army unless a man in an American uniform was in sight. Cantor and Friedlander, smelling the approaching pogroms on every wind, tried to reach Pilsudski's headquarters to ask for the appropriate discipline as the troops fell back. They were caught by Russian raiders between the two armies. They were robbed and shot and buried where they fell. Far more surprising than the vicious crime is the fact that the rest of the First Unit survived.

The serious fighting was over in this Russo-Polish imbecility by the autumn of 1920. Less than a year later the work of the First Unit was finished and the Joint was preparing to turn from direct relief to reconstruction, and then to retirement[8] after re-

---

[8] This was the first of many such innocent illusions on the part of the Joint, which has always thought, like Sisyphus, that it was about to get the rock to the top of the hill. But the rock always rolled down again.

construction. The speed with which the first part of the work was done, in spite of the two wars and the wide desolation, was due partly to the ancient tradition of self-governing communities which we have mentioned, and partly to a number of modern international organizations for Jewish self-help. The machinery was all there; the Joint had only to produce fertilizing ideas and fertilizing money—and to refrain from being "bossy" or otherwise irritating, because Jews are stubborn people who would often rather starve than be ordered about.

Among these organizations, with which the Joint has collaborated in all corners of the world during its forty-six years of life, the most important for the early days in Eastern Europe were the ORT (Russian initials for "Sociey for the Encouragement of Handicraft"), which was founded by Baron Horace de Günzburg in 1880, and the OSE (Russian initials for "Jewish Health Society"), which was founded in 1912. Both of these have become world-wide unions since the First War, and there is scarcely a country on earth where (with subsidies from the Joint) they have not taught skilled trades and agriculture on the one hand, and modern medicine on the other, to Jewish settlers or to Jewish refugees waiting forlornly for a place to settle.

The members of the First Unit were inheritors of the immemorial tradition of Jewish communities, and of course they knew all about the ORT and the OSE.[9] And of course they had sense enough not to annoy the recipients of their aid—unlike governments, which can scarcely save a man from drowning without making him wonder whether he wouldn't rather be thrown back. Thus the miracle of 1920-1921: the end of relief and the beginning of the doomed hope that the Joint could soon go out of business.

The first step, during that *annus mirabilis,* was to set up eleven regional offices to coordinate the work of a thousand Jewish

[9] Confusingly enough, this was later to be called the TOZ in Poland—a difference of initials, like NATO vs. OTAN.

communities. Thereafter, with the help of these communities, the unit attempted five main tasks:

1. Child care, which meant everything from milk stations to rebuilding ruined schools, from creating summer camps in the country to supplying clothes for the schools, and fuel. Four hundred thousand children were soon being helped, including seventy-five thousand orphans.

2. Medical aid. This meant rebuilding and re-equipping hospitals and old-age homes which had been carefully destroyed or ransacked by successive waves of anti-Jewish armies. It also meant the provision of forty trucks to follow the Polish armies forward and backward and forward again, carrying milk, hardtack, and medicine for the sad civilians. In each truck were a nurse and a doctor.

3. The creation of a system of credit banks (known as Loan Kassas), so that small merchants might start again in business and artisans might acquire tools and raw materials. The latter were frequently unavailable, so the Joint had to supply these from abroad. (When possible, the local communities raised at least a small part of the money for these Loan Kassas.)

4. The rebuilding and support of Yeshivoth.

5. The care of refugees returning homeless and penniless from deportation to Russia, or from any dark corner where they had found a place to hide. This involved mess halls, tea stations, fuel, cash, and medicines. Also matzoh, the unleavened bread for Passover—because, as we have already seen, many Jews are not necessarily keen on being kept alive if they cannot live according to their ancient ritual.

In those days—which were already grim but not yet totally cruel in our modern sense—such luckless refugees could still, if aided, find haven in America. The Joint became the patron of many who took this long road of escape. The Joint also handled remittances from American relatives to destitute Polish Jews,[10] and set up a bureau to help such Jews get in touch with their more fortunate transatlantic kin. As an adjunct to this service, the Joint imported food in bulk and then sold food drafts to American Jews, who could send them to their Polish friends or relatives for presentation at JDC warehouses. This plan, invented by Boris Bogen, was copied by Herbert Hoover's American Relief Administration in Russia during the great famine.

We have mentioned that the Joint raised $16,583,996 between 1914 and 1918. From 1919 to 1921 it raised $33,422,351. Small change again, in the light of subsequent history; but the Joint still believed that it would soon be out of business. A few more wise, imaginative, but not too extravagant efforts might be needed; then the Jews of Central and Eastern Europe would be rehabilitated and could at last begin to live in their ancient homelands with the security which (for almost a century) had been taken for granted by French, Dutch, British, and American Jews.

Es war ein Traum. It was more: it was a daydream, which may be more dangerous than a dream which takes place during sleep. No one outside of Germany, in 1921, could foresee the rise of Hitler; but almost anyone might have foreseen, as some of the Zionists had done, that the vast civil war in Europe, plus the Russian Revolution, plus the American immigration act which was clearly about to be passed, would prove disastrous for the concentrated Jewry of the old Pale of Settlement.

Neither social nor economic conditions were favorable to the survival of a Polish Jewry. The Jews were hated, and the Polish economy was squeezed between revolutionary Russia and resentful Germany. The same warnings could be seen in the Balkans, in Hungary, even in Austria, where hatreds were rising

[10] Between January and September 1920, $5,225,000 was transferred to Poland under this scheme, a relaxation of the financial burden of the Joint.

because there had been too many pitiful refugees from the battlefields of Galicia.

In all these places—and also in North Africa and in other broken bits of the Ottoman Empire—the Joint was using its thinly stretched funds to rehabilitate Jewish life in countries where the Jews would no longer be able to live. Yet what else was there to do, even had the future been foreseen with accuracy? How could the Joint tell the Jews of Europe, who were often the most ancient inhabitants of their several countries, that they must now prepare to leave home? And where could they go? The old tides of hatred were rising fast and there was scarcely a place left on earth which would accept huge Jewish immigration—except Palestine, had the British been induced to open wide the doors. But not all the money of American Jewry could have made Palestine (even mandated Palestine, which was far bigger than Israel today) able to accommodate the threatened masses. In a grim and brutal sense, before Israel could become the answer for the Remnant, the Germans had to exterminate their millions.

In any case, the stated purpose of the Joint was to help Jews to live their own lives in their own way wherever they might be found. So the work of rehabilitation began. The measure of the success was the measure of the subsequent heartbreak, for, horribly enough, one result was to keep many Jews exactly where the Germans could collect them most conveniently for burning.

Let us take three examples of the saving work which could not save because the world was going mad and the geography was wrong: two chiefly in Poland-Lithuania, and the other in Russia.

Chapter Two

1.

By the end of 1921, after seven years of repeated attacks on their spiritual and bodily well-being—and after the resuscitation of such physical assets as schools, hospitals, bath houses, synagogues, and credit facilities—the Jews of Poland needed most of all a long-term project for building the health of child and adult alike. Tuberculosis, favus, and trachoma were epidemic. The decay had gone too far to be arrested by a mere succoring of the decrepit—and even that was too expensive for the resources of the local communities. The Poles themselves were not much interested. They did not necessarily object to the Jews' improving their health if they could; but for the most part the government did not choose to use public money for such a purpose.

The time had come for the Joint to organize a permanent medical service to protect the healthy, to guard the children, and to do what was possible for the half- or wholly ruined. So the Joint promoted the founding of TOZ, a Polish analogue of the

Russian OSE, or Jewish Health Society.[1] "The cure of the sick is a great good deed (*mitzvah*), but the prevention of sickness is a greater one," was the motto.

Although TOZ was an initiative of the Joint, within eighteen months of its birth it was wholly in the hands of Polish Jews, only money and creative, non-dictatorial advice coming from New York. At first the Joint paid for everything; but by 1939, just before the Germans returned, the Joint was paying only 15 per cent, and meanwhile the work had increased twenty-fold. The infant-mortality rate had been halved. The general mortality rate had been lowered by 33 per cent. Twenty-seven thousand cases of favus had been cured. And the Joint had been able—for the first time ever in Poland—to persuade the rich Jews and the poor, the free-thinking intellectuals and the synagogue groups, to work together closely.

Then the armies of the Third Reich arrived. By this time, however, the Jewish Health Society—under its original Russian initials, OSE—had become a world-wide movement. From Poland it had spread first to Romania and the Baltic States, then to Western Europe, South America, North Africa, and Palestine, usually receiving financial aid from the Joint. During the Second World War, workers for the OSE saved thousands of Jewish children in Germany, France, Holland, and Belgium from falling into the hands of the Gestapo.

A few years after founding the TOZ, the Joint had joined forces with the Jewish Colonization Association to carry on other work of reconstruction in Western Europe. The Association had been founded in 1891 by Baron Maurice de Hirsch, who in the course of a few years gave it almost $50,000,000. The original purpose was to help Jews escape from Russia and Romania and settle on the land in Argentina and Brazil; but after the First War ICA (as the Association was commonly called) turned some of its funds to helping the Jews who did not wish to move. Hence the amal-

[1] The Russian OSE had been outlawed in 1919.

gamation with the Joint, for the purposes of this part of ICA's work, under the title of American Joint Reconstruction Foundation (1924). Funds were to be provided by both agencies, and six directors apiece were to be appointed, with another eight to be chosen from among the leaders of Eastern European Jewry.

The most important work of this Foundation was the extension of credit cooperatives throughout Europe, especially in Poland and Lithuania. The cooperatives were not a new invention. They began among German Jews in the middle of the nineteenth century and spread throughout the Pale of Settlement. They were a useful device for an economically weak minority, but they were ruined by the war. The Joint chose to re-establish them for two reasons. First, if they were properly run, the money supplied by an outside agency would become a revolving fund. Over the years it would acquire twenty or thirty times its original value. And second, the cooperatives seemed the best way to stimulate self-help, which was always one of the chief purposes of the Joint. It lived in perpetual fear of weakening the wills of its clients by doing too much, which is one reason why it lived with the perpetual illusion that it could soon go out of business.

The Foundation might supply a large part of the first funds for a cooperative. In the early days it often supplied from 70 to 85 per cent. And the Foundation might act as a coordinator and supervisor, auditing books, setting up correct accounting procedures, stimulating in towns and villages the formation of new cooperatives, organizing the little ones into district groups and the district groups into large cooperative unions. But in the end it all depended on the local people. This was not charity. It was a way of stimulating business so that the communities could look after themselves.

Loans were made on a strictly business basis, the debtor's credit rating to be determined, the purpose of the loan to be justified, and interest to be paid. Loans were made only to members who contributed regular, fixed sums. The proof of the wisdom of the operation is that by 1939, when the German armies returned, credits from the Foundation were only about 10 to 18 per cent of the operating funds of the cooperatives, instead of 70 to 85 per cent.

The figures are impressive. In 1924, 323 cooperatives had already been born, with a membership of 115,000. In 1930, 767 cooperatives had a membership of 320,000. They had $3,500,000 of their own money, $12,000,000 on deposit from their members, and $2,500,000 of credits from the Foundation. They granted over fifty thousand loans in that year, totaling $65,000,000—mostly for tools and merchandise. (Assuming five to a family, two and a half million people must have benefited). And in the eight months up to September 1939, when the Germans arrived, loans of $57,000,-000 had been arranged.

Although the majority of the credit cooperatives were in Poland, some towns in Lithuania had 80 per cent of their families enrolled. Many of the cooperatives had 15 per cent of gentile membership, and in Bessarabia the percentage was sometimes as high as 25. For the desperately poor, who had no credit and could pay no interest, the Joint revived the Gmilath Chessod, or free-loan societies, an ancient Jewish charity. Two million loans, worth $40,000,000, were granted between 1926 and 1939.

Meanwhile, in the year of the partial amalgamation with ICA, the Joint undertook an even larger effort in Russia with an even more surprising short-term success.

2.

In 1924 the United States passed an immigration act which closed a momentous chapter in American and European history. The open-handed, world-minded policy ("I lift my lamp beside the golden door") gave way to a policy of closing all possible doors. Russia, for example, was thenceforward to have an annual quota of 2697 immigrants. Since the Russians had already forbidden emigration, they did not take this as more than a minor insult, but the Russian Jews took it as a calamity. They were not only forbidden to leave Russia; they were well-nigh forbidden to live if they remained in Russia. And now, even if they escaped in large numbers, there was no place left on earth where they could go. France and England remained, as always, generous to exiles; but they thought in thousands, whereas the United States had thought in millions. Almost nine million immigrants entered the United States between 1901 and 1910, and between 1911 and 1920 almost six million.

In Russian Europe and Russian Asia the doors had closed on an enormous prison. In North America the sign went up that there was no more room. What was the status of the immobilized Russian Jews?

The Revolution had an unintended, grievous effect upon the Jews. As we have said, Czarist Russia had insisted that the Jew be exactly the type of man which the Revolution insisted upon eradicating—the petty trader, the moneylender, the self-employed artisan. He had long been barred from productive work on the land or in heavy industry; but now the Revolution said that only such producers could be true citizens. By necessity, the Jew had been the purest type of petty bourgeois; but now the bourgeois was an outcast who could count himself lucky not to be dead. He was told by the new government that all the heavy legal restrictions had been removed from the Jew and that he now enjoyed freedom, including the famous freedom to sleep under bridges and to starve. The outside world blamed the Jews for having started the Revolution; inside Russia they were blamed for having opposed it.

Added to his old, inherited distaste for the Jews, the Russian peasant soon after the Revolution had a new grievance: a number of ruined Jews took jobs as civil servants under the Soviet Republic. Some of them became tax collectors, which meant, in fact, expropriators of the peasants' grain. The government had to feed the cities if possible, but it had nothing with which to pay farmers except printed pieces of paper which were laughably described as money. So the grain was seized, either as a so-called tax or in return for so-called cash. And the Jews were blamed.

Meanwhile, in the Ukraine, came the worst outbreak of pogroms since the seventeenth century—sheer malice on the part of anti-revolutionary forces. They raged from the end of the war until the end of 1919, and again during the Polish-Russian war.

More than a hundred and fifty thousand were killed, and about four times as many were wounded. The loss of property in the small towns was very nearly total. And all this was accompanied by little civil wars of revolt against the great civil war which was the Revolution. Petlyura, the Ukrainian nationalist, stormed through southern Russia with the troops of the "Independent Ukrainian Government." Denikin raised his White Army in the Don country, won the Caucasus in 1918 and the whole of the Ukraine the next year. And bandit leaders, whose followers believed in nothing but the ancient doctrine of plunder, roamed and marauded.

> Now days are dragon-ridden, the nightmare
> Rides upon sleep.

The institutions of civilization had broken down, and, according to custom, the Jews suffered most.

The forlorn survivors of the shtetl felt that their best hope was a large-scale movement back to the soil. Even with government encouragement, which was forthcoming because of the need for food, this was a forbidding task: to transfer masses of people who had never been allowed to live even in a village, let alone on a farm, to self-sufficient agriculture on the lonely Russian steppes. Nevertheless, as early as the Russo-Polish war (and subsequently urged on by the famine of 1921-1922), thousands of young Jews began to train themselves for the land and hundreds of families left the ghettos for any unused spot where they could grow a little food.

Until the spectacular rebirth of Israel, the world had long believed that Jews were averse to the agrarian life; but nothing in Russian history supports the view. Whenever a Czar relaxed to the smallest degree the prohibition against Jews on the land, the Jews enthusiastically occupied every permitted acre. This was true under Alexander I, under Nicholas I, and most notably under Alexander II after the emancipation of the peasants, when the Jewish colonies near Odessa were formed.

Alexander II was assassinated in 1881 by a Russian nihilist. Savage pogroms occurred, widespread, with the connivance of the government. The old regime in Russia, when trouble came, responded automatically, like Anatole France's penguins: "Put some socialists in jail and kill some Jews." These pogroms led to a mass emigration to the United States, and also to the formation of the Hibbat Zion ("Love of Zion"), the first effective step toward the Return. In spite of Turkish opposition, money was raised in Russia, Poland, Romania, and England to buy land for Jewish settlers in Palestine. Fifteen years before Herzl's First Zionist Congress, these colonies were building a practical, physical background for the political Zionism of the twentieth century. Without them the Balfour Declaration would scarcely have been possible.

In 1921, in the midst of the great famine, Dr. Joseph Rosen went to Russia with the American Relief Administration as a representative of the Joint. (Dr. Rosen, a famous agronomist, was a native of Russia who had gone to the United States at the age of twenty-seven.) He reported to the Joint that many Jews desperately needed, and wanted, to settle on the land, and that the Russian government was ready to help. If the Joint, he suggested, could provide money, machines, seeds, and supervision, hundreds of thousands of Jews might find salvation, for in this important field the Revolution provided a lucky, albeit a short-lived, opportunity. In 1924, owing to a lack of water, six million acres of good land in the Crimea lay vacant. At the moment neither the government nor the potential Russian settlers could afford to sink the necessary wells. But the job could be done with American money and American Keystone drillers. And the Russians would give any land thus redeemed to the Jewish settlers, since the success of the Revolution might depend on increasing the supply of food.

These potentially fruitful plains along the shore of the Black Sea would not long remain empty. The chance had to be seized at once or lost forever, yet there was divided opinion in the United States. Some did not choose to cooperate with a Communist government. Some argued that the millions which would be needed might better be spent in Palestine, where at least the settlers could hope to be free from pogroms. Some insisted that Jews could never make a living as farmers. In Russia, however, there were no doubts. The Zionists, the Orthodox, the left-wing intellectuals, all begged that the experiment should be made—though all agreed that the Joint should also, as in Poland, provide medicine and technical training for those who preferred the factory to the farm. The little businessman had been abolished, but the handworker, if healthy and well trained, could survive in the new society.

The best argument was supplied by Dr. Rosen: Under the land-settlement scheme many Jewish families might become self-sufficient. "The settlers," he said, "do not depend on anybody but themselves to supply them with work." In 1924, therefore, the Joint decided to experiment in a small way. It set up the American Jewish Joint Agricultural Corporation (known as the Agro-Joint) to act as its agent in Russia, and endowed it with $400,000. Within a month the Soviet government formed a Committee for the Settlement of Jews on the Land (Komzet). Agro-Joint and Komzet, between them, chose sites in the Ukraine and

The Saving Remnant

the Crimea, which the government agreed to donate. Dr. Rosen found a staff of young Jewish graduates from agricultural schools. Farms for the first group of settlers were surveyed and planted. When families arrived in the spring of 1925, they had a grain crop to harvest and sufficient food (if wisely handled) to last them until the following season.

Success was immediate and beyond all reasonable hopes. By the time of the first harvest Dr. Rosen could report: "With the exception of one tractor mechanic, the Agro-Joint has no American staff in Russia. All the work is being done by local people." And "all the work" was indeed heavy work, even by early American frontier standards.

"I was in the colonies last year," wrote the legal adviser to the Agro-Joint in October 1926, "when the Jews started to come to the steppes in large numbers. Imagine the endless Russian steppes, miles and miles, on which you will not find a single soul or a house. To such steppes, where a man can be lost as easily as a canoe on the ocean, came the Jews. They did not know how to harness a horse, how to handle a plow. They felt absolutely helpless. It seemed impossible to harmonize them with the steppes to which they came. A year passed, and I visited the steppes again. Instead of desolate, wild, deserted prairies, we found villages. Instead of the former hopeless small traders, storekeepers, who were afraid of a horse, we found farmers. The Jewish fields can compete with the best in Russia. The Jewish wheat is of such quality that it can now be used for seeding purposes, and not merely for consumption."

The Russians were pleased with these results. In 1926 they asked the Joint to stop experimenting and do the job on a big scale. They promised to do more than their own share. So the president of Agro-Joint (James N. Rosenberg of New York) went to Moscow with Bernhard Kahn (whom we last met with Ludendorff), to confer with Dr. Rosen and the head of Komzet. The Russians offered $8,000,000 worth of 5-per-cent Soviet bonds to

49

the Joint, asking that the Joint place the bonds in America. The
$8,000,000 would then be given entirely into the hands of Dr.
Rosen to use as he saw fit. And the Soviets promised to match
the $8,000,000 with another $10,000,000 of their own, which
would also be turned over to the Agro-Joint. And they offered
as much free land as was needed in the Crimea, and lumber
from the northern forests.

Here, seemingly, was an opportunity for salvation which was
limited only by the amount of money which could be raised.[2]
The first step was to market the bonds of the Soviet Union; so
the Joint formed a corporation called the American Society for
Jewish Farm Settlements in Russia. Mr. Rosenberg was president
of this as well as of the Agro-Joint. The money was raised with
the help of a subscription of $5,000,000 from Julius Rosenwald,
a subscription of $1,000,000 from Felix Warburg, and $500,000
contributed outright by John D. Rockefeller, Jr.

Mr. Rosenberg estimates that by 1938—when, with war threatening, the Russian government suddenly called a halt to the work
and Dr. Rosen returned home—almost 300,000 Jews had been
settled on more than 3,000,000 acres of land in the Crimea, the
Ukraine, and White Russia. Mr. Rosenberg gives the overwhelming share of the credit for this startling achievement to Dr.
Rosen, but Dr. Rosen was always inclined to pass on most of it
to the Soviet government. In 1936 he reported as follows to the
Joint:

> In a problem of this kind and magnitude, it would have
> been impossible to accomplish any results without the active
> cooperation of the government in the country. In contrast to
> the passive resistance, not to speak of the active opposition of
> governments with which the JDC has frequently been con-
> fronted in other countries, the Soviet government has not
> merely actively cooperated in the work, but has actually
> taken the lead officially, recognizing the solution of the

[2] In the end, excluding the value of the land, more than $40,000,000 was
spent, the major part contributed by the Soviet government.

The Saving Remnant

Jewish questions as a state problem. . . . In the Agro-
Joint colonies Jews enjoy Jewish cultural autonomy; Yiddish
is spoken in the schools and courts, thus transmitting Jewish
national tradition to the younger generation through Jewish
communal life, the study of Jewish literature, etc.[3]

The story of these Jewish settlers had as unhappy an ending
as possible. The Germans appear to have killed them all. World-
wide efforts have been made to get some news of somebody who
belonged to the Agro-Joint colonies; but with the possible exception of one man (who claims to be the sole survivor) there is no
news. In 1956 James Rosenberg wrote to Edward Warburg, who
had succeeded his father as chairman of the Joint: "We have
never been able to find one bit of information as to what happened to the 300,000 Jews who were settled in the Crimea and
the Ukraine. Four or five years ago I tried and was utterly baf-
fled, and unable to learn anything. My fear is that the whole
wonderful work has been destroyed."

3.

The Joint has been heavily criticized, especially by Zionists,
for squandering money and brains on this work which merely
settled the Jews in the path of their destroyers. Chaim Weizmann writes of the Joint:

Their faith in the ultimate restabilizing of European Jewry
was a tragedy. It was heartbreaking to see them pour millions into a bottomless pit when some of the money could
have been directed on to the Jewish Homeland and used for
the permanent settlement of those very Jews who in Europe
never had a real chance. . . . An outstanding example was
the project of the creation of an autonomous Jewish settlement in Soviet Russia, which began with the Crimea as the
chosen area. . . . I believe the Crimean scheme was a sin-

[3] In 1938 the Russian government redeemed the twenty-year bonds on
generous terms.

cere attempt on the part of the Russian government to "normalize" certain Jewish elements which did not fit into the reorganized economic life of Soviet Russia. . . . But for a great many non-Zionists, at that time at any rate, the peculiar merit of the Crimean scheme was precisely that it had nothing to do with Palestine and Jewish nationalism, and could in fact be used to deflect from Palestine the attention of Jewish groups.

Weizmann is here complaining of a deep division, not only within American but within world Jewry. The Joint, as we have seen, was for the most part non-Zionist. Its contributors were for the most part suspicious of "Jewish nationalism." They were Jews and totally American, just as their friends were Jews and totally British, French, Italian, or Dutch. In fact, when the Agro-Joint was launched with such high enthusiasm, men still believed that they could be Jews and totally German. Few of these deluded souls had been born and brought up in the Pale of Settlement. They were not weather-wise, and unlike Weizmann they did not see the menace of the dark clouds rising.

The Joint was nonpolitical, devoted simply to making the lives of Jews as dignified and worthy as possible in the lands of their own choosing. Furthermore, the Joint could well point out to Chaim Weizmann that the Jewish homeland had no room for most of its clients. Julius Rosenwald used to say to Weizmann, "If you can convince me that Palestine is a *practical* proposition, you can have all my money." But it never was a practical proposition for the nine million Jews of Eastern Europe. They were too many and Palestine was too small. Who was to help these oppressed people, if all available funds from the West were poured into the renascent desert? The argument was never settled until the terrible Kristall Nacht in Germany, November 9-10, 1938. At that point, sadly but courageously, the Joint accepted Rabbi Hillel Silver's message: "You can no longer separate the problems of Palestine and Europe." Let us look at a few "problems of Palestine," beginning with the brief but incoherent Balfour Declaration of November 2, 1917, from which stemmed the hopes and the frustrations of thirty years.

"His Majesty's Government," wrote Arthur Balfour to Lord Rothschild, "view with favour the establishment in Palestine of a national home for the Jewish people, and will use their best endeavours to facilitate the achievement of this object, it being clearly understood that nothing shall be done which may prejudice the civil and religious rights of existing non-Jewish communities in Palestine, or the rights and political status enjoyed by Jews in any other country." Anyone who can tell what that means would find the Delphic oracle as lucid as Voltaire and could unriddle the Sphinx. The fault, however, does not lie with the author.

Balfour was prepared (on the evidence available today) to sponsor an earlier draft of the declaration which said in part: "His Majesty's Government . . . accepts the principle of recognizing Palestine as the National Home of the Jewish people to build up its National Life in Palestine under a protection to be established at the conclusion of Peace. . . . His Majesty's Government regards as essential for the realization of this principle the grant of internal autonomy to Jewish nationals in Palestine, freedom of immigration for Jews and the establishment of a Jewish National Colonization Corporation. . . ."[4] This, since we know that the author was a master of the English language, could only have meant that Balfour looked forward to the early creation of an autonomous Jewish state with Great Britain as a friendly, protecting policeman. Oddly enough, the change between the two drafts seems largely to have been the work of bitter anti-Zionist British Jews, led by Edwin Montagu, Secretary of State for India.

This tiny group of comfortable Jews—comfortable, after all, only since Cromwell's time, which to Weizmann would seem like yesterday morning—set themselves, in all good faith and convic-

[4] No Arab was consulted about either draft.

tion, to thwart the seemingly impractical but pain-bred and faith-bred longing of the Jews from the Pale of Settlement for the Return. And the British dissidents very nearly succeeded. For a brief moment only, in 1917, the world was willing to listen to the Zionists. One of the Great Powers had conquered Palestine and stood ready, for reasons of her own, to invite Jewish settlement. Two other powers, France and the United States, had expressed their benevolent but worried interest. And then the Jews fell upon one another—assimilationist versus Zionist—with a rage which put the British government in an odd position. An argument in favor of the declaration was that it would rally world-wide Jewry behind the cause of the Allies; but if it merely divided the Jews against themselves, it was scarcely worth while. If, on the other hand, what the Jews really wanted was a declaration which meant nothing—or possibly everything, depending on which light one saw it in—Balfour was the man to draft it.

Weizmann himself called the vague permission for "a national home for the Jewish people" an "act of restitution." Historically, this is not an easy position to defend. As Robert Graves wrote in 1948: "There are no modern title-deeds to Palestine except the Mandate which the British are now surrendering. They seized the country from the Turks, who had seized it from the Arabs, who had seized it from the Crusaders, who had seized it from the Arabs, who had seized it from the Romans, who had seized it from the Jews, who had seized it from the Canaanites, Perizzites, Philistines and others."

Perhaps the Jewish title to Israel rests most convincingly on three points—aside from the all-important point that the Jews are in possession. The first was stated by Arthur Balfour: "The position of the Jews is unique. For them race, religion and country are interrelated as they are interrelated in the case of no other race, no other religion and no other country on earth." The second point is that Jews are making the ancient land into a garden, whereas the Turks and the Arabs between them made it into a desolation. And the third point is the exceedingly bad conscience which the Western, Christian world must suffer in its relation to the Jews—a bad conscience which may stand the Jews in good stead when the next effort to destroy them is made. Unfortunately, none of these points has any great appeal to the Arab.

In a recent book[5] Arthur Balfour is described as a "ruthless dilettante, whose languid interest was caught by the spectacle of an intellectual and spiritual intensity so foreign to his own fastidious detachment." And it is said that he "appears to have taken up Zionism as a kind of hobby." This seems unlikely. Balfour's most favored disguise was that of "languid interest" and "fastidious detachment"; but he never behaved in keeping with this disguise when the interests of his country were at stake. His mind was flexible and ingenious ("devious," therefore, to his opponents), but he did not have "hobbies" in foreign affairs. His declaration seems to have been aimed at getting the British more deeply entrenched in the Middle East and at getting the French out. If, incidentally, it got the Jews back into their ancient home, this would be a pleasing by-product of his craft.

Weizmann, the prophet-politician plus man of science, who always knew which mask to wear on which occasion, might talk to Lloyd George about cultural regeneration and the Old Testament; but he would talk to Balfour about imperial policy. "It is one of the 'ifs' of history," he wrote, comparing the emasculated final version of the declaration with the original, "whether we should have been intransigent, and stood by our guns. . . . Or would the government have become wearied of these internal Jewish divisions, and dropped the whole matter? . . ."

> Our judgment was to accept, to press for ratification. For we knew that the assimilationists would use every delay for their own purposes; and we also knew that in America the same internal Jewish struggle was going on—complicated by

[5] *The Seat of Pilate: An Account of the Palestine Mandate,* by John Marlowe (London: Cresset Press, 1959).

the fact that President Wilson, who was wholeheartedly with us, considered the publication of a declaration premature, in view of the fact that no state of war existed between America and Turkey.

The declaration, as Weizmann clearly knew, was partly a war measure and partly a by-product of Franco-British rivalry in the Middle East. Because of this vain, reciprocally destructive conflict, the Zionists were given their chance and took it.

As early as March 1915, T. E. Lawrence of the Cairo Intelligence Department wrote that the danger to British interests in the Middle East did not come from Germany but from France and Russia. "The French insist upon Syria," he wrote, "which we are conceding to them: there remains Alexandretta, which is the key to the whole place. . . . If Russia has Alexandretta, it's all up with us in the Near East. And in the next war the French will probably be under Russia's finger in Syria. Therefore, I think it absolutely necessary that we hold Alexandretta." And a week later he wrote: ". . . we can rush right up to Damascus and biff the French out of all hope of Syria. It's a big game, and . . . one worth playing."

Thirty years later, while the Second World War was in progress, the British at last removed the French from Syria and Lebanon. "A second Fashoda," said General Catroux. Meanwhile countless promises, to Arabs and to Jews, had been made and broken. The making and the breaking had little to do with Lawrence and his Arabs, or with the Balfour Declaration; they had to do with a struggle for possession which was out of date. The upshot is that the French are out, the British are out, the Jews are in Israel, and the Arabs are in an uproar. Nobody planned it that way—not even the Zionists, who were alert enough to take advantage of the accumulating chaos. So it seems fair to say that the Joint was not the only institution which failed, during and after the first war, to foresee the future of Palestine.

"Few countries," writes Jon Kimche, "have been blessed with

such servants as the Englishmen who worked in the Middle East during the First World War and afterwards; they loved the people among whom they worked, they liked their job, they believed in their destiny and in the righteousness of their cause; they were endowed with abilities far beyond those normally found in colonial officials; they had vision, imagination and ability—and they failed in their allotted task more completely than the simplest, crudest, most inexperienced or self-seeking bureaucrat. They lived fifty years too late. The Russian Revolution had overtaken them and they had not noticed it; the Arab was waking up, filled with the heady wine of Western nationalism, and they did not realize it. In short, the British administration of the Middle East after the First World War took no account of the most potent factors which British intervention and the war itself had produced: the reality of the Russian Revolution, the growth of Arab nationalism, and the firm establishment of Zionism." [6]

4.

Palestine became a theater of war in the spring of 1917. By the end of the year General Allenby had taken Jerusalem and the British were in possession. The census was inaccurate under Turkish rule, but there seem to have been about 90,000 Jews in Palestine, 600,000 Arabs, and 75,000 Christians.

We have seen the first efforts of the Joint to send relief in terms of money, food, and medical supplies—the latter being perhaps the most scarce. Malaria and a virulent form of dysentery and typhoid fever were widespread. Cholera was not unknown. Since none of these diseases is anti-Semitic the population was afflicted impartially. What little the Joint could do, therefore, was done on a nonsectarian basis. An anti-malaria team of doctors and technicians drained swamps, discouraged mosquitoes, and

[6] *Seven Fallen Pillars*, by Jon Kimche (New York, British Book Centre, 1952), page 27.

made large tracts of land habitable for Jews, Christians, and Arabs. The Joint has always been nonsectarian when Jews and gentiles have been similarly afflicted: with Herbert Hoover's Relief Administration after the First War, in Shanghai and during the battle against typhus in Romania after the Second War, and today in Agadir.

During the three years of fighting before General Allenby conquered Palestine, the Franco-British blockade of the Mediterranean became increasingly troublesome. With the help of the French ambassador in Washington a shipment of medicine was allowed into the port of Jaffa in the autumn of 1916. And with the help of the Zionist organization the Joint could sometimes get money into the country, either for direct grants to the needy or for the maintenance of schools and the promotion of agriculture. This, incidentally, was the first cooperation between the Joint and the Zionists.

In the spring of 1918 the official British Zionist Commission, which included Chaim Weizmann and which we mentioned in Chapter One, arrived in Palestine to prepare the way for making the Balfour Declaration come true. As quickly as possible this commission took responsibility for emergency relief, leaving the Joint free for such works of rehabilitation as the care and training of the war orphans. As usual, an independent committee was set up, sponsored and supported by the Joint, but run by people on the spot: the Palestine Orphan Committee under the chairmanship of Norman Bentwich, an Englishman.

Although local Jewish communities and the Hadassah (the Women's Zionist Organization of America) were also active in this work, the Joint's committee was in charge of 4039 orphans in 1920. So far as possible, it avoided institutional care, seeking to place each child with a relative or a foster parent and supplying the necessary money for board and education, clothes, books, and health services. Sometimes "group homes" were organized, with seven or eight families agreeing to look after fourteen or fifteen children. Two children's villages were established, where all the daily tasks of life were carried out and supervised by the children themselves. By 1928, all but 151 of the original 4039 orphans had been absorbed into the general life of the community, and the committee was disbanded. The remaining work was taken over by Hadassah.

At the height of this work Sir Herbert (later Viscount) Samuel, High Commissioner in Palestine, paid his tribute to the Committee. "When the tide of war ebbed," he said, "it left lying helpless thousands of Jewish orphans. The American Joint Distribution Committee came to their rescue. For five years it has cared for them with the greatest devotion, by methods that were well considered, frugal, and sympathetic. Three-fourths of the children have now been permanently provided for, almost all in the land of Palestine itself."

In 1918 Zionists throughout the world were rejoicing over the British defeat of Turkey and the Balfour Declaration. They thought—especially if they had never visited Palestine—that the new day had already dawned. In fact, after exactly four hundred years of misrule,[7] the Turks had left behind them a waste of sand, a few overcrowded towns wherein no effort had been made to relate housing to population, sanitary conditions which would have seemed inadequate to a nomadic tribe of Mongols, an Arab population whose education (for the masses) was still at the stage where people tried to cure typhoid and dysentery with amulets and charms, and a few cases of Jewish settlements where the healing color of green was returning to the land. In their inefficient way, the Turks had done their best to keep these Jewish farmers out.

The British, therefore, with all their tergiversations and their inability to decide what they wanted in Palestine, had no easy task during their days as the mandatory power. But in the early years—before Arab threats and the mounting need for Arab oil

[7] Sultan Selim I conquered Syria and Palestine in 1517.

confused their purposes—they took seriously the promise to "favor the establishment of a national home," even if they could never make up their minds what "national home" meant. (Neither could most of the world's Jewry, for that matter.) Between 1920 and 1935, under British auspices, about 240,000 Jewish immigrants were admitted to Palestine, more than half of them during the last three—the Hitlerian—years. Hence the Arab Conference in Syria, presided over by the Prime Minister of Iraq, which resolved that "we must make Great Britain understand that it must choose between our friendship and the Jews. Britain must change her policy in Palestine or we shall be at liberty to side with other European powers whose policies are inimical to Great Britain."

This was not a small threat, with world war looming and with a surfeit of "other European powers" who would be eager to add to the dangers and embarrassments of the mandate. The unhappy soldiers and civil servants who were seeking to administer a turmoil which could not be administered, in the name of a policy too changeable to be defined, must often have been reminded of Yeats's Irish Airman:

> Those that I fight I do not hate,
> Those that I guard I do not love.

5.

While history was thus preparing to involve the Joint inextricably in the affairs of Palestine-Israel, the Joint was involving itself in the most unexpected corners of the earth, including Abyssinia and Vladivostok. As soon as the news went out that an organization was prepared to help all suffering Jews anywhere, the demand for beneficence became world-wide.

Abyssinia was a small but interesting example of how far the work of the Joint can reach. Legends of Jewish tribes in Ethiopia had been current since the Middle Ages. In 1790 a traveler brought authentic facts: north of Lake Tana lived an isolated group of about twenty-five thousand people who called themselves Falashas ("strangers") and who claimed descent from the Jewish people. Their customs and their rites, it was later discovered, made the claim seem irrefutable. They observed all the older Biblical feasts, and their religion was a literal obedience to Old Testament injunctions. Since they knew nothing of post-Biblical Hebrew literature (and only a smattering of Hebrew after all these centuries), their ancestors may well have been converted to Judaism before the Christian era.

In 1904 a group of European Jews with headquarters at Frankfurt formed a Pro-Falasha Committee to help these "strangers" preserve their culture and their religion. The First War brought the work to an end, but after the war an American Pro-Falasha Committee was formed to send medicine and physicians, books and teachers. The Joint made a small contribution toward the first expedition. Later it heard that the results had been encouraging and that plans were afoot to build a Jewish school at Addis Ababa. So for a number of years the Cultural Committee of the Joint voted minor subsidies. Since the Second War the Jewish Agency has taken over the work.

Siberia was a far larger and more critical commitment. Among the masses of Jews expelled from western Russia at the start of the First World War, with nowhere to go and no orders except to get out of the way, a surprising number penetrated that far country. Herman Bernstein, an American journalist and diplomat who was luckily in Siberia in the autumn of 1918, called the Joint's attention to these unhappy people. He said there were at least a hundred thousand Jewish refugees straggling forlornly along the route of the Trans-Siberian railway from Omsk to Vladivostok. Some were headed west in an attempt to get home, some east in an attempt to forget Europe and all its pain. Others were living in abandoned cattle cars and forgotten railway stations. Thousands had already died of hunger or of cold. And since very few Jewish families lived in that vast land, organized relief did not exist.

Furthermore, among the 160,000 prisoners of war scattered among Siberian camps in 1918, at least 10,000 were Jews. The first representative of the Joint to reach these grim places was told that another 20,000 had died during the years of captivity. These were the Austrian-Jewish soldiers taken by the Russians in Galicia and Bukovina. The death rate in some camps was as high as 25 per cent. Escape was easy; but it was also an invitation to death in those desolate wastes.

Added to its other shortcomings, Siberia at the time was the seat of countless small revolutions. For example, the Kerenski Government had freed all Czechoslovak prisoners on their promise to form a legion to fight at Russia's side. The legion won high honors at the battle of Zborov. Then the October Revolution intervened; fighting against the Germans became a bourgeois activity. The Czechs were told to head for Vladivostok, whence they might find their way home via Japan or the United States. This was a long trip for men devoid of transport, and the legion can scarcely be blamed if it was inconsiderate in seizing what few goods it found along that endless ghost-railway.

The plight of the legion was made no easier by Admiral Kolchak, whose counter-revolutionary armies in Siberia had suffered a defeat which turned into a rout. These disgraced armies also headed for Vladivostok, only rather faster than the Czechs, whom they overtook at Irkutsk. The Czechs were annoyed, and since they still maintained their military discipline they were more formidable than this rabble. They handed Kolchak to a local Social revolutionary committee, which handed him to the Bolsheviks, who shot him in February 1920. And all this time, in every corner of Siberia, provisional republics and local soviets were being created and overthrown and restored—to say nothing of the half-dozen monarchist movements, in addition to Kolchak's, which kept the pot boiling.

The Saving Remnant

Such was the background for the hundred thousand wandering Jews and the ten thousand who remained in camps. If we assume the normal rule that when other people are suffering the Jews are suffering more, the Joint and all other agencies of mercy were clearly needed in the Far East.

Here was a new type of work for the Joint. In the Pale, in the Levant, even in Abyssinia, it had sought to repair and strengthen an existing Jewish life so the people could stay where they were. But Siberia was emergency rescue work—and, as such, good training for the future which nobody yet foresaw.

Joining forces with the Hebrew Immigrant Aid Society of the United States (HIAS), the Joint sent money, clothes, and workers. Wherever, as in Irkutsk and Harbin, they found an organized Jewish community, they worked in its name and with its help so far as possible. This was not often possible, since the collapse of the Russian currency had destroyed what little Jewish capital existed in Siberia. The recently well-to-do, who would have helped the Joint to help the others, were themselves in need.

When the workers of the Joint arrived, the rot was just beginning in Kolchak's army. This failure, and all the other failures of the counter-revolutionaries, had to be blamed on somebody other than those responsible, so naturally the blame went to the Jews. The hope was to persuade the people of Siberia, and especially the unpaid soldiers, that the Revolution was a strictly Jewish invention. Then the soldiers might stop killing monarchists and bourgeois and concentrate on killing Jews. Kolchak's foreign minister told a representative of the Joint that the only way to save the Jews of Siberia was to induce the United States to recognize the Kolchak regime. Since the regime, including Kolchak himself, was about to be annihilated, this could not be arranged. The Joint had to struggle with other means, and without too much success, against the tide of anti-Jewish hatred.

Here is an example of the troubles they had: in June 1919, Kolchak's troops evacuated Ekaterinburg and the town was taken over by General Anenkov, chief ataman of the region. His Cossacks set briskly to work and killed some three thousand Jews. The British consul at Ekaterinburg, an eye-witness, said the streets were "filled with Jewish blood."

All the Joint could do, in the midst of such chaos and counter-chaos, was to put money in the hands of any local communities which could be found or founded, and to get clothes and money to some of the prisoners of war as far west as the Urals. Also, the Joint set up a Far Eastern branch in Vladivostok, the committtee consisting of five local Jewish leaders plus two prisoners of war elected by their comrades. Thereafter the Joint supplied money to this committee and to the branch it had established in Manchuria, leaving to HIAS the duty of helping those who were lucky enough to be allowed to emigrate.

After the execution of Kolchak, the Bolshevik troops took control of Siberia and Vladivostok. Benevolence was no passport through the Red Army's lines; so the Joint could only hope for the best in the shut-off areas whose needs were sparsely served through the Jewish Council of Irkutsk, which got occasional help from the Joint. When the Vladivostok Joint got permission to send Dr. Kahn with funds to Irkutsk, the breakdown of the railway system was so complete that the trip took him several months.

On the credit side for the Bolsheviks, the nine or ten thousand remaining Jewish prisoners of war were now allowed to leave their camps and look for jobs. They could also look, surreptitiously, for a chance to escape from the Soviet empire and return home. Here the Joint could not help, at least in the first stages. The American Department of State took the view that repatriation of prisoners must wait upon an agreement with the governments of the countries from which the prisoners came. This was reasonable, for there could be no point in moving a man at great expense and effort from Harbin to Krakow if, on arriving "home," he was to be put in jail as a counter-revolutionary.

The Saving Remnant

The Joint has always boasted that in its manifold world-wide activities it has never gone counter to a directive, or even a request, from the Department of State. No middle course is possible. Either a private group of citizens operating abroad in peacetime and in war obeys its government, or else it becomes a form of conspiracy. By making the wise—the only tenable—decision, and by never openly deviating from it during forty-six years, the Joint has become trusted in Washington beyond most private agencies with an ax to grind overseas.

Even when the country from which a prisoner came was glad to have him home, it could not always arrange for his return. The postwar shuffle of boundaries, and the prolific birth of new nations, was confusing. A country which had not existed a fortnight before could scarcely start its new life by sending to the ends of the earth for "citizens" who might or might not approve of its existence. On the other hand, it might well announce that it would welcome these citizens if they could make their own way home. Thus the Siberian War Prisoners Repatriation Fund was created by nine American charitable groups. The Red Cross and the Joint gave $250,000 apiece, the others according to their means. In the end, $700,000 was spent—the Joint contributing more than its original pledge. Nine thousand men were repatriated, of whom 2000 were Jews.

6.

These are merely scattered illustrations of the Joint's work during its early years. Excluding the Siberian adventure, which was forced upon it by revolution and the breakdown of a society, the pattern of its operations was now set and its philosophy clarified. The Joint strove always for reconstruction and sought always to minimize the period of relief. The Joint put as much of the burden as possible—both financial and managerial—on the local community and on the many international Jewish organizations devoted to special aspects of Jewish welfare. The Joint would supply ideas, occasional experts or administrators, and a part of the money needed for a long-term project. As soon as possible it would pull out, leaving the local people or the international organization, or both, to carry on. Above all, the Joint stood for the absolute right of Jews everywhere to live their own Jewish lives in their own communities, different but equal, like any other national, racial, or religious minority.

This was to become a daring stand in the days toward which Western civilization was moving.

Chapter Three

1.

What is meant by Jews' "living their own lives"? What is meant by the demand to be "different but equal"? If we could answer these questions we might come close to understanding the age-long, haunting problem of anti-Semitism. And in order to face the questions at all, we must forget for the moment the assimilated Jew, the man who remembers he is a Jew only when someone is rude to him socially.

Most Jews are steadily conscious, and intensely proud, of their Jewishness. A few even go so far as to regret the completeness of their emancipation in the West, fearing that the end of their tragic, timeless struggle may be to win recognition as equal human beings and to disappear as Jews. But what does the phrase mean, "to disappear as Jews"? So far as an outsider can see, which is a very small way, this means in part to lose the intimate memory of Jewish history, the intimate knowledge of Jewish books, and the belief that the Jews either chose, or were chosen,

67

to be "the suffering servant," the witnesses of the one God. No matter how attenuated the belief may have become over the centuries, it still sets the non-assimilated Jews apart, not in vainglory but in the acceptance of difference and thus of pain.

People who have been chosen—or who chose themselves—to bear witness must continue to exist. They dare not disappear. Thus the Jewish clannishness, the customs and rituals which make them seem strange, the distaste for intermarriage. And thus, perhaps, the superstitious fear they have so often inspired among their neighbors—the fear leading to hate and the hate to pogroms.

This same sense of dedication (unconscious, perhaps, in most cases), this unspoken faith that sometime, somewhere—but probably in Israel—the Jews will once more be called on for a special contribution to mankind, this must be related to the Jewish passion for learning. "When most of the world was illiterate," writes Rabbi Bernstein, "every Jewish boy could read and by thirteen was advanced in the study of a complex literature." And we have already seen that many Jews prefer not be rescued unless their schools can be rescued with them. Yet, strangely, they are the least ascetic of people. They do not flee to monasteries, and we have no record of Jewish hermits. Learning, endless learning, is to them a high pleasure and not a discipline. And it is written that "on the Day of Judgment, a man will be called to account for every innocent pleasure and enjoyment he has denied himself."

This "innocent pleasure" of learning has been of great service to mankind. Brooding over the destruction which the Germans inflicted, Chaim Weizmann wrote: "Our great men were always a product of symbiosis between the ancient, traditional Talmudic learning in which our ancestors were steeped in the Polish or Galician ghettos or even in Spain, and the modern Western universities with which their children came in contact. There is, as often as not, a long list of Talmudic scholars and Rabbis in the pedigrees of our modern scientists. . . . Now these great places of Jewish learning in Vilna, Warsaw, Kovno, Breslau, Vienna, Pressburg, have been wiped off the face of the earth; the great Jewish archives have been plundered or destroyed, and we have to reconstruct them fragmentarily page by page. We have suffered not only physically; we have been murdered intellectually, and the world scarcely realizes the extent of our affliction."

All this may help to explain the Joint's troubles in dealing with the cultural life of East European Jewry. After the First War came a burst of cultural renewal throughout the old Pale. Schools, rabbinical seminaries, and learned societies representing all shades of opinion were set up or were rescued from oblivion, many of them with help from the Joint. The Joint's policy was to withdraw support from elementary schools as soon as possible, leaving them as a charge on the local community, and to give as much as possible to institutions of higher learning—including, of course, the Yeshivoth. Between the wars more than two hundred and fifty Yeshivoth received money for building and repairs, for teachers and salaries, and for feeding and housing the students. This heavy outlay in a field which could affect only a small part of the community caused grumbling both abroad and at home. The Joint explained its generosity to the Yeshivoth by pointing out that while they represented only one aspect of Judaism they also, in a larger sense, nourished the whole of world Jewry. More than anyone, the Yeshiva scholar poring over his Torah and his Talmud has kept the Jewish spirit alive during millennia of suffering. "The Torah through the ages was the portable spiritual fatherland of the Jews."

The Joint's case was a good one, but the grumbling continued. So in 1921 the JDC in New York set up a special cultural committee to be responsible for all the money spent on schools and religious institutions. The committee represented each of the three groups which had come together to form the JDC: the rich business and professional group, the Orthodox religious groups, and labor. Fifty-five per cent of the cultural budget for each year was assigned to the Orthodox group (which explains why the Yeshivoth and the schools for rabbinical study remained the major beneficiaries), and 17½ per cent to labor.

Labor was chiefly interested in helping the schools maintained by the working class to teach secular subjects in Yiddish. The third group, the opulent, assimilated Jews, spent most of its 27½ per cent on libraries, research foundations, and schools in which the teaching was in Hebrew. Rabbi Judah Magnes—the orator who had raised his million a night for the Joint in its infancy —made a tour through six countries to examine every institution which received support. And he persuaded the local communities to give even more liberal help to these chosen institutions, in spite of their own want.

Between 1921 and 1926, $2,500,000 was spent in Eastern Europe on this program; but the line of demarcation is of course illogical, because when the Joint paid the tuition of a scholar, or supplied him with food and clothes, this too was a "cultural activity."

The report which led to the founding of this cultural committee in 1921 shows the problems which the Joint had to face among its own members and officers in New York, and throws light on our observations about the Jewish character. After pointing out the difficulty of reaching an agreement between ardent socialists and bearded Orthodox rabbis (to say nothing of cosmopolitan New York bankers) on the meaning of such words as "education" and "culture," the report adds:

> On the other hand, the view was very strongly expressed by all the members of the committee that cultural activities, meaning specifically religious and educational activities, had a particular claim upon our funds. It was felt that it is only by maintaining the spirit of our brethren in Eastern Europe that their life is worth preserving to them, and that education and the provision for a continued leadership is as essential as food and clothing. . . .

The Saving Remnant

Hand in hand with the medical assistance we hope to provide, the child-caring plans that we anticipate being able to inaugurate, and the stimulus toward the reconstruction of economic independence, we must not overlook the fact that the Jewry of Eastern Europe has for many centuries maintained itself against almost overwhelming odds only because the people placed their spiritual and cultural aspirations above their material welfare and physical comfort. . . . The reports that have come to us are unanimous in expressing the hope of the people, one that many of them place even above providing them with bread, that means shall be forthcoming to maintain their spiritual life.

The committee therefore urges that in view of the ultimate benefit to the whole Jewish people, and especially to the people in Eastern Europe, who are in danger of sinking into a state of degradation from which it may take generations to elevate them, that, though they may continue for a long time to be undernourished and in rags, its recommendation to allow the Jews in America to foster the cultural aims of the people . . . shall receive favorable consideration.

The request was granted, and no further dissension troubled the home office, although overseas the non-devout still fretted about so much money spent on people who did nothing but sit and read books.

2.

Even after agreement had been reached as to what each of the three groups should do, the cultural work remained the most complex and difficult of all the Joint's tasks. A program for feeding children or housing the aged is much the same whether one is dealing with Poles, Lithuanians, or Austrians. But education is more complicated. Not only does everyone have his own ideas about what he or his child should learn, but every government has its own exclusive system, so that nothing which works in one country is likely to be useful across the border.

The Saving Remnant

After the First War the Polish Government recognized attendance at the Yiddish and Hebrew schools as equivalent to attendance at a state school, so a complete secular education had to be provided in addition to the desired Jewish subjects. In Austria (aside from Galicia) all children went to state schools, and the Jewish schools were extra, teaching Biblical history, Hebrew, and religion. Hungary was half-and-half, and in Romania all Jews were legally foreigners, and no foreigner was allowed in a state school. This was confusing enough, but it was nothing compared to the problem of promoting Jewish culture in Russia.

In the first place, no religious instruction was allowed for any children of any denomination up to the age of eighteen. To the majority of Jews, for whom education and religion are scarcely separable, this was discouraging. And in the second place, Jewish traditions, history, literature, and religious customs were treated with greater severity than were those of other faiths. The new government—especially the Jews in the new government—wished to stamp out Jewishness, knowing that it was the most persistent of all traits. Jews must be Russians, exactly like everyone else, and as soon as there were no more unassimilated Jews there would be no more anti-Semitism.

A third handicap was that Hebrew was declared to be a counter-revolutionary language, and was thus forbidden. This again was the work of Jewish Communists, who had to prove themselves more Russian than the Russians and who disliked Hebrew for two reasons: it was the language of religious instruction; and it was the language of Zionism, an intolerable heresy which preached that people should leave the Bolshevik paradise for a fairer land.

Literature, history, and religion were all discouraged; according to the rules, the Joint could do nothing for Jewish culture in Russia. Yet with a combination of ingenuity and impudence it did a lot. In Petrograd the Institute for Higher Learning was reborn with the help of money from the Joint, also the Jewish Ethnological and Historical Society. Ethnology, one would have thought, was the most dangerous of subjects for a Jew in the new Russia; but strange things escape scrutiny in a revolutionary chaos.

Even more venturesome was the Joint's support of the Jewish Art Theater, Habimah. This was a minor triumph, for Habimah dared to present plays in Hebrew, the forbidden language. The Jewish Communists, ardently proving their non-Jewishness, saw to it that the theater's subsidy was abolished. Lunacharski, head of the Moscow Art Theater, and Madame Kamenev, wife of the president of the Moscow Soviet, protested in the name of art, and with help from the Joint the theater struggled on until 1926, when it left Russia for a tour of Europe and America. In 1928 it settled in Palestine, and by 1945 it had its own building at Tel Aviv.

Elderly rabbis and teachers, whose lives were given to Jewish scholarship and religion, had no place in the new Russia. They were not allowed to leave and they were not allowed to work. Partly they were cared for by their neighbors, and for the rest by food packages and cash remittances from the Joint in co-operation with the *Landsmannschaften*—associations of Jews who had emigrated to America (or whose parents had emigrated) from the same town or province abroad. These were first formed out of loneliness in a foreign land, and the deep need to keep in touch with others from the old country. Later they became societies for giving aid to the former home town. In 1923 the Joint set up its own Landsmannschaft Bureau in New York and in Moscow to insure that this good work went forward smoothly. Within a few years the bureau was in touch with 336 towns in the Ukraine and northwestern Russia. Three-quarters of the towns had been visited by representatives of the Joint to make sure that the packages and remittances reached the correct address.

The Saving Remnant

We have now given a sketch of the pre-Hitlerian Joint: its philosophy, its methods of work, its world-wide scope, and its persistent illusion that life would soon become sane enough and stable enough for the Joint to resign from business. This illusion reached its height between 1930 and 1932—the birth years of the first agency on which American non-Zionist Jews could work amicably with Zionists of all countries.

Article IV of the British mandate over Palestine provided that "an appropriate Jewish agency shall be recognized as a public body for the purpose of advising and cooperating with the administration of Palestine in such . . . matters as may effect the establishment of the Jewish national home," and that "the Zionist Organization . . . shall be recognized as such agency." We saw that the Joint worked in Palestine with the Zionist Organization, briefly, toward the end of the First War. But wholehearted cooperation was difficult between those who deplored "Jewish nationalism" and those whose hearts and lives were given to establishing not merely a national home but a national state.

Three approaches to "the problem" divided world Jewry before and after the First War. One was that of Baron Maurice de Hirsch, whose total gifts to his Jewish Colonization Association (ICA) and to other rescue work came to more than $100,000,000. The purpose of ICA was to get the Jews away, out of Eastern Europe, to some less deadly countries overseas. But not even the Baron's wealth could move millions of families to safety. And when they were moved—to the Argentine, for example—what then? Herzl, whose relations with the Baron were unsatisfactory, was brutal on the subject. "You breed beggars," he said. "You believe that you can export poor Jews. I say that you are only creating new markets for anti-Semitism."

The second approach was that of the Joint, which wished to

74

enhance the life of Jewish communities wherever they were—
not to transport them unless they asked for it, but to improve
their lot. Herzl died ten years before the Joint was born, but he
would probably have deprecated this spending of money all
across the world rather than on his own cause. Yet in the days
before anybody had imagined Hitler, most Jews wanted what the
Joint offered: they wanted to be helped to live better, and with
greater dignity, in their own homes. And many of them shared
the Joint's distrust of Zionist nationalism. As late as 1930, for
example, the Jews of Germany still wanted proudly to be Germans. Several hundred leaders of their communities signed an
advertisement in the *Vossische Zeitung* of Berlin: "We profess
the Jewish religion, but reject any sort of Jewish nationalism. We
regard ourselves, along with the overwhelming majority of German Jews, as members of the German, not of the Jewish, people.
In the establishment of the national Jewish homeland we see an
error which is bound to jeopardize the work of emancipation of
the champions of German Judaism, and the ethical-religious
task for humanity."

The third approach was Zionism, which Herzl made passionately alive as a form of poetry, and which Weizmann over the
weary years molded into politics. Could even Weizmann have
done it, without Hitler? When they told Herzl he was dreaming,
he said that "if you will it, it is no dream"—a noble answer, but
untrue. It ignored the main problem: too many Jews and too
little room. Even today, might not Russia hope to break the
economy of Israel by letting loose her millions of Jews, assuming
that the millions are discontented and would like to move? Herzl
himself, in his less romantic moods, saw that he was somewhat
ahead of time. "We are not yet desperate enough," he wrote in
1895. "We shall have to sink still lower, we shall have to be more
widely insulted, spat upon, mocked, beaten, robbed, and slain
before we are ripe for the idea."

In view of the speed with which all these requirements were

to be met, the sooner the three groups came together the better: the emigration-philanthropists, the rehabilitation-philanthropists, and the lovers of the homeland.

As early as 1923 steps were taken to broaden the base of the Jewish Agency so that those who believed in Hirsch and his ICA and those who believed in the Joint could join hands with the Zionists in the building of Palestine. The Jewish state was the stumbling-block, not the homeland, which was acceptable to all since nobody could define it. The Zionists always intended the state (as Balfour himself may well have done), and many of them disliked working with Jews who intended anything less. Here the wisdom of Weizmann was decisive. If he could get the world's leading Jews working together in a "Jewish Agency for Palestine," he foresaw that history would solve the problem of the homeland versus the state. In 1930—just in time—a new Jewish Agency constitution, which had been ratified at Zurich the previous year, was approved by the British Colonial Office. The Agency included such non-Zionists as Louis Marshall,[1] Léon Blum, and Lord Melchett. They thought they could now keep the "nationalists" from making trouble, but trouble was to be the order of the day for eighteen years.

This unhappy fact had not yet become obvious in New York. In the year of the birth of the new Jewish Agency, Bernhard Kahn (then European director) was called to New York to present arguments as to why the Joint should not abolish itself. "A new Jewish economic structure is in the making," he pled. "The JDC in all these years has done a piece of work such as is unheard of heretofore in Jewish history." In the end, he had to call upon

---

[1] Marshall died after the Zurich Conference and before the ratification by the Colonial Office. Benjamin Cardozo, soon to be a Justice of the Supreme Court of the United States, wrote of Marshall: "One feels that he has somehow been transformed into a great civic institution . . . so that with all his intensely human traits he has acquired, in his own life, a new and, as it were, a corporate personality."

the great Albert Einstein to attend a meeting and insist that the Joint must not die. Yet by 1932 it seemed to be dying of inanition. The depression was at its worst; Franklin Roosevelt was campaigning, and later cabinet-making; little banks were closing, and big ones showed signs of wobbling. Few people (except some journalists, who were dismissed as scaremongers) foresaw that Hitler would become chancellor in January 1933, and that the Third Reich, complete and terrible, would be proclaimed within three weeks of the first inauguration of Roosevelt.

In ignorance of the approaching horror, the Joint had grounds for believing that its work was largely done. It also had grounds for knowing that money was almost impossible to raise. Already in 1929 income had fallen from the $3,500,000 of 1928 to $1,600,-000. And each year thereafter it had diminished, reaching $385,000 in 1932. Mr. Paul Baerwald (about to become chairman) had already warned the executive committee that Jews who still had money to give felt more and more strongly that they should use it at home.

By June of 1932 appropriations for Eastern and Central Europe were reduced to less than one-third of the figures for 1931. The organization was barely ticking over, and if it had not been for the eruption in Germany it would probably have accomplished its heart's desire and ticked itself quietly into the grave. Yet following the eruption, and in spite of the fact that in many fields the American depression was at its worst in 1933, the Joint's income increased threefold that year. Thereafter the climb was steady (with a slight falling off in 1935) until the astonishing three years following the Second War, during which the Joint received $193,597,279. These were years when American taxation seemed high to those who were paying it.

4.

No time was lost by the Germans in carrying out their promises to the Jews. The declared object was to get rid of them all, relieving them of their property en route. In the early days of the new regime it was not thought necessary to kill them, except for a small minority of well-placed people *pour encourager les autres* to get out. But *les autres* needed more than this sharp push from behind. The little people had nowhere to go. The outside world was quick to pass resolutions disapproving of the German "cold pogrom," but it was not quick to amend immigration acts or to offer employment to men and women who arrived with nothing but a suitcase of old clothes. And many Jews of world fame, who were needed and wanted everywhere, remained stubborn German patriots. Weizmann records two examples of this fidelity in spite of all abuse.

The first was Richard Willstätter, winner of the Nobel Prize and professor of chemistry at Munich University. A proud Jew, he resigned his professorship in the middle twenties because of the mounting anti-Semitism of his colleagues. The Bavarian government begged him to return, but he would not. He carried on his work through the Munich Academy of Science. Weizmann asked him repeatedly to move to Palestine. Sir Simon Marks offered him the directorship of the Daniel Sieff Research Institute at Rehovoth—from which has grown the majestic Weizmann Institute of Science, one of the centers of world scholarship. He was happy to preside at the opening of the Sieff Institute in 1934, but even in the shadow of the impending Nuremberg Laws he would not desert his country. "I know that Germany has gone mad," he said, "but if a mother falls ill it is not a reason for her children to leave her. My home is Germany, my university, in spite of what has happened, is in Munich. I must return." He stayed with his ailing "mother" until the Second War started. Then he was expelled and went to Switzerland to die.

The second was Fritz Haber, also a winner of the Nobel Prize for chemistry. Haber, unhappily, may have prolonged the First World War when he was head of the German war chemical services. His process for producing ammonia from the nitrogen in the air gave unlimited supplies of fertilizer to the blockaded Germans. He was not a proud Jew. He was a convert to Christianity, and his family with him. But he was a proud German and had no use for Zionism, which kept reminding him of a history he chose to forget. He was head of one of the greatest institutes of science in the world, at Dahlem, and felt himself as thorough a patriot as any man alive. Yet when Hitler came to power he was thrown out at once, stripped of money, honors, and job. His Christianity was considered a worse insult to the Reich than the Judaism of Willstätter. Or perhaps it was his immense renown which destroyed him. In the new German philosophy Jews were Jews, whatever religion they professed, and they had no business to be more important than other people.

So Haber turned up in London, broken, reformed in his views on Zionism, and asking Weizmann for help. He gladly accepted the offer to go to Palestine. "You will find a modern laboratory," said Weizmann, "and able assistants. You will work in peace and honor." But Haber died on the way, in 1934.

Pity the nation which can find no use for such patriots. Over sixteen centuries of Jewish life in Germany, and Jewish contributions to civilization, were now repudiated. Why? In their times of pride and frenzy, which have been numerous, the Germans have always tended to desert not only Christianity but the classical mythology of Greece, for the bloodthirsty pessimism of the Nordic gods. Why? We can only answer that Hitler was not the first to prefer the *Götterdämmerung* to the Day of Judgment, and that Heine was not the first to be scared of his own country.

Such questions may be fanciful; but the fact remains that eighty million people do not go mad, enthusiastically mad, overnight. Depravity cannot be a simple accident, like an airplane with a dead pilot crashing into Times Square.

If this seems too melodramatic, let us take the careful words of a great public servant, James G. McDonald. In October 1933, Mr. McDonald was appointed by the League of Nations as

"High Commissioner for Refugees (Jewish or other) coming from Germany." [2] After the Nuremberg Laws of September 15, 1935, he submitted his letter of resignation, partly because of what was happening in Germany, but also because nothing was happening (except for private initiative such as the Joint's) in the outside world. First he recapitulated, for those who still insisted that the whole thing was a Jewish exaggeration, the story of the cold pogrom. "More than half a million persons," he wrote, "against whom no charge can be made except that they are not what the National Socialists choose to regard as 'Nordic,' are being crushed. . . . Except for those prepared to sacrifice the whole or greater part of their savings, the official restrictions on export of capital bar the road to escape, and the doors of most countries are closed against impoverished fugitives." He referred to the Nuremberg Laws, which deprived all Jews (and "non-Aryan" Christians such as Haber) of their citizenship and of the hope of earning a living. "Though less than one hundredth part of the total population," he said, "the Jews are held responsible for all the adversity which the German people had to undergo. As in the Middle Ages, when they were massacred and expelled from German States as the cause of the Black Death, so today they are eliminated from the economic and cultural life of Germany and degraded on the ground that they were the cause of the German humiliation. . . . The names of the Jewish war dead may no longer be engraved on war memorials."

He then makes the legal point that in discriminating against "non-Aryans" the government of the Third Reich was violating the express terms of a solemn pledge given at the Peace Conference in June 1919. In other words, grounds existed not only for supplications from the outside, but for interference, if anyone cared.

In conclusion, Mr. McDonald said:

Pity and reason alike must inspire the hope that intercession

[2] Felix Warburg persuaded him to accept the appointment.

will meet with response. Without such response, the problems caused by the persecution of the Jews and the non-Aryans will not be solved by philanthropic action. . . . Convinced as I am that desperate suffering in countries adjacent to Germany, and an even more terrible human calamity within the German frontiers, are inevitable unless present tendencies in the Reich are checked or reversed, I cannot remain silent. . . . I should be recreant if I did not call attention to the actual situation, and plead that world opinion, acting through the League and its Member-States and other countries, move to avert the existing and impending tragedies.

"World opinion," however, was busily pretending that Hitler was not too bad and that the Germans as a whole were good companions, even if a few sadists were taking advantage of the revolution which created the Third Reich. Six months after the Nuremberg Laws Hitler put his troops into the demilitarized zone of the Rhineland. Nobody moved, and few people complained. If Germans on the march across the Rhine were to be treated as agreeable neighbors returning to their own garden, the nations were clearly in no mood to fret about what Germans were doing deep within their borders. "All our countries gave lip service," said Mr. McDonald; "but nobody would do anything. I had to resign."

The ability to do nothing was shown at its finest in the summer of 1938, when President Roosevelt convened the representatives of thirty-two governments at Evian, on the French side of the Lake of Geneva, to discuss whether anyone could help the beleaguered Jews, since the League could not, and since the problem was too vast for voluntary bodies. Such an invitation from America, the historic home of the immigrant, sounded hopeful; but the United States had nothing to offer, aside from the rather niggardly promise to accept immigrants up to the limit fixed by existing law. In other words, though the world might be on fire, America would abide by the isolationist decisions of 1924; but she graciously undertook not to do worse than that.

The Saving Remnant

Australia agreed to receive 5000 refugees a year for three years, which was kind but unlikely to solve any problems. Only the Dominican Republic made a proposal on a scale equivalent to the emergency. General Trujillo said he would take 100,000 Jewish refugees from Germany, and promised land, citizenship, and all religious and civil liberties.[3]

Unhappily, this lone gesture of good will did not come to much. The Joint was wary from the beginning, chiefly because of the climate (and perhaps because it feared dictators *et dona ferentes*). Town-dwelling Jews had become good farmers in the Crimea, but could they survive in the semi-tropical island of Hispaniola? Nevertheless, the Joint asked Joseph Rosen and James Rosenberg—the team which had planned and accomplished the miracle of the Agro-Joint—to go to the Caribbean and explore the chances. The Joint's mild hopes for the plan became yet more mild when Dr. Rosen caught a virulent malaria.

One great good, however, came from this Dominican Republic Settlement Association, which Mr. Rosenberg, in spite of all discouragements, took to his heart. President Trujillo allowed the association, on its own authority, to issue a limited number of Dominican visas to Jews in Germany. Four thousand were issued —equivalent to four thousand permits to go on living. A man with such a visa would be admitted into any neighboring country because he did not appear to be a long-term charge. This may seem a small thing in the midst of wide catastrophe, but it is not given to many to save even four thousand lives.

In the end only a few hundred people remained in the Dominican Republic, at the cost of about five thousand dollars per family. And a few hundred more used it as an escape route to the United States or Canada. The settlers are still there, self-

---

[3] The conference also set up an intergovernmental committee for the resettlement of refugees, with headquarters in London. The chairman was Lord Winterton, who found himself handicapped by the same apathy in high places which had astounded Mr. McDonald.

sufficient nowadays, and doing well enough to contribute to the United Jewish Appeal in North America. General Trujillo has built them a community center, at his own expense, in Ciudad Trujillo, the capital city (better known as Santo Domingo).

Mr. McDonald had been painfully right when he said that "the problems caused by the persecution of the Jews will not be solved by philanthropic action. . . . The efforts of the private organizations can only mitigate a state of growing gravity." French, British, and American Jewish money was available in increasing and surprising quantities, and also the long experience in self-help of international Jewry. But what can private money do when governments declare, "We do not want your victims; take them somewhere else"—and when the foreign offices of the world are intent on placating Germany?

Politicians enjoy talking about "the conscience of mankind," which they tell us is repeatedly wounded by the behavior of other politicians. A study of these years raises the question whether such a thing exists. Let us take an example which has a happy ending but which is none the less a sad comment on our frightened and unbrotherly way of life.

In January 1939, Mr. Morris Troper was in Paris as chairman of the European Executive Council of the Joint. He heard from New York of a plan to charter a steamer from the Hamburg-America Line to take Jews from Germany direct to Cuba. He consulted the leading Jewish emigration association (a combination of the Hebrew Immigrant Aid Society and Hirsch's ICA) and was warned that any Cuban visas held by these Jews would not be honored. A lively black market existed for visas to any corner of the earth, and many consuls—or self-appointed consuls —were not above selling visas which they knew their governments would disavow.

The warning was later confirmed. No permanent visas had been issued for Cuba. And no Jews could land on transit visas unless they were obviously on their way to a country which had al-

The Saving Remnant

ready accepted them. And the same was true, so far as the emigration association knew, of Central and South America. Nevertheless, plans for all this ill-omened journey went forward. The Hamburg-America Line was more than willing. It would charge the Jews everything they possessed for the passage—a round-trip passage, so that if nobody would receive them they could be dumped back into Germany at their own expense. This, of course, would mean a concentration camp and death, for although Jews were still allowed to leave Germany if they could find a place to go, they were not allowed to return without meeting the worst fate.

On May 13 the *St. Louis* sailed from Hamburg with 907 Jews— and a few Christians who had married Jews. On June 4, as anticipated, they were refused admission in Havana Harbor. All but 194 of the passengers were awaiting American visas which would admit them to the United States within six months to two years. Two hundred children were on board. Nevertheless, no one was allowed to land.

After waiting a reasonable time for some nation to suffer a softening of the heart, the Germans ordered the ship back to Hamburg. Mr. Troper in Paris received a cablegram of utter despair from the "Passengers' Committee." Unless the Joint could help, they were doomed. They well knew that in the camps Jews starved like cattle who have been turned out to browse in dry sand. So did the world know this, but the knowledge had no immediate effect. The Joint promised to pay board and lodging for the passengers of the *St. Louis* in any country that would accept them until a permanent home could be found. In addition, it offered a security bond of $500 for each person. This was all it could do, except for Mr. Troper's urgent pleadings with almost every government in Europe. And still nobody acted.

In desperation, Shanghai was suggested as a possible port. But the Germans would have none of this; why waste fuel on Jews? The one concession they made was to order the ship to steam slowly, in case Mr. Troper found a customer for his human cargo. So the anguish was prolonged, while the passengers organized themselves for suicide and Mr. Troper appealed to the foreign offices and even to the kings and queens of the Continent. His appeal was somewhat weakened by the conspicuous inaction of the government of the United States. After all, the *St. Louis* had lain at anchor within a few miles of Miami and other American harbors. And four-fifths of the passengers would end in the United States anyway, if the Germans did not kill them first. The head of the Sûreté Nationale in Paris mildly remarked that it seemed a pity "that our American friends were not able to direct them to one of their own ports instead of urging them upon us." To this the Joint had no answer.

At last the cruelty came to an end. Holland agreed to take 194 of the passengers, the Joint guaranteeing maintenance and posting a bond for each person. Belgium took 250. France, on the same evening, offered room for 250, and the next day England agreed to match France's offer. Mr. Troper joined the small group of men who have been responsible for saving a great many lives. When he went on board off Flushing, to prepare for the sorting-out process at Antwerp, a girl of eleven said to him, "We regret exceedingly that flowers do not grow on the ship; otherwise you would have had the largest and most beautiful bouquet." They had been at sea for thirty-five days.[4]

5.

The Joint had moved its European headquarters from Berlin to Paris when Hitler became Chancellor, and had prepared to

---

[4] In the end, when Mr. Troper had dealt with the problems of keeping family groups together, of not separating lifelong friends if possible, and of trying to place refugees in countries where they had relatives, the figures were: England, 288; France, 224; Belgium, 214; Holland, 181; the United States, o.

start again from the beginning—back to emergency actions, back to relief, farewell to Bernhard Kahn's happy boast of 1931: "A new Jewish economic structure [for Eastern and Central Europe] is in the making." With the help of the world-wide economic depression the infection of the Third Reich's policies spread eastward rapidly onto fertile soil. By 1935 a million Jews in Poland had been driven from their jobs. "The hope of gradual recovery for the Jewish masses has gone," said a report to the Joint. In Romania the rot was almost as sudden and complete.

The Joint, however, could still send money and goods and encouragement to these countries. And the cultural institutions, which it had helped to rebuild, still survived. (The United Polish Appeal of Great Britain raised £50,000 in 1936 and handed it to the Joint for such use as it saw fit.) But in Germany the synagogues were mostly closed. The community centers were mostly destroyed. And the one thing the Joint could not bring itself to do was to nourish the Third Reich with dollars.

At least four hundred and fifty thousand Jews remained in Germany at the end of 1935, more than a hundred thousand having escaped. The Joint, of course, could help the émigrés once they left Germany. Indeed, it bore more than sixty per cent of the costs of this migration—to Palestine or to lands of temporary refuge. But the money and the vigor of those who stayed behind were ebbing fast. The chances for escape were diminishing—not because of the Germans, who still wanted to get rid of them all, but because no nation would receive them penniless. And the life of a Jewish child in a German school— even if he was allowed to attend—had become intolerable. So the children had to be taught at Jewish expense, by communities whose members were no longer allowed to earn. Clearly, the Joint had to invent a way of helping the communities without helping the Reich.

This was a new problem in the long Jewish fight for survival. The million Jews who fled Russia after the pogroms of 1881 and

1882 found the doors of the world open, especially the doors of the United States. But in 1935 no room could be found for the half-million who should have fled Germany. If admitted to refuge at all, in any large numbers, they were expected to "move on." The Joint could often postpone the move by paying for the refugees' keep. In 1934 and 1935 it spent a quarter of a million dollars on this delaying project in France alone. Yet far too many of the refugees knew that in the end there was nowhere to go. They were left without home or hope. If they returned to Germany—as ten thousand, in their desperation, did—they went straight to a concentration camp, which in those days, as we have said, meant painfully slow death, since the machinery for efficient slaughter had not yet been devised.

The first invention of the Joint, to meet the problem of how to help Jews without helping Germany, was to promise repayment in dollars for marks deposited in Germany—either with the local communities or with the Central Committee for Jewish Relief.[5] If children could be smuggled out, the Joint would then pay in dollars for their education. If adult emigrants could acquire visas for any country, near or far, the Joint would care for them in transit and pay their passage in dollars. Meanwhile the marks they left behind would be a contribution from the Joint to the work of the Central Committee. And if the donors did in fact escape, they would get their money back in the currency of any country not dominated by Germany.

This system, begun tentatively as a modest, hopeful experiment, grew to great importance during the war. World-wide, in lands conquered by the Germans or the Japanese, Jews gave all they had to local organizations which had been approved by the

[5] "Zentral Ausschuss der deutschen Juden für Hilfe und Aufbau," set up in 1933, after Hitler became Chancellor, for the purpose of "supporting the Jewish economic position in Germany" (vain hope), "supporting groups which intend to emigrate . . . and supporting those who intend to establish themselves in Palestine." The Joint and the Central British Fund for German Jewry made this committee a chief beneficiary.

Joint, against the promise of the Joint to repay later. About thirteen million dollars were thus raised, for work behind the enemy lines. Occasionally the local or central committees would be raided and burgled by "Aryans"; but on the whole the committees were good at concealing their assets.

Sometimes records could be kept of the gifts or loans; but often, as in Poland, the only record would be the word of some stray survivor. In 1959 claims were still being made, and honored, on behalf of participants in these most unorthodox deals.

A second method for helping the Jews with dollars without helping the Reich was the Transmigration Bureau. Even after the war began—until the "final solution" was proclaimed early in 1942—Jews were allowed, almost encouraged, to leave Germany and some German-occupied countries, so long as they took nothing with them. But the prospective emigrant, if traveling overseas, could buy his passage only in dollars, which of course he did not possess. The steamship companies would accept no other currency. So the Joint's Transmigration Bureau provided the dollars in return for local funds deposited with approved committees. Thus, again, the Joint's work was financed in the homeland while the emigrant had his chance to get out—at an average cost of $500.

The bureau also welcomed deposits in New York from friends and relatives of would-be emigrants, whether from Germany or from occupied Europe. Five or six hundred people a day would besiege the office, offering money and the last known address of the person or family to be saved. Twenty-two thousand deposits were accepted, amounting to $5,500,000. Some 40,000 lives might have been saved by these gifts; but in the end the Joint sadly refunded $3,850,000, representing the men and women who never got out.

The bureau did not deal with the refugee directly, but only with the local Jewish Emigrant Aid Committee in Germany, Austria, Czechoslovakia, Holland, Belgium, or Luxembourg. The committee would notify the bureau that a deposit had been made, or the bureau would send word abroad that a friend had put up the money in New York. The committee in Europe would then make the arrangements, and the bureau would pay the bills.

The Transmigration Bureau, a wise and good invention, came to an end on the day of Pearl Harbor.

Chapter Four

All during the thirties the Joint was learning, painfully and reluctantly, "with many farewell pious looks behind," that its great
work of reconstruction in Eastern and Central Europe was not to
endure, and that after the Hitlerian upheaval, and a second
desperate effort at rescue, most of the non-Zionist Jews would
come to recognize Palestine as the haven for the large majority of
survivors. In view of the difficulty in persuading non-Jewish
Americans, as late as 1941, that the nation was in danger and
must help to win the war or else find itself the next victim on
Hitler's list, one cannot wonder that American Jews during the
thirties (who lived just as far from the Rhine as their gentile
neighbors) would not take to heart the gory promises of *Mein
Kampf*. The delusions of the members of "America First," who
protested until the last hour that Hitler had no unkind thoughts
toward what he called "the mongrel race of Americans," were
more inexplicable than the delusions of the assimilated Jews
who feared Zionism. Had there been any place on earth where

the door was even ajar, the Joint would probably have admitted that at all cost the Jews of Eastern and Central Europe must be removed from their encroaching prison.

In 1933, 8,000,000 Jews lived in the old Pale of Settlement in Hungary and in Galicia. What could the tiny British mandate do for them? How could the Joint resist the hope that they might still be made secure in their own homes? The policy of flight, since there was nowhere to flee, was a policy of despair. When the ship is unquestionably sinking, or when the pass has indubitably been sold, the officers in charge may decide to die where they stand and to issue the dreadful order, *sauve qui peut*. But the Joint was not in charge. It was the friend from far away who had come to help. Perhaps the only effective help was to join the Zionists in seeking to force the door of Palestine. But since the British government was pushing the door tighter shut each year, and showed signs of locking and bolting it once and for all, a group of private citizens in America might be excused for not declaring war on the empire. Nevertheless, the Joint was mildly criticized by its friends and fellow workers in England for not saying *sauve qui peut*.

We have mentioned the Central British Fund for German Jewry, which was founded in 1933 with the same sense of urgency that had inspired the birth of the Joint in 1914. The title of the British organization suggests that it too had little perception of the impending horror. The Jews of Germany were insignificant in number, though great in scholarship and in knowledge of finance. East and southeast of Germany lived the time-honored Jewish civilization and the largest Jewish community on earth. The Joint knew this of old, from the First War—knew it in its bones, just as Chaim Weizmann from the Pale of Settlement knew it. The Joint thought in terms of the nine millions, not of the five hundred thousand. Thinking on that scale, it had to think of supporting the millions where they were, not of getting them out to nonexistent havens. Only in desperation could it abandon the majority to save the few. The Joint never consciously, deliberately, reached that stage until the Germans made the decision simple by killing the overwhelming majority and leaving the few.

"Simply because the JDC exists," said Joseph Schwartz, who became acting European Director in the gloomy year of 1941, "the Jews it cannot reach take hope." And Paul Baerwald, the second chairman of the Joint, wrote in 1936 of "the difference between their feeling that we are standing by them and the crucial hopelessness of feeling themselves forsaken."

In that same year of 1936 the Central British Fund sent three emissaries to New York to enlist the Joint more strongly in the effort to help Jews escape from Germany: Sir Herbert Samuel, Lord Bearsted, and Simon (later Sir Simon) Marks. They wanted an international Council for German Jewry, with a fund of £3,000,000. The Joint was glad to give money and to lend the Council such renowned members as Felix Warburg and Paul Baerwald. There, on the Council, the Joint worked with the leading American Zionists, such as Rabbi Stephen Wise and Morris Rothenberg. But the old question rose at once to trouble them: Where were the emigrants to go? If Palestine was the only answer (and a very small one), the Joint would help in so far as it did not feel committed to Jewish nationalism. "In view of the later developments of Jewish-American opinion in relation to Palestine," wrote Norman Bentwich when describing the problems of the Council, "the emphasis which at this time it [i.e., the Joint] laid on the help of European communities and on emigration to other countries [i.e., not Palestine] appears remarkable."

Thus the debate continued, not only across the Atlantic but among the directors of the JDC in New York. We can establish the exact moment when the policy changed by reviewing, over the years, the diverse schemes for raising money. At first the three groups which invented the JDC made their separate contributions. Then for a decade the funds came from national campaigns for Jewish relief. In 1930, when the Jewish Agency was broadened to include non-Zionists, a united appeal was launched to serve both the Joint and the Jewish Agency—the Joint to receive about 60 per cent of the take. For the next seven years the Joint either went to the public on its own or joined in a united appeal —always wary lest it become tarred with Zionism. The crisis came in 1938, when the Joint was asked to take part in a United Jewish Appeal which would become the sole support of the Joint and of the uninhibited Zionists.

The Joint was unhappy and self-divided. In the executive committee some members argued lukewarmly that this was the surest way to raise money. Others argued heatedly that they would rather forgo the money than be associated with those who preached that Jews were a nation rather than a religion, or rather than an assimilated secular group within each nation. James Rosenberg pointed out that under this new plan no contributor could know whether he was supporting what he approved or what he hated. And the division of funds was unfair: too much for Palestine, too little for Europe. Rabbi Jonah Wise said that if helping the Jews of Europe meant imposing Zionism on American Jewry, he might rather not help.

On November 9, 1938, the committee accepted in principle the Rosenberg-Wise position—but not for long. That night, November 9 to 10, was Kristall Nacht in Germany, the Night of Broken Glass. Within forty-eight hours the hopes and plans of world Jewry were changed forever. The old game was up. Too late to defend all the ships; the time had come to tell the convoy to scatter. Nobody could foresee precisely how many million Jews the Germans would soon have at their disposal, but everybody who was interested (or perhaps "disinterested" is the word) now knew that *Mein Kampf* meant exactly what it said.

At 2 A.M. on November 10 a planned attack was launched against the Jews of Germany. All night and all the following day were given over to burning, beating, and looting. The SS men were organized in squads and armed with picks, crowbars, and axes. At the Dachau concentration camp ten thousand smocks ornamented with the Star of David had been prepared for the neighboring Jews who were awaited.

The "spontaneous" riots were systematic in the best German fashion. Nine out of the twelve synagogues in Berlin were burned; the remaining three were close to "Aryan" buildings that must not be endangered. Stores, offices, cafés, and homes were demolished throughout the land. Personal effects were stolen, furniture smashed, cemeteries desecrated. Orphanages, old-age homes, and hospitals were evacuated and the buildings turned to rubble. Meanwhile, as an incidental pleasure, Jews were beaten and murdered. Many committed suicide. Damages for the eighteen hours were estimated at a billion marks.

The next day Goebbels announced that Kristall Nacht was "an intensive expression of the justifiable and understandable anger of the German nation." He was referring to the murder, by a young Jew, of a minor German diplomat in Paris.

On November 12 the Jews were fined a further billion marks, on the ground that they were responsible for the riots. And they were ordered to repair, at their own expense, all the damage done. Insurance payments were to be confiscated by the government. And after January 1, 1939, no Jew was to operate his own business, and no Jew was to enter a theater, a museum, café, or other place of assembly. All Jewish males between the ages of seventeen and sixty were to be arrested and sent to concentration camps. Most of them were released within a month, but thirty-five thousand were not heard from again.

Kristall Nacht inspired Rabbi Hillel Silver's message to the Joint: "You can no longer separate the problems of Palestine and Europe." James Rosenberg, the most articulate of the non-Zionists, agreed. History demanded that there be no more dissension. The executive committee reversed the decision of November 9. In 1939 the Joint merged with the United Palestine Appeal to form the United Jewish Appeal, which from that day to this has raised more than $1,250,000,000. Rabbi Jonah Wise and Mr. Rosenberg become devoted friends of Israel and of the UJA.

Ironically, during the very year of this reconciliation the British issued the White Paper which in effect made Zionism an illegal conspiracy. The paper declared that only 75,000 Jews could enter Palestine during the next five years. Thereafter Jewish immigration would be subject to Arab control—which meant no Jews at all. The sale of land to Jews would be forbidden or closely restricted over most of the country. And in 1949 the British would set up an independent Palestinian government, in which Arabs and Jews would be represented in proportion to their numbers.

The Balfour Declaration was thus formally buried. The Jewish national home was to be governed by Arabs, and the national state must not be discussed. But here too history intervened. In the not-so-long run, the launching of the United Jewish Appeal proved more important than the British White Paper. The relentless postwar insistence upon the birth of Israel might have been defeated without this union of the two main groups in America. And incidentally, the fight for the national state called the world's attention to the "new" Jew who has been such a surprise to people who are ignorant of history. The "typical Jew" is no longer "the suffering servant" or the starving scholar in a Yeshiva, but Yehuda Arazi,[1] a combination of the Scarlet Pimpernel and the most dangerous pirate on the Spanish Main. The gentle, unconquerable scholars kept Judaism alive through twenty centuries; but when the time came to build the third commonwealth of Israel the renascent Maccabees took charge. Neither the Germans nor the British foresaw or comprehended the Arazis of the postwar world.

2.

The story of the Joint, and of world Jewry since 1914, cannot be told without an occasional note of unkindness toward British

[1] See pages 297-307.

The Saving Remnant

policy in Palestine. Let us, however, pay tribute to the work of British Jews (side by side with the Joint wherever possible), and to the generosity of British governments at home. These governments may well have had troubled consciences over the mandate; but they also had the Arabs and the Arab oil to consider, not to mention the Germans, the Italians, and the ambiguous Russians. Who can say—at least until the Second War had been won—that their decisions were not forced upon them?[2]

In 1935 the Central British Fund promised the Home Office that no Jewish refugee who was allowed into England would ever become a charge on public funds. This led to many relaxations of harsh rules. Yet when the war began the fund was released from half of its obligation, because the government knew that thousands of Jews who had been brought to Britain in all good faith "in transit" were now necessarily residents "for the duration."

The Central British Fund (with its offspring, the Council for German Jewry) helped about twenty thousand Jews a year to emigrate from Germany—some to Palestine and the rest overseas or to their East European countries of origin. "It is a tragic reflection," writes Norman Bentwich, "that so near to the outbreak of the Second World War, the fatal insecurity of East European Jewry was not adequately recognized." The reflection is at least as tragic for the Joint as for the Central British Fund. Worst of all, perhaps, is the reflection that while Jews were being saved from the Third Reich on a retail basis the Germans were acquiring new ones wholesale: 210,000 in Austria, in March of 1938;

[2] The efforts of the British Jews to save Germans, Austrians, and Czechs, and the helpfulness of British governments, have been told by Professor Norman Bentwich in an excellent book: *They Found Refuge* (London: Cresset Press, 1956). Here we can only summarize a few points. The close relations between the Central British Fund and the Joint—especially after the war, when the Joint opened a branch office in London—are made clear by Professor Bentwich throughout.

230,000 in Czechoslovakia, in March of 1939; and then, when the war began, the majority of the Jews in the world (including at least 350,000 in Western Europe plus another 130,000 refugees waiting helplessly in Vichy France).

The day before Kristall Nacht only 5500 Jewish refugees had reached England from Germany. Nine months later, at least 80,000 had arrived—a higher proportion per capita than any other country accepted in that year of dread.[3] A large number of the British sponsors for these rescued people were non-Jewish. The Home Secretary, Sir Samuel Hoare (later Lord Temple-wood), lifted the passport restrictions for children, and also for adults who were offered bona fide jobs as servants or as minor employees in business firms. (The "minor" has to do with trade unions, not with the government.)

Long afterward, in his autobiography, Lord Templewood lamented that he had not coaxed the medical profession into accepting more German and Austrian doctors and surgeons. "When war came," he wrote, "how great was the country's gain from the new diaspora. How much greater it might have been if professional interests had not restricted the scope."

Three million pounds were spent by the Fund in five and a half years—not including the many thousands of guarantees by British citizens (Jew and gentile) to take full responsibility for immigrants. Each guarantee was a life saved, and it is written that he who has saved one man is as if he had saved the world.

Most heartwarming of all the British efforts was the Children's Movement, under the chairmanship of the Protestant Lord Gorell. With the help of the Home Secretary, between the spring and the sad September of 1939, 9354 children were brought from Germany and Austria into so-called safety—mostly Jews, but with a scattering of "unreliable" Aryans, both Roman Catholics and

[3] The Jewish Refugees Committee had 60,000 on their list. More than an additional 20,000 were privately sponsored—excluding the Children's Movement.

Protestants. They had no prospect but the grave, had not England opened her arms. Some were hopefully en route to friends and relatives in other countries; but the war stopped that.[4]

Oddly, according to British law, children could not be scattered among private homes all over the island unless each of them had a guardian. So Parliament passed the Guardianship (Refugee Children) Act in record time, and much to his surprise Lord Gorell found himself the custodian of the lot. "It is simple," he wrote, "unusual—and also, as it happens, truthful—to be able to say that I have had more children, legally, than any man since Solomon."

The quiet, generous kindness of British families made the Children's Movement a triumph. Almost every child snatched from the edge of Belsen or some equivalent hell was rehabilitated and made whole in the course of a fierce war—though "child" was not always the appropriate word by the time Lord Gorell got one of them off his hands. Many were married by 1946; many had changed or abandoned their faith; and in each case Lord Gorell, as guardian, had to say "yes" or "no." Yet there can scarcely have been a more rewarding task than to preside over the salvation of so many boys and girls who had been carefully, methodically doomed.

3.

The war began early for the Joint. During the first few days of September 1939, the Luftwaffe half destroyed its office building in Warsaw and wholly destroyed one of its schools, where 120 students were working. Then, while the brief war of annihilation proceeded, the Joint and the Jewish cultural agencies moved to Pinsk. They returned clandestinely after the surrender of Warsaw on September 27—and, as we have seen, during the eight months

---

[4] Twenty-six escaped overseas in 1942, and 138 in 1943.

The Saving Remnant

before Pearl Harbor the Germans allowed the Joint to have an official headquarters in the Warsaw Ghetto.

This decision seems truly eccentric. Within a fortnight of the invasion of Russia the *Einsatzgruppen* of the SS were practicing for "the final solution" on all Jews available in the conquered territories. During the next four months they killed about three hundred and fifty thousand—mostly by shooting them into mass graves, although for children and for the inmates of hospitals and asylums they tried the newly invented gas-vans which made use of the carbon monoxide from their own exhausts. This sounds a convenient and economical device, but it proved disappointing. The motors stalled,[5] the vans leaked, and in too many cases the victims had to be shot anyway. Soon the Germans realized that it was pointless and expensive to murder the same person twice, so they turned their ingenuity from gas-vans to the hydrogen-cyanide chambers and the enormous ovens of Auschwitz. Yet these too were unsatisfactory.

Rudolph Hoess, the commandant of Auschwitz, never stopped complaining to Heydrich (and later to Himmler) that he was asked to produce first-class results with third-class tools. And we can see what he meant when we reflect that his best day, on his own boastful estimate, was 16,000 dead, burned, and with the bones ready for grinding to powder. But meanwhile 20,000 new Jews from all over Europe had detrained in the marshaling yards at Auschwitz. So even Hoess, falling far behind in turning raw material into the desired product, was compelled to resort to mass shootings into mass graves. This, of course, wasted the bones, and since Germany was short of fertilizer, Hoess felt him-self rebuked.

Auschwitz, however, was the second stage. The first stage was Russia, and the amateurish gas-vans, and the consequent mass extermination (or "resettlement," as they called it) under the

[5] Any garage mechanic could explain why the motors repeatedly stalled, but the reason is too unpleasant to appear in print.

The Saving Remnant

eyes of the Wehrmacht. And what does appear unusual is that the Joint was allowed to operate openly in Warsaw at a time when the elimination of Jews was on such a scale, and of such notoriety, that Field Marshal Walter von Reichenau and Generals von Küchler and von Monstein all felt obliged to post the following order of the day:

> The soldier in the Eastern Territories is not merely a fighter according to the rules of the art of war but also the bearer of a ruthless national ideology . . . therefore the soldier must have understanding of the necessity of a severe but just revenge on subhuman Jewry.

The meaning of those words, "severe but just," was clarified by Göring in an instruction to Heydrich on July 31, 1941:

> I herewith commission you to carry out all preparations with regard to the organization, the material side and financial viewpoints, for a total solution of the Jewish question in those territories of Europe which are under German influence. . . . I furthermore commission you to submit to me as soon as possible a draft showing the administrative, material, and financial measures already taken for the execution of the intended final solution of the Jewish question.[6]

How can we explain a policy of killing all Jews in conquered territory while permitting the Joint to foster and encourage the Jews of Warsaw? First, we should remember that "the final solution" was not proclaimed by the Führer himself until early in 1942, after America was in the war. Perhaps Hitler, in 1941, was still thinking of dumping his Jews into a far-off penal camp—Madagascar, or some uncomfortable corner of Russia after he had conquered it. Schacht had proposed this, at least for the Jews in Germany. And Alfred Rosenberg had proposed it for the entire 15,000,000 of the world's Jewry: an ambitious project, since

[6] For the German text, see Gerald Reitlinger, *The Final Solution* (New York: Thomas Yoseloff, 1953), page 83, footnote.

the first step must be to conquer the United States and export her 5,000,000.

The Schacht plan was to blackmail all the Jews of the outside world into paying for this migration. In December 1938, he proposed to Lord Winterton and Lord Bearsted that the assets of German Jews should be seized and used as security for an international loan. These stolen marks (perhaps 1,500,000,000) would thus be translated into foreign credit, and in return Germany would finance a gradual emigration from the Reich over a period of five years.

In other words, the Germans got the money, the democracies got the Jews (propertyless, but with their tickets paid at least as far as London), and then what happened? The French were to provide Madagascar, and the hundreds of millions of pounds and dollars that would subsequently be needed would come from Lord Bearsted's committee in London, the Joint in America, and all Rothschilds everywhere. This may sound demented, but compared with the so-called logic of "the final solution" it shows a form of intelligence.

If such notions were still simmering in Hitler's brain as late as 1941, he might seek to have his minions remain on speaking terms with the Joint, the only reservoir of rich Jews to which he still had access. And he would not think it inconsistent to allow Göring (the Reichsmarschall who would be in charge of the permanent "resettlement," if it came to that) to test the latest death-traps meanwhile.

Furthermore, as Gerald Reitlinger points out, two "Jewish problems" were nagging at Hitler's mind, although he never distinguished them with clarity. The first was "the conspiracy of world Jewry" as outlined in his favorite forgery, *The Protocols of the Learned Elders of Zion*. This "conspiracy," he reiterated, had beaten Germany in the First War, had imposed the Treaty of Versailles, had robbed his country between the wars, and was also a skillful combination of capitalism and communism at their worst. Again, in order to deal with this sinister affair he would have to conquer the United States either in his present war or in his next.

The second "problem" was that of the 9,000,000 Jews to the east and the southeast of the Reich: the Yiddish civilization. This, at least, was not a myth. Hitler had met members of this civilization and he hated them as the purest examples of the "non-Aryan." They were the "subhuman Jewry" of Reichenau's order of the day. And Hitler had grounds for his distaste: these cultivated people could never—even after his favorite "thousand years"—find the Third Reich respect-worthy. Killing them, however, would have no effect on his imagined "money-power," since the Elders of Zion must reside in Moscow and Wall Street.

Hitler's predicament, caught between his real Jews and his invented demons, is shown in a favorite statement which he made to the Reichstag early in 1939 and which he proudly repeated five times during the war: "If the international Jewish financiers inside and outside Europe should again succeed in plunging the nations into a world war, the result will be not the bolshevization of the earth and thus the victory of Jewry, but the annihilation of the Jewish race throughout Europe."

Here was his unresolved quandary. The "Jewish race throughout Europe" meant mostly the 9,000,000 of Galicia and the old Pale of Settlement, whereas the "Jewish financiers," whose machinations explained every German setback, lived mostly—if at all—in the United States. Perhaps it was a comfort to Hitler to declare war on America and get all his Jews—men, women, and ghosts—into the same basket. This declaration of war was almost the only promise to an ally which he ever kept.

In any case, the Führer's divided mind, or something equally confusing, gave the Joint eight months of protected life in Warsaw. Thus the Joint became part of the new Ghetto. It was still there and still at work, underground, in May of 1943, when the last building collapsed on almost the last Jew.

The Saving Remnant

During the first war year the Joint in Warsaw continued its work much as usual, concentrating on trade schools, orphaned children, and medical aid. It also supported centers for the repair of shoes and clothes, and sent money for artisans who had lost their tools during the twenty-six-day blitz. The chief innovation was that the Joint now ran soup kitchens for children and for refugees from the surrounding countryside, bewildered and terrified people who had been expelled from their homes by German or Russian troops and who sought to lose themselves, and perhaps to gain some animal comfort of propinquity and warmth, by merging with the hundreds of thousands of their fellows in the capital city. They should not have swarmed into Warsaw. They should have hidden in the country and lived on grass, or starved, rather than present themselves, so conveniently gathered together, for Treblinka.

Until September of 1941, when the Ghetto post office was forbidden to handle foreign mail or parcels, large sums of money were collected by the community leaders against the credit of the Joint. Even those Jews who did not admit that they were to be killed were well aware that they were to be robbed. Many of them, therefore, turned in all they possessed, naming somebody in the non-German hemisphere as beneficiary. The Joint would pay the "somebody" in dollars. The Jewish community of Warsaw would spend the zlotys in buying food and policemen. And not an extra penny became available for the Reich to steal.

Meanwhile, in October 1940, the Ghetto had been proclaimed. The 80,000 Christians who moved out of the area found themselves comfortable in the houses of the 150,000 Jews who moved in; but the comfort was not reciprocal. The best efforts of the Joint from now on were described by an inmate as "a pebble thrown into a bottomless pit." Yet the pebble had a spiritual worth which does not normally attach to pieces of stone; it was the last contact with world Jewry, with the community that suffers together and that always tries to help.

The Saving Remnant

Needless to say, since "non-Aryans" are not necessarily saints, this influx of recently rich Jews, loaded with such wealth as they could lay their hands on, was not an uplifting event. Most of them refused to give their goods to the community. They preferred a final fling. The police at the gates were still Poles, and easy to bribe. In the midst of the dissolution and the hunger, therefore, excellent black-market restaurants sprang up, and excellent brothels.

> Let molten coin be thy damnation. . . . [said Timon of Athens]
> This yellow slave will knit and break religions.

Yet in a strange way that last flowering of human sinfulness in the midst of high tragedy provides the Aristotelian note of pity and terror.

Even the poor gave evidence that Jews share the common faults of man. "Hysterical competition for a crust of bread and a place to sleep, under the constant threat of death from starvation or a German bullet, can destroy humanity in human beings," wrote Bernard Goldstein, who was present. "There were signs that we might become a mob in panic, each individual rushing for safety for himself, trampling anyone who stood in his way." [7] Here too the faraway Joint had the privilege of helping. Tenement committees were set up, elected by the residents, to relieve the most needy, to prevent evictions when possible, to staff kindergartens and communal kitchens, and to care for the sick. The committees also collected small, pathetic lending libraries of religious books and of legal and illegal literature. The tenement committees, a thousand strong before the days of Treblinka, became the chief agencies for the work of the Joint.

Food parcels were of course sent abundantly, and until the closing of the Ghetto post office many of them were delivered. Thereafter they were allowed to accumulate in the old building, so that the half-starved Jews could have a look at them. They

[7] *The Stars Bear Witness* (New York: Viking, 1949).

then were collected and removed in German trucks. Yet even after Pearl Harbor, as we have said, the Joint got almost a million dollars into the Ghetto—and money meant food so long as the SS and the Polish police remained normally corrupt. Four hundred thousand of these dollars were dropped by the Royal Air Force in packages of a hundred thousand-dollar bills. (In 1947 the Joint learned that $340,000 of these had in fact reached the Ghetto underground.) The rest of the money came either through a secret route established by the Polish government-in-exile in London, or through the ingenuity of a heroic Swiss, Saly Mayer, without whom much of the Joint's wartime work would have been impossible and who has a section to himself later in this book.

At first the food-smugglers, if caught, were fined a thousand zlotys or jailed for six months. Then the price was raised to ten thousand zlotys or a year. Finally, in October 1941, the death penalty was decreed. Since the official food ration was 800 calories a day, none of these punishments was effective: either you died quickly by a bullet, or you brought your family something to eat. So long as the money lasted—and mysteriously it did last—smuggling thrived. At one point, according to Emmanuel Ringelblum, the smuggling was so efficient that it caused a shortage of bread on "the Aryan side," as the Jews called the non-Ghetto Warsaw. This was the situation that made Hitler lose his easily exhausted patience and decree the "resettlement" at Treblinka.

According to Ringelblum, the Ghetto had 430,000 inmates in the summer of 1941, and 380,000 were still alive when the deportations began. At the time of the first tentative uprising, in February 1943, Ringelblum believed that only 40,000 Jews remained. These figures must be approximations, although the Oneg Sabbath made as careful a census as possible. SS Major General Stroop, who was in charge (after the major uprising of April 1943) of destroying the Ghetto and all its inhabitants, denied that he had such a paltry enemy. In his official report, which reads like the most biting sarcasm of Swift or Voltaire, he wrote:

> The resistance put up by the Jews and bandits could be broken only by energetically and relentlessly using our raiding parties by day and night. . . . The longer the resistance lasted, the tougher the men of the Waffen-SS, Police, and Wehrmacht became; here, too, they fulfilled their duty indefatigably in faithful comradeship, and resisted as models and examples of soldiers. . . . Only through the continuous and untiring work of all forces did we succeed in catching a total of fifty-six thousand and sixty-five Jews whose extermination can be proved. To this figure should be added the number of Jews who lost their lives in explosions, fires, and so on; but those numbers could not be ascertained.[8]

This message of self-congratulation was written by a soldier who had flame-throwers, armed cars, and artillery at his disposal and who was fighting starved men, women, and children equipped with pistols, a few hand-grenades, and an occasional Molotov cocktail. The German casualties were sixteen dead and ninety wounded. The Wehrmacht, with all its faults, has a record of dangerous bravery. Perhaps it was not too pleased by this flattery from a mere SS General.

Some of the pistols and grenades, incidentally, may redound to the credit of the Joint—or of the cash which the Joint had smuggled in. The chief source of supply for the Ghetto's armament was an Italian division which had been withdrawn from the Russian front in February but which was still resting in Galicia in May of 1943. Combining humanity with business, the

[8] See "The report of Jürgen Stroop, Concerning the Uprising in the Ghetto of Warsaw and the Liquidation of the Jewish Residential Area (including photocopies of Stroop's daily reports and some photographs of his pictorial report)" (Warsaw, 1958), pages 24-26. Stroop thought so highly of this report that he had it bound in leather and typed on the most rare and expensive paper.

The Saving Remnant

Italians sold pistols to the Jews, and also transport to the lucky few who had escaped from Warsaw. The price of an Italian pistol in Lvov was 2000 zlotys, or about $150.

Whatever we may think of SS Major General Stroop, he was right in claiming that "there were no more Jewish dwellings in Warsaw." And he was almost right in claiming that there were no more Jews. Such a hopeless last stand, wherein everybody must infallibly be killed, may sometimes be regrettable—but not this time. The Jews had done a deed of the same symbolic importance as the Alamo—where, as in the Ghetto, everyone was doomed, but where everyone chose to die grandly rather than seek terms with an implacable foe. The uprising in the Ghetto, as Gerald Reitlinger says, was "the first national military struggle of the Jews since the rebellion of Bar Kochba in the reign of Hadrian." It was also the world's introduction to the "new" Jew who has proved so surprising.

Two out of the three leaders of the Joint in Warsaw were dead by the time the Ghetto was destroyed. The Germans had murdered Isaac Giterman and Leo Neustadt; but David Guzik remained. And while Guzik lived, some shadow of the Joint lived with him. Yet Guzik, who survived the unsurvivable, was not the fighter type. Nor did he seem tough enough to surmount all plagues, including typhus, starvation, and the Germans. He represented that side of the Joint which insists on accurate accounts and careful use of Other People's Money.[9] Bernard Goldstein gives an amusing description of him at a time when he and the Joint were being importuned for more money to buy more arms. "He had worked in a bank," said Goldstein, "and had never lost the habit of measuring all organizational problems in terms of money. . . . He . . . had no markedly 'Jewish' features, but he was extremely pious. . . . He had a weakness for Orthodox Jews, and they seldom left his office without getting what they wanted if it was in his power to grant it. A long black coat, a gray

[9] See page 150.

107

beard, and sideburns always made him forget his banker's training." This pious bank clerk does not sound like a man who "rides
in the whirlwind and directs the storm." Yet Guzik is one of the
two enduring and recurring types which the Joint breeds.[10]

All over the world, in bizarre outposts during the war and in
capital cities during peace, a fruitful struggle, or dialogue, takes
place between the two types. The first is impatient and impetu-
ous. "Our people are being killed and kicked about." (At all times
this will be true somewhere.) "We must rush to their aid at any
cost and do the accounting later." And the other character in
the dialogue is equally ardent but more in the habit of "measuring organizational problems in terms of money," especially when
it is other people's money. He likes to know, first, that the money
is in the bank or at least pledged, and second, that every penny
is squeezed until it squeaks and that none of its usefulness is lost.
Perhaps "dialectic" would be a better word than "dialogue," because out of this struggle comes the synthesis: the job gets done
and the pennies get squeezed. So much is this true that when the
donors—the "other people" who provide the pennies—are told
that no explanation can be given for an expenditure, they say
confidently, "Much good must have come from that money,
since they do not dare tell us how it was spent."

Mr. Gitler-Barski of Warsaw had worked since the First War
on many projects sponsored by the Joint. During the abortive uprising in the Ghetto of February 1943, he escaped to the outside
with his wife and child and was given shelter by a Polish family.
In April the Germans decreed that all families hiding Jews would
thenceforth be put to death. So for the sake of his friends Gitler-
Barski fled, and was captured and sent to Belsen. At Belsen the

---

[10] The terrible years in the Ghetto changed Guzik, bringing out qualities
of leadership and imagination which Bernard Goldstein never divined. By
the end of the war he had become a militant Zionist of the type which has
made Israel. Yet the prudent accountant, as seen by Goldstein, is an authentic character in the panorama of the Joint.

The Saving Remnant

Jews of different nations were kept in separate but contiguous pens. One day some Hungarians in the next pen heard that Gitler-Barski had worked for the Joint. They asked to speak to him through the barbed wire. They had nothing much to say; they merely wanted to gossip about Joseph Schwartz, the European Director of the Joint whose name had become a legend because he always attempted the impossible. They found consolation merely in talking about him. Fifteen years later Mr. Gitler-Barski still marveled at the power of a good man's name, even in that seventh circle of hell.

After his time in Belsen, Gitler-Barski returned to a dead Warsaw which was almost empty of Jews. There he found Guzik, whose first words were, "We must restart the Joint." This they did, and at first all went well. The provisional government in Poland, not yet Communized, not yet purged of all associations with the old government-in-exile in London, was informal and helpful. It granted visas readily; it encouraged the Joint to start once more to rebuild the remains of the Jewish community. Teams of doctors and dentists were sent from America, not only to care for the survivors but to give refresher courses to those who had been totally cut off from world science since 1939.

The Russians had occupied Warsaw in January 1945. A few naked, half-starved Jews emerged from the bunkers—about two hundred in all. Others, like Gitler-Barski, returned from the concentration camps, still in their prison stripes. A few trickled in from hiding places in nearby villages and forests. And a surprisingly large number were allowed, in the first days, to return from Russia. It was a pitiful community, nevertheless, the remains of a once great civilization. And immediately this remnant was made aware of a vicious anti-Semitism among the Poles. "What, still so many Jews? We thought the Germans had been more efficient." This was the recurring greeting from their neighbors. Bernard Goldstein was arrested and taken to a police station for speaking Yiddish in public.

The Saving Remnant

"Who had cheated the Nazis?" wrote Goldstein. "Those who rotted beneath the broken stones or were ashes in some charnel pit, or I, sentenced to live out my days and nights with the tortured memories of what had been?

"This was the end. This was the sum total of hundreds of generations of living and building, of religion, of Torah, of piety, of free thinking, of Zionism, of Bundism, of struggles and battles, of the hopes of an entire people—this, this empty desert."

In fact, for a Jew, the whole of Poland was worse than a desert; it was a huge shallow graveyard wherein the Germans had barely taken the trouble to shovel dirt over the innumerable corpses. Twelve years later mass graves were still being uncovered throughout the land. In the outskirts of Lublin the author saw an old man and a very young girl pulling a cart. The child was waving a human thighbone in one hand as she pulled with the other. Those who were too old or too young to work were moving bones, day after day, from a nearby ditch to a Jewish cemetery. The ditch was half a mile long, so they would be busy for many weeks.

Perhaps a hundred and fifty thousand had returned from Russia during the first chaotic days. About two hundred thousand Jews had assembled in Poland by the time the death camps were emptied. They set up a Central Committee, representing all political views from Right to Left. Through this committee the revived Joint could work effectively, and for a time it seemed that the old community, at least in miniature, might return to life. Schools were organized, and cooperatives, and even Yiddish theaters. The Joint was pouring in food, clothing, and medical supplies.

Then came the Kielce pogrom, on the Fourth of July, 1946, in a town where only a few hundred Jews had survived, or had crept home from camps. Forty-one were killed, and sixty wounded, and the Jewish Youth Center was wrecked. The mob was outstandingly vicious and bitter and might well have finished the job except for a halfhearted intervention by the police. The number of dead was small compared to what Jews have often suffered in Poland, but this time the indignity was too much to bear. The Kielce pogrom did what not even the Germans had accomplished: it convinced the Jews that Poland was uninhabitable for them, that a thousand years of work and homemaking must be abandoned. The reborn community melted away—to the displaced persons' camps in Germany, to Palestine for the lucky few, or to the open road. By the end of the year 120,000 had left the country. And most of the rest were waiting for Palestine. waiting for the birth of Israel, the only place on earth they could hope to go. Nothing was left of what had been the most important segment of world Jewry, except those who could not yet escape and a few militant Jews in the Communist ruling caste.

"The remaining Jews of Poland act out the epilogue to the great national tragedy which began in September 1939," wrote Goldstein. "Those of us who survived that holocaust are freaks of nature, testimony to the dogged human will to live. But we are as surely dead as our more fortunate brothers who have found peace. We have our lives, but our life is gone."

The Joint, however, remained faithful to those "remaining Jews of Poland." Everything must be done to rescue their bodies and to nourish their culture, to protect them from the combined pressures of despair and of communism. The Communists only wanted them to cease being Jews; the Joint only wanted to maintain their community life until some way could be found to get them to Palestine. The Joint was too successful for its own good; so in 1949 the government of Poland expelled the whole organization, confiscating schools, medical and community centers, old-age homes, Yeshivoth, everything that for the second time had been painfully reconstructed. The curtain did not rise again until 1957, when the Russians let another trickle of Jews—perhaps thirty thousand—return to their Polish homes. Nobody wanted them; they did not want this death-stained Poland; but Moscow would not allow Warsaw to send them to the West. So the Joint was invited back to take care of them until the ban on travel might be lifted. And of course the Joint returned, with no hope now of rehabilitation, but merely to show that the world community still longed to help until such time as this pitiful remnant could go home.

Chapter Five

1.

Early in the Second World War Jewish emigration from Germany and some German-occupied lands was permitted, and at times encouraged. The limit was set partly by shipping facilities, but chiefly by the world's refusal to accept refugees in quantity.

Later, when Germans were killing 400,000 Jews from the Warsaw Ghetto within a few months, the more humane nations refused to believe this awe-inspiring fact. Bernard Goldstein wrote: "The first news of the early deportations, which we had sent to the outside world with such difficulty, had been met with indifference, with disbelief. The world was cynical and suspicious of 'atrocity stories.' The empty stillness mocked us. We were completely, utterly, unbelievably alone. . . . Through the underground radio we received the news that brave and loyal Artur Ziegelboim, our representative with the Polish government-in-exile, had given us the only aid within his power. During the night of May 12 [1943] he committed suicide in London as a gesture of protest against the callousness and indifference of the world."

If this indifference was true in 1942 and 1943, when the German tide had been halted and the Allied armies had reached what Sir Winston Churchill called "the end of the beginning," it was far more true in the days when the British Commonwealth stood alone, when Stalin was Hitler's friend, and when the United States was pretending that the war was no concern of hers. Britain and occupied Europe could not, and nobody else would, make room for the millions who were about to be killed. Yet strange routes of escape were established for the fortunate few who had found some country, somewhere, to receive them.

Until Mussolini's "stab in the back" of June 20, 1940, the Italian ports were open; Lisbon was open; the Black Sea ports were mostly open to anyone who could reach them—but in all cases with the proviso that steamship fares should be paid in dollars. In effect, even those who possessed visas could not take advantage of their good luck unless they were backed by the Jewish Agency if on their way to Palestine, or by the Joint if on their way elsewhere.

We shall return to these diverse routes later, but let us start with the oddest one of all, the route across half the land-mass of the earth, from the Baltic Sea to Shanghai. Those who took this journey became, immediately on their arrival, the charges of the Joint.

Some twenty-five to thirty thousand Jews were already resident in Shanghai, mostly Sephardim from Baghdad who arrived shortly after Shanghai became a Treaty Port in 1842. They were attracted by the glitter of the immensely rich Sassoon interests which had spread from Baghdad to Bombay and thence all over the Orient. Shanghai became one of the most prosperous Jewish communities in the world. After the Revolutions of 1917, a number of Russian Jews and non-Jews found their way to this haven. And since Shanghai was free from the twin curses of passports and visas, another wave of Jews who were rich enough to pay for the long passage arrived during the years before the Second War. Most of these settled in the Japanese part of Shanghai. Then, when Russia absorbed Lithuania in 1940, she gave permits to any Jews in that territory (including refugees from Poland) who wished to try the bitter hazards of the trans-Siberian route. Moses Beckelman of the Joint was in Lithuania and organized the trek.

Four thousand Jews thus crossed the world to Japan, where they found only about a hundred of their fellows. They were given transit visas. The few who had access to America proceeded happily. The rest made for Shanghai—the last 1500 of them arriving just before Pearl Harbor. Even so, they were lucky. The Germans, when they stormed into Lithuania in 1941, would have killed them all; the Japanese, at worst, only half-starved them. Also, to their great good fortune, the Joint had sent one of its truly remarkable characters to Shanghai in July of 1941, to see what was happening and to suggest what should be done. This was Laura Margolis, who had taken a six-month leave from her job with the Jewish Welfare Society of Buffalo to help the Joint in Havana at the time of the *St. Louis* affair. The six months dragged out to seven years.

The war, even in its early years, had not been propitious for the rich Jews of Shanghai. When Miss Margolis arrived she found 8000 people on relief and a community spirit that was disturbingly grudging. No desire was shown for the pooling of the resources of this desert island. So she went to Manila—of all places—to set up a Far Eastern Office of the Joint. She returned to Shanghai with an aide, Manuel Siegel, late in November, just in time to start serious work on the day of Pearl Harbor.

Shanghai had been effectively in Japanese hands ever since 1937, when the last Chinese troops were driven out; but the International Settlement had so far remained unmolested. Now, however, Japan was at war with the nations which had established the International Settlement; Jews were anathema to Japan's allies; and Americans were anathema to Japan. So American Jews should have been in the worst possible way. Nevertheless, for more than a year the Japanese were conciliatory even to Miss Margolis.

The Joint had told Miss Margolis to use the now tried and trusted device: to borrow to the hilt from all Jews who still had money, against the promise to repay in any desired currency at the end of the war. The Japanese said, "Go ahead. Borrow all you can from the community and look after these refugees. We don't want to bother with them." By "refugees" the Japanese meant every Jew who had arrived since Japan took control of the city in 1937. But at first the reputation of the Joint did not seem to work. In this far corner of a convulsed world the wand of the magician had lost its potency. Having made her offer, Miss Margolis waited for eight days. Nobody came forward with money, and since she was cut off from home there was no other large source of supply. The poorer Jews, the new refugees, were already semi-starved. Dysentery, typhus, and meningitis had appeared.

At last one man gambled on the credit of that distant office in New York. At once the dam broke, and the money began coming in. The problem now was how to use it wisely in the beleaguered city. Another problem, which may have discouraged potential givers, was that Miss Margolis had to tell the Japanese the names of her contributors. Yet most people would prefer possible future backmail to a probable immediate disease. And disease was spreading on the wings of poverty.

The next step was to organize the Jews in camps, with an elected spokesman from each camp to form a Central Committee. The committee was made up mostly of Poles and Lithuanians from the latest immigration, and White Russians from that of 1917. The older Sephardic community, which had given most of the money, did not yet choose to associate with the indigent newcomers. Doubtless they were glad of this decision when Miss Margolis's newcomers "liberated" some idle and expensive machinery in the Sassoon plants and transformed it into camp kitchens. Yet the kitchens and the Central Committee, between them, were what kept the Jewish community alive until the end of the war. The committee could take over the Joint's credit and money-raising powers when Miss Margolis and her assistant were removed. And the kitchens could turn the most repulsive rations into something vaguely edible.

Throughout the whole of 1942 the Japanese left Miss Margolis and her lonely Far Eastern Jews unhindered. But in January 1943, after three months' warning, she and Mr. Siegel were interned in isolation, and most of their charges were removed to a "designated area." This was a concentration camp. And, at first, most of those who were "designated" were the Jews who had arrived since 1937—about seventeen to eighteen thousand.

Miss Margolis set herself at once to become as unhealthy as possible, so as to be sent to hospital, whence she might get in touch with her committee. With the help of very little food and lots of sleeping pills she attained a state of advanced emaciation and was transferred to the Italian hospital. With her usual unlucky timing, she arrived just as Italy withdrew from the war, and thus from the Axis, and thus became an enemy of Japan. But she was now on a repatriation list—1500 Japanese exchanged for 1500 Americans. She left on the *Gripsholm,* changed ships at Goa, and reached New York via the Cape of Good Hope on December 1, 1943. Since even the most underground communications with Shanghai (except for money through Switzerland) had been cut off since the day of Pearl Harbor, and since she had pledged the Joint to half a million dollars without consultation or renewed authority, she was mildly worried when she walked into the offices of the Joint. She found her welcome reassuring: "Please, were you able to borrow every last penny in the community?"

Within three weeks of V-J Day in 1945 the Joint was back in

Shanghai, and by November of that year Charles Jordan, today the Director-General of Overseas Operations, had arrived to deal with the problem. About sixteen thousand of the Joint's special charges were still alive. As usual, the first need was for cash and food and medical supplies. Then a home for the aged was established, and a hospital with two hundred beds.

After the emergency relief, in this case, came emigration rather than rehabilitation. The gathering Communist revolution in China did not encourage the Jews of Shanghai to rebuild their community. With the help of UNRRA, some reached the United States. Some made for South America, and a few for Australia. But the majority could go nowhere until the birth of the State of Israel and the call for the ingathering of the far-scattered Jews. Even after Israel, the problem of transport remained. As the Chinese Communists moved toward the port cities in 1949, the rush to escape from Shanghai became a desperation. The Joint found passage for thousands, by ship, and sometimes by special aircraft. The difficulties are illustrated by the strange case of the Sealed Train—an unhappy name, suggestive of the German death trains, a name which the Joint in its own publicity changed to the "Liberty Train."

Passage for 475 Israel-bound Jews had been secured on the SS *General Gordon* of the American President Line, sailing for San Francisco. The plan was to take the refugees across the United States by train. At New York they would be met by another ship and taken to Israel. Then the Department of State intervened: it would grant a transit visa to an individual, or perhaps to a family, but not to this indiscriminate mass. Furthermore, the United Nations was at that moment trying to maintain a truce in the Arab-Israel war. If men of military age were included in the group, might not that violate the terms of the armistice?

In the end the Department of State agreed to grant transit visas on the following conditions: the refugees were to be taken across the country in a sealed train, and no men of military age

The Saving Remnant

were to be included without the approval of the truce mediator, Ralph Bunche. The latter condition might have made the whole scheme impossible, but Mr. Bunche ruled that the terms of the truce would not be violated if the group contained no members of the armed forces of Israel and if the number of young men was reassuringly small. So at last, with the Communists at their heels and the bureaucrats on their flanks, the Jews set sail, reaching San Francisco on February 21. There, under a legal fiction which sounds as absurd as that prevailing at the Mandlebaum Gate in Jerusalem today,[1] the refugees were all declared inadmissable by the Immigration Service, and the American President Line was ordered to deport them *from New York*. They were put into a special train for Ellis Island, which was sealed and under guard —rather as Lenin was taken by the Germans from Switzerland to Russia in 1917. (In fact, a few people were allowed off the train, humanely, for reasons of illness.) The train reached New York the last of February, and after a short stay on Ellis Island the refugees at last sailed for Israel. The legal fiction, of course, had been a kindly act; but the whole operation was nerve-racking for the Joint, suggesting that Jews had to be subjected to a special form of quarantine, like cattle with foot-and-mouth disease.

In spite of such inconveniences, about fourteen thousand Jews had left Shanghai for Israel by the end of 1949. Since the war the Joint had spent $4,236,000 on Shanghai. Always a few stay behind, no matter what the danger or what the impending squalor of their lives. The Joint calls these the "hard core" cases; it has dealt with them in every corner of the earth. Today the Jewish community of Shanghai numbers about fifty.

[1] If a non-Jew wishes to cross from Israel into Jordan—Jews, of course, are *verboten*—he must have two passports: the one which got him into Israel, and another which is without the hated stamp of the Israeli government. Presenting the innocent passport, while still standing in Israel, one demonstrates to the Arab official that one has never put foot on Jewish soil.

The Saving Remnant

2.

The eccentricities of dictatorships are inscrutable. Why should the Russians have given safe conduct across their vast empire to the Jews they found in Lithuania, while the Polish Jews who were acquired by the partition of 1939 and who refused Soviet citizenship—and also the Ukrainian Jews who subsequently fled before the Wehrmacht—were incarcerated in Asia?

More than three hundred and fifty thousand were consigned to the bleak Asian borders of Persia during 1939 and 1940. They were joined by some of the lucky ones who escaped the ravening German armies in the summer of 1941. The Russians meant them neither harm nor good; as in the First War, they were a nuisance because they cluttered up the ground where the fighting took place. And, as in the First War, most of them died of cold or hunger—not because the Russians planned it that way but because they were too busy being killed by Germans and learning how to kill back.

About a hundred and fifty thousand of these Jews were still alive in 1942, gathered into small towns along the frontier of Persia and struggling to set up their own communities. The chief problem for this remnant was that it had no money, which meant that it had almost nothing to eat. Early in 1942 letters began to reach friends and relatives—in the United States, in Palestine, in South Africa. They all said the same thing: "Send food." All agencies of relief began forwarding parcels to the addresses given in the letters—but the Russian government collected a high and arbitrary duty before the parcels could even be opened and assessed. Since the recipients were mostly penniless, they now wrote plaintively, "Don't send parcels. We can't afford them." But at least the silence had been broken; the world knew where to find some of the myriad Jews who had vanished into Russia.

The Polish Red Cross tried to help, since the Red Cross is accustomed to crossing frontiers without paying duty. Their parcels got as far as Teheran, but the Russians would not let them beyond the border. Then the Joint was asked to take over. In June of 1942 it sent Charles Passman[2] to Teheran and then to Moscow to work out a plan with the Russians. Mr. Passman found that a direct relief program was impossible. Russian pride would not allow it, although the same pride was not impaired by the starvation of citizens and refugees. Yet the Soviet Union made one all-important concession: parcels, up to twelve pounds in weight, might be sent to individuals if the addresses were correct and if the Joint would pay the duty in advance. The parcels could be insured with a Russian company, so that postmasters should know that their own freedom was at stake in case the parcels were stolen. Throughout the next two and a half years there was no pilfering, although a few parcels were returned as misdirected.

How was the Joint to find the names and addresses? Seven thousand were already available, and indexed, as a result of the first wave of letters crying for help. As soon as parcels went out to this group, with return-paid receipts and postcards attached, new names came flooding in by the tens of thousands. So the Joint hired bonded warehouses in Teheran and began combing the world for supplies. These were not easy to come by, or to deliver in far-off Persia, during the summer of 1942. The Persian government agreed to charge no transit duty for goods that passed through the bonded warehouses, but it did charge a road tax which, added to the Russian duty and the stamps and the cost of the articles themselves, made the parcels expensive.

The American Lend-Lease Administration for the Middle East, with headquarters in Cairo, allowed the Joint to buy a rich variety of its goods. German and Polish Jews who had escaped to Bombay rounded up tea and blankets. In Persia itself, with luck and diligence, tobacco could be bought, and soap, and more

[2] Mr. Passman is an American who moved with his family to Palestine after the First War.

blankets. Shoes and clothing came from Palestine, and also dried fruits. And from anywhere and everywhere the Joint collected needles, pins, shoelaces, and razor blades—precious articles of exchange in Russia. Meanwhile the Jewish Agency uncovered many new addresses and contributed $700,000 to help the good work. And from time to time some lucky Jew escaped from Russia into Persia, bringing more names and addresses and more priceless information as to the market value of needles or tobacco or soap or tea—the latter being the best of all goods for bartering, but also one of the hardest to find.

Mr. Passman quickly discovered that a twelve-pound package of food was of little use to his starving clients. They needed goods which were in scarce supply and which they could sell or exchange. Asiatic Russia did not lack food, but the Jews had no money with which to buy it and the government was not concerned with their fate. Luckily for them, almost everything except food was lacking; so with their razor blades, shoes, tobacco, tea, and the like, they became tiny capitalists, tolerated by their Communist masters, who were eager for the goods that poured in from Teheran. So Mr. Passman found himself running a huge general store—a Sears, Roebuck in miniature—with a hundred and fifty thousand customers to keep alive. He was also running a strange parody of a stock exchange wherein the law of supply and demand worked inexorably. If he sent too many needles or too much soap to a given town, the price would drop and his Jews would go hungry.

A quarter of a million parcels went out from Teheran, and the hundred and fifty thousand people were saved from sure death. After the war most of them escaped—either through Persia or via Poland and the DP camps—and are now in Israel. For once, a rescue operation really rescued and did not simply keep the Jews together for the Germans to catch. The whole parcel service cost $5,000,000, of which $1,700,000 went to the Russian customs, and $322,000 was spent on stamps. This seems a small sum to save so many lives for two and a half years, but the goods in the parcels were worth about five times their market value when they reached Asiatic Russia.

The Joint did all the work on this parcel service and paid more than half the cost—the rest coming from the Jewish Agency, the Jews of South Africa, the Polish Red Cross, and the Poles of London. Throughout the war the Polish government-in-exile in London was most helpful to the Joint, being eager to show that it, at least, was not anti-Semitic. This helpfulness, oddly enough, almost caused a breakdown in the parcel service toward the end of the war.

Shortly after the conference at Yalta, the Russians set up the so-called Russian Committee for Polish Liberation, which became the Lublin Government. Bitterly opposed to the Polish government in London, which had a representative at Teheran, the Russians tried to use the Joint to discredit London and enhance Lublin. The Russian ambassador to Persia told Mr. Passman that he would remit all duty on the parcel service if the Joint would mark each parcel "Sent by the Lublin Government." The answer was that the Joint knows no politics, deals only with Jews who are in need of help, and can take no part in the internal affairs of Poland or any other nation. This harmless statement of fact annoyed the Russians, who threatened to seize all the supplies in Teheran—or at any rate all the ex-Lend-Lease supplies—on the ground that they should have gone straight to Russia in the first place and should never have been sold to the Joint. They went so far as to send their trucks to the warehouses and load them with the Joint's precious goods. The American Embassy temporized, but pointed out that the United States government, after all, had a right to decide what it did with its own Lend-Lease equipment. After a few hours, and considerable bluster, the Russian trucks were unloaded.

A by-product of the parcel service was the bringing together of thousands of separated families. In 1941, when this particular group of Jews was hurriedly dumped into Asia, the action was helter-skelter. Members of a family had no way of keeping track of one another, or of getting in touch subsequently. The immense card index of names and addresses, on which the whole of the parcel service depended, made possible the sorting-out of these scattered families. And in many cases, once the Joint knew exactly where everyone was, it could put its clients in touch with relatives in distant lands. The mere fact of being in touch, of being thought about and prayed for, can be most useful in keeping people alive during hard times. So Mr. Passman's mail-order-emporium-plus-stock-exchange had the maximum of beneficial results.

3.

We have seen what happened to the Jews who fled across Asia and to some of those who were imprisoned within Asia. The other chief routes of escape, for the few who eluded the Germans, were through the Black Sea ports of Romania and through Lisbon.

The first route was used only by people bound for Palestine. The British White Paper of 1939 was still in effect: only 15,000 immigrants a year could be admitted legally. The Joint and the Jewish Agency had arranged that within these narrow limits anyone who got to Istanbul would receive a transit visa to Palestine. To reach Istanbul refugees had first to cross the whole of Romania (an Axis satellite, and anti-Semitic to boot) and then acquire illegally some wretched ship which was too far gone for normal commerce. These vessels became known as the "coffin ships." Yet in spite of the hazards of the route, the legal quota for Palestine was almost filled in 1939 and 1940, whereupon the Turkish government, under Arab pressure, began to refuse landing facilities.

In 1940, SS *Salvador* cruised forlornly throughout five months, was admitted to no harbor, and finally struck a rock in the Sea of Marmara. Two hundred were drowned, which was at least an improvement on returning to Romania and to the mercy of the Germans. In 1942 came the famous incident of SS *Struma*. This was a tiny ship—fifty feet on the waterline—packed with 769 Jews. She sailed in February from Romania to Istanbul. Turkish officials ordered her to leave the harbor at once and to make her own way to Palestine. No passenger could be given a transit visa, since the Palestinian quota was allegedly exhausted, and no passenger could stay in Turkey. The captain of the *Struma* protested that she was unseaworthy and could not make Palestine. And even if she did, the British were waiting for her and had declared they would arrest her passengers. The only hope for any of these Jews was to go overland through Turkey, Syria, and the Lebanon, and then to slip across the border.

The Joint provided $10,000 to feed the passengers, while it pled with the British to relax the law. *Struma*, meanwhile, had managed to develop "motor trouble" and thus lingered in the harbor for three months. Then Turkey insisted that she must leave. Having no other place to go, the captain headed back for Romania. Luckily, perhaps, *Struma* hit a mine and sank with all hands. One woman was picked up alive.

Struma had become famous during her wait at Istanbul. Great imagination was not needed in order to feel sorry for those 769 Jews who had come so far on their flight toward freedom under such difficulties, and who were being sent back to the death trains for Auschwitz. When *Struma* sank she became a convenient symbol of the inhumanity of our times. Thus she may have saved more Jews than her frail hulk could carry, for the British people were shocked at the catastrophe. The rigid restriction on immigration into Palestine was somewhat relaxed.

The Danube-Constantsa-Istanbul-Palestine route was inauspicious; yet in the end more Jews escaped in that direction than in any other. The Lisbon route was far safer, and was well organized by the Joint. But the Lisbon route led westward. The Joint could see to it (at least until the "final solution") that anyone with a visa could get out, and on a ship that was not likely to sink. But where, in the West, could Jews in any quantity take refuge? The British, fighting for their lives, and with the Arabs prepared to welcome the Axis, are harshly criticized for their policy of exclusion in Palestine. But who else, among safer nations, allowed half as many Jews into any territory under their control?

Before turning to the Lisbon route, we must pay a tribute to the nations of Western and Northern Europe. So far, in both wars, we have dealt mainly with the problems of Eastern Europe. Poland, Galicia, Hungary, Romania, Lithuania, Russia—these were the regions which harbored the civilization of the shtetl. In this they might seem to the historian to have been fortunate. But they did not think so. They were all brutally anti-Semitic— not all the people, by any means, but most of the people throughout these districts. So when Germany caught the ancient plague in its most virulent form, they were all willing, on this one point, to let Germany have her way. "What—still so many Jews?" That spine-chilling comment from the returning Poles in 1945 could not have been made west of the Rhine or north of Schleswig-Holstein. Instead of collaborating with pleasure in the German crimes, most citizens of the West were horrified and many of them made gallant efforts to circumvent the murderers. The efforts, no matter how slight, were truly gallant, since the penalty for harboring, or even helping, a Jew was to be hanged on the spot, your body left dangling for several days as a warning to the neighbors. And if you had a wife and children, they too would dangle. On the other hand, anyone who informed on a Jew, or on a Jewish hiding-place, was rewarded with brandy, sugar, cigarettes, or money.

The point of view of the West at its finest was expressed in 1942 by the Archbishop of Toulouse: "There is a Christian morality . . . that confers rights and imposes duties. These duties and these rights come from God. One can violate them. But no mortal has the power to suppress them. Alas, it has been destined for us to witness the dreadful spectacle of children, women, and old men being treated like vile beasts; of families being torn apart and deported to unknown destinations. . . . The Jews are our brethren. They belong to mankind. No Christian dare forget that!" A good many Christians have forgotten it, during two thousand years; but this was a brave moment for the archbishop to reaffirm the truth.

Such words are more easily spoken than acted upon. Absolute terrorization is well nigh impossible to confront. Nobody can tell how he would behave in the shadow of an omnipresent Gestapo. Yet in spite of the Gestapo, in spite of quislings and collaborators and men of feeble will, the peoples of Western Europe did not do badly. More Jews escaped the "final solution" through their help than through all the routes to the world overseas. "Every Catholic family shelters a Jew," complained a pro-Nazi paper in Lyon. "The French authorities provide Jews with false identification papers and passports. Priests help them across the Swiss frontier. In Toulouse, Jewish children have been concealed in Catholic schools; the civilian Catholic officials receive intelligence of a scheduled deportation of Jews, advise a great number of the refugees about it, and the result is that about fifty per cent of the undesirables escape."

The angry editor was doubtless exaggerating these Catholic crimes against the Third Reich. No group on earth will ever be as brave as he accused the French Catholics of being; if it were, the Joint might at last be allowed to go out of business. But at least the citizens of the Western nations committed some of these "crimes," and on a considerable scale. In the East of Europe, they were committed also (Emmanuel Ringelblum and Mr. Gitler-Barski were both hidden by "Aryans" in Warsaw); but in the East the "crimes" were so rare that they scarcely bothered the Gestapo. In the West they half frustrated it—no small achievement against naked terror.

In Holland opposition to anti-Semitic rules and practices became a badge of patriotism. When the mass deportations to Auschwitz began, in 1942, thousands of Dutch families risked execution by hiding Jews. Forty thousand were given refuge, and fifteen thousand survived—so the Gestapo doubtless killed as many Dutch benefactors as Jewish "undesirables."

In Belgium, which had 45,000 Jews, 20,000 were saved. The Belgian police, when asked for lists and addresses, could not remember having seen any Jews. The Germans would have had to hang half the population if they had followed their rule of destroying everyone who could be suspected of helping a "sub-human." When the Belgian ambassador in Washington told the Joint that thousands of Jews were being sheltered by the Underground, the Joint sent $60,000 by parachute—not specifically for Jews, but for the national Resistance.

The northern countries were equivalently brave—including Norway, which, to its misfortune, contributed an unattractive noun to all languages. Finland, with 2000 Jews, was perhaps the only country on earth that had not heard about anti-Semitism, or, if it had heard, it had forgotten. The Jews were simply Finns who happened to be Jewish. The only discrimination practiced was that of the more religious Jews who did not choose to marry gentiles. Yet Finland was in an awkward position: she was the ally of Germany in the war against Russia, an alliance which suggests a cat collaborating with a tiger. Wholly dependent on the Germans for arms and even for food, the Finns refused to surrender their Jews, or even the few Jewish refugees who had fled northward from Germany and Austria. In the summer of 1942 the terrible Himmler went to Helsinki to insist on exporting the whole lot to Auschwitz. "Finland is a decent nation," said Foreign Minister Witting to Himmler's negotiator. "We would rather perish together with the Jews. . . . We will not surrender them!"

The Finnish government made endless delaying actions, or constitutional grounds: nobody could hand over a citizen, or even a refugee, until Parliament agreed. And Parliament seemed always to be either in summer recess, or busy with vital legislation while preparing for the Christmas recess, or just plain lazy. In the end, not a Jew was surrendered—although four were arrested by the Germans on criminal charges and shipped off to death. This was a long way from the "final solution."

Denmark, led by her King, was the shining hero of resistance to the death gangs. The Jewish population was a little over 6000, plus some 1200 refugees from Germany. All Jews had been full citizens since 1814, and the disease of anti-Semitism had long been outgrown. After the spring of 1940, Denmark belonged to Germany as completely as Belgium or Holland, although for a time she was allowed her own government. Yet no pressure could induce the Danes to impose the anti-Jewish laws of their masters. In 1943 the frustrated Herrenvolk decreed the immediate establishment of ghettos, the enforcement of the Jewish badge, and the preparation of lists for the death trains. King Christian said he would move from his palace into the first ghetto and that he would be proud to wear the Star of David. The experts of the SS, however, were confident that they could solve this tiny, peripheral "Jewish problem": there was only one way of escape—by sea to Sweden—and the German Navy was guarding that route. So they sent their troops in to arrest all Jews. Yet more than 6000 did escape—by sea to Sweden, in spite of the German Navy, which suggests that the Vikings are still better seamen than the land-based Master Race.

In Norway, with the help of Vidkun Quisling's friends, 770 Jews were caught and deported by ship, via Stettin, to Auschwitz; but 1700 escaped into Sweden, with the combined help of their fellow countrymen and the Swedes. This too fell far short of the German ambition to make Europe "clean of Jews."

In the far south the majority of the Italians, who fought reluctantly on both sides during the war and who never quite knew what slogans to paste on their walls in what year, were not reluctant in their efforts to protect Jews. Fascism, with all its faults, was not in itself an anti-Jewish heresy. "Fascism means unity," said Mussolini in 1927; "anti-Semitism means division. To us in Italy, German anti-Semitism appears ludicrous. . . . It is barbarism." The subservient Caesar had to eat his words after signing the German alliance; but his people, for the most part, held to the view expressed by their dictator two years after the March on Rome: "Anti-Semitism is an alien weed that cannot strike roots in Italy."

Anti-Jewish laws were first imposed on the 57,000 Jews of Italy in 1938—but not the ghetto, and not the Jewish badge, which the Italians found unacceptable. No deportations occurred during the first years of the war. But in 1943, when Mussolini fell and Badoglio made an armistice with the Allies, the Germans took over most of Italy and the horror descended. Yet the Italians, who never really put their hearts into the killing of Englishmen, or even of Germans, saved 40,000 Jews from Hitler's death trains, as compared with 15,000 whom they could not save. "Thirty centuries," as Mussolini used to boast, had taught the Italians many things, including the simple fact that all governments are inefficient, as well as being a nuisance, and that they can generally be circumvented.

The puppet government established by the Germans in September of 1943 was unusually inefficient and widely hated. The sabotage of the "final solution" was so successful that Ribbentrop himself went to Rome to demand more Jews for the gas chambers. He was strongly supported by his ambassador, von Mackensen, and by Prince Otto von Bismarck. Not even this impressive combination of the old, aristocratic Germany and the barbarous upstarts could induce the Italian people to cease hiding Jews. Even the Army took part in this anti-German activity. In the South of France, in the Italian zone, the Jewish population rose from 15,000 to almost 45,000. This was after the abolition of "unoccupied France," when the Germans were hunting Jews along the Côte d'Azur. The Gestapo officer responsible for catching Jews wrote plaintively: "The attitude of the Italians is incomprehensible. The Italian military authorities and police protect Jews." He could not have been more bewildered had he stumbled upon a primitive tribe which made pets out of typhus-bearing lice.

4.

After the war, the Italian friendliness was all-important to the Joint and to other rescue groups. During the war, however, France was the scene of the most important work in the West; France was the route to Lisbon and to Switzerland, and the home of 350,000 Jews (including the refugees from Belgium and from Holland), of whom less than 130,000 perished. The number of Jews saved is all the more striking because France—*"mère des arts, des armes et des lois"*—had become a self-recriminating country wherein cooperation on any major effort was difficult. These proud people should not be divided, with over-simple logic, into Gaullists and Pétainists, for most men were half divided within themselves. Many who served General de Gaulle had nagging at their hearts the Vichy doctrine that France had somehow sinned and must expiate. Many who served Marshal Pétain longed to go on fighting Germans to the last ditch. The whole tormented land might have prayed, with Keats:

> Do gently murder half my soul, and I
> Shall feel the other half so utterly.

Yet France, with the exception of the sad few who can never refrain from flattering a conqueror, was active in helping Jews.

The Saving Remnant

This is noteworthy, because ever since the days of Dreyfus France has been dishonored by a hysterical Jew-detesting propaganda from such writers as Céline and Maurras. From the first days of the Occupation a Nazi-sponsored press worked diligently to fan these smoldering hates into a bright flame. And the Vichy government was quick to sell Jews in return for the smallest contribution to its self-esteem—except Laval, the least-loved man of Vichy, who sometimes indulged his genius for evasion by cheating the Germans out of thousands of Jews. One can scarcely imagine that he did this from kindness. Perhaps he wanted to reassure himself that even the Führer could be double-crossed. In any case, only about 30 per cent of the French Jews were killed —a poor performance for the SS, whose commander for Northern France and Belgium complained: "It is almost impossible to cultivate in Frenchmen an anti-Jewish feeling on ideological grounds." He could only suggest that more money, and "other economic advantages," should be offered in exchange for Jews.

The Vichy government, cringingly, set up a Commissariat Général aux Questions Juives under Xavier Vallat, who boasted to an SS captain, "I am an anti-Semite of much older vintage than you. On that score, I could be your father!" Yet Vallat was a disappointment to the Gestapo: he would not impose the Jewish badge—not, presumably, because he would not like to, but because he knew that the French could still be most formidable, for any governing group, if they were ordered to disgrace themselves by aping Germans. Vallat was dismissed under pressure from the SS; but his successor was also uncooperative, and for the same reasons. The badge was not worn in the "Free Zone" until Germany invaded in November of 1942.

Even in Occupied France, where the badge had been enforced in the previous June, the Gestapo was vilified, ridiculed, and made uncomfortable in a fashion that only the French can achieve and in the face of which only the Germans are defenseless. Somewhat unimaginatively, the SS arrested their tormentors and sent them to concentration camps wearing white armbands with the inscription *Ami des Juifs*—sweet words which, for the time being, were becoming a code of honor throughout Western Europe.

Before turning to what the Jews and the Joint were doing for themselves in France, let us give an example of French Christian aid. Father Marie-Bênoit, a Capuchin monk and a Hebrew scholar, turned his monastery at Marseille into a Jewish rescue center. In the cellar he set up a factory for making passports, identification cards, certificates of baptism, and other useful forgeries. He organized a smuggling service for Jews, into Switzerland and Lisbon—and here the Joint could help with money, because good smugglers are expensive. After the occupation of the "Free Zone," these routes were blocked. The good Father got in touch with the Italians, and thousands of Jews began to cross into their zone. This was awkward for the Germans, who could not start hanging their allies for protecting the "subhumans." They appealed to Mussolini, and Father Marie-Bênoit was summoned to Rome. There he appeared before the Pope with a plan to transfer fifty thousand French Jews to Morocco and Algiers, where the Allies were in possession. The British ambassador, and the United States representative at the Vatican, agreed to interest their governments. Then Mussolini fell, on July 26, 1943. The Badoglio government promised to supply four ships, and the Joint promised to finance the scheme. But the Germans took over Italy, and the plan was frustrated.

Undeterred, Father Marie-Bênoit moved into Italy, where he became Padre Benedetti and turned the International College of Capuchins into a new factory for documents which made Jews into "Aryans," complete with food-ration cards. Although the Gestapo knew all about him, and killed most of his co-workers, they never caught this priest, who was revered in France and

Italy as "Father of the Jews." [2] They complained to the end that "the clergy continues, as in the past, to disapprove of the anti-Jewish laws, under the pretense of Christianity."

5.

We have seen that the Joint moved its European headquarters to Paris in 1933. At first only a small American staff was needed: to keep in touch with the local Jewish communities and organizations which the Joint had sponsored all over Europe, and to help with funds when necessary. As late as 1937, the Joint was spending less than three million dollars a year. During the twelve months after Kristall Nacht, it spent more than eight millions; but the enormous expenses did not come until after the Second War, until the rescue operations and the rush for Palestine-Israel.

When the war began in 1939, the Joint opened an office in Amsterdam, hoping to keep in touch with Germany. This proved a vain hope, so the office was moved to Brussels for the benefit of the Low Countries. On May 11, 1940, the staff in Brussels was lucky to escape to Paris, where Herbert Katski was temporarily in command. (Most of the Joint's workers were of course European Jews, frequently stateless persons. If the Germans caught them, they would be on the first train to a camp. Saving Jews "under the pretense of Christianity" was bad enough; but saving Jews under the banner of Judaism was an abomination.) By the time the group from Brussels arrived in France, the country was overrun by Dutch and Belgian refugees.

At the time of Munich the Joint had taken a provisional office at Angers, and subsequently at Bordeaux. So in June of 1940 Mr. Katzki had a nice problem on his hands. His duty to save the

[2] Cp. *Contribution à l'Histoire de la Résistance Juive en France*, by David Knout (Paris, 1947): *"Pour la première fois depuis des siècles, le nom de chrétien devenait pour un Juif une garantie, un vrai chrétien—un frère, un prêtre chrétien—un protecteur naturel."*

European staff was absolute; but his duty not to contribute to panic was equally clear. The Joint, by this time, had been at the storm center of so many crises in so many countries that non-Jews kept a close watch on its movements. If the Joint got out, this was a dark sign, because sometimes (as in Poland) it stayed as long as any Jews were still alive. But in Poland, from the beginning, all work was underground, and everyone who stayed (or who, like Ringelblum, returned) did so in order to die with his friends. In France there was no such certainty of doom. Mr. Katzki—warned by the American Embassy that the Joint could do no more work in Paris, even though its American members would be safe—shipped the last of his European staff off to Angers, whence they quickly moved to Bordeaux. He himself waited in Paris for Mr. Troper, the director of European operations, and for Joseph Schwartz, his assistant. These two men had been in Hungary for a month, to canvas the hopes for illegal immigration into Palestine.

The Joint has always claimed that it never touches anything "illegal," as defined by the Department of State. This may be largely true: the Joint did not often pay directly for illegal traffic; it merely kept Jews alive when they got into trouble en route. Since they almost always did get into trouble, this was a genuine contribution. In the case of the Troper-Schwartz mission to Hungary, the Joint found funds for Jews from Germany, Czechoslovakia, and Austria who were planning to travel toward the Black Sea ports. Unhappily, the travelers did not complete their journey. They got only as far as Yugoslavia, where the Germans overtook them and "resettled" them.

On June 10, Mr. Troper and Mr. Schwartz reappeared into the light of day in Switzerland. They were warned not to go to Paris, but they did. They arrived ahead of the Germans and joined forces with Mr. Katzki and three American secretaries. At the Prince de Galles Hotel, they were the only customers. Robert Murphy at the American Embassy told them to leave. The

Joint still had two automobiles in Paris, so the six of them headed south. Four days later, after the customary horrors on the refugee-crowded roads, they reached Bordeaux. The Germans were overtaking them, so they did not linger in the beautiful wine country but made for Lisbon, which was almost the only remaining town in Europe where American citizens could work at saving Jews.

At Lisbon the Joint began chartering ships to sail for Cuba and the United States—or buying all the berths on regular passages. These were still the days when some Jews with visas, and with dollars from the Transmigration Bureau or other sources, could leave Germany and her vassal states. Trains ran regularly to Lisbon from Berlin, Vienna, and Prague. The Joint (or the Joint's Transmigration Bureau), working through the Jewish emigrant aid committees of the several countries, and even through German tourist agencies, planned the schedules for these astonishing trains and was ready to meet them at Lisbon.[3] At least as far as the Spanish border, the trains were supervised by armed German guards. Then the Joint took care of the passengers until they boarded the chartered ships.

The ships were Portuguese, and unlike the Black Sea hulks they were proper passenger ships with reasonably good service. They were of course, and quite properly, overcrowded—with bunks built into every spare hold—and the cost per passenger was very high; but no complaint was made about any vessel chartered by the Joint from a Portuguese shipping line.[4] This was

[3] The story of some of these trains reads like a version of *Alice's Adventures in Wonderland* which happened to be written in hell. One train, organized by the North German Lloyd in Berlin, found on reaching the border that the visas for Portugal were not in order. But if a long delay ensued, the American visas for the whole trainload would expire. The agent of the North German Lloyd stormed into the office of the Joint, insisting that something be done at once to clear his passengers for Lisbon. "Don't you people realize," he said to the astonished Joseph Schwartz, "that the lives of these refugees are in danger!"

[4] The Joint often put pressure on the shipping line to build in more bunks and to sacrifice even minimum comfort.

not the case when private profiteers took advantage of the world demand for any form of passage and sold built-in bunks on decrepit freighters at the price of a de-luxe cabin on the *Queen Mary.*

Anyone who passed frequently through Lisbon during the war on government missions will have felt a sense of shame at moving so easily through a town oppressed with such fear. Year after year the refugees waited for a door to open somewhere in the cold-hearted world. Year after year they expected the Germans to sweep through Spain and Portugal any day, any hour. There they stayed and prayed, on the Atlantic verge of Europe, holding their hands

> in suppliance with desire,
> With stretched desire for the ulterior shore.

Meanwhile numberless people went smoothly to and fro in the most comfortable airplanes—who may not have been doing anything useful.

The extent of the fear, of the passion to get away, is made clear by the story of SS *Navemar.* This was a wholly undesirable ship, almost an SS *Struma* on a large scale. She had been privately chartered to sail from Spain to the United States. She was an ancient freighter with no facilities for passengers, not even toilets. Tiers of bunks had been fitted into the airless holds. Passengers took turns on the meager deck for a breath of air. There they found themselves in competition with five live oxen, the commissariat for the voyage. The captain had vacated his cabin in return for $2000 per head for everyone who could squeeze into that single ventilated space.

By the time *Navemar* sailed, the American visas of the passengers had expired. She might have wandered forlornly like *Salvador* or *Struma,* from harbor to unwelcoming harbor, until she too ran into a mine or a rock. But Joseph Schwartz in Lisbon cabled New York to ask the Department of State to extend the visas, and told *Navemar* to drop anchor in the River Tagus—the

Joint paying the demurrage. Mr. Schwartz then induced a reluctant Portuguese government to allow the passengers on shore, so long as the Joint was responsible for the full keep of all of them. But when he boarded *Navemar*, and pointed out that no one could live long in such conditions, and promised to take care of anyone who went ashore until the next regular sailing to the United States, nobody would leave ship. The Joint, as they well knew, could not possibly promise that another vessel would ever sail from Lisbon with a passenger list which had not been vetted by the Gestapo.

Then came a macabre version of something by Gilbert and Sullivan. The Department of State had generously sent word to the American consulate at Lisbon to extend the visas. But this proved impossible because the consulate did not have enough typewriters to make out the new forms in time. *Navemar*, with slave-ship conditions below decks, could not lie indefinitely off Lisbon. Yet the passengers were still too frightened to disembark. Here is a problem which no government is equipped to solve. If you do not have typewriters you cannot do the necessary paperwork for hundreds of new visas—a pity, but, come what may, the forms must be completed. The Joint, however, could spend money without asking permission from Washington. It provided the typewriters and even the typists. In the end *Navemar* did sail, and did not sink.

This shortage of typewriters in the Iberian Peninsula was a recurring absurdity that would have cost the lives of many hunted people had it not been for the Joint. In Seville, for example, some hundreds of refugees found that their visas were expiring before they could sail. Again the Department of State was willing, humanely, to extend the time. But again the American consulate was helpless for lack of a few simple machines. So the Joint in Lisbon sent two Portuguese Jews, with money to acquire typewriters at any cost, to the rescue of the American officials.[5] No one was to blame. Only a private agency can break the rules. If a civil servant were to buy typewriters on the black market, how could he justify such riotous good sense (in triplicate) to his superiors?

The ships which finally sailed to the United States met with no further trouble: they did not founder, like some of the Black Sea horrors, and the visas of the passengers were real visas. But the ships which sailed to Cuba had a percentage of unlucky men and women who bought visas at a high price and who found on arrival that the visas had never been cleared with the Cuban government and were therefore useless. These immigrants were placed in a camp near Havana, where the Joint looked after them and sooner or later arranged for their release.

Another problem in Lisbon was the reasonable caution of American Naval Intelligence. How could the Joint know that all these people moving from Germany to the United States were in fact Jewish refugees? Might not some of them be German spies? The questions were inevitable; Intelligence was right to raise them; but obviously the Joint could not "know" the answers, in the absolute sense of that word. By good luck and good sense, however, the Joint avoided mistakes: no one who reached America under its auspices was ever accused of being an agent. In the occupied countries of Europe, on the other hand, where suspicions and recriminations became an epidemic disease, many of the brave servants of the Joint were later accused of collaboration. They had dealt with Germans or with German agents; they had disappeared on inexplicable errands; they must have been up to no good. Why were they alive, anyway? If they were patriots, would not the Germans have killed them? This was the question which everyone asked about his neighbor after the terrible years of occupation. The question was leveled at some of

[5] Portuguese citizens could cross into Spain without visas. Unofficial Americans were not welcome in the country.

the Joint's workers who had made their way in great danger to strange places for consultation with Joseph Schwartz and who returned home to the lion's den in spite of being offered sanctuary at Lisbon.

6.

The headquarters at Lisbon maintained branches at Casablanca, Tangier, and even (unofficially) at Barcelona, where the office was a hotel bedroom. Occasional refugees kept straggling into all these ports, and the Joint took care of them with board, lodging, and medicine.

A most ambitious plan, which almost succeeded, was to bring 5000 children from France through Spain into Portugal and then send them to the United States. The American government approved. A ship, with nurses and doctors for the children, was en route for Lisbon when Vichy got wind of the operation and closed the border. Laval, who enjoyed robbing the Führer of Jews, did not choose to rob Unoccupied France. The Pyrenean smugglers in the pay of the Joint had previously been most successful with children; but now the traffic ended abruptly. Instead of 5000 children, 300 got away.

Although these operations through Lisbon saved many precious lives, they were not numerically important against the background of European Jewish tragedy. This was the fault of the world, not of the Joint. Money was available on a scale to keep any number of Jews alive anywhere. And during 1940 and 1941 Jews were available in large quantities. But nobody would take them, except in derisory numbers. Ships could be bought, smugglers could be bought, policemen and SS troops could be bought, but no free government could be either bought or wheedled into giving the necessary refuge. So the Joint at Lisbon took care of such Jews as it could find, and tried to comfort itself with the thought that the news of this effort would spread through Central

and Eastern Europe, bringing to those Jews the meager encouragement of knowing that they were not forgotten and the diminishing hope that something might be done in time to save them.

Late in the summer of 1942 the first word of the mass deportations to Treblinka was smuggled out of the Warsaw Ghetto. The
official world, as we have seen, dismissed this as an "atrocity
story." But the Jews did not dismiss it. A last great effort was
made to get food into the Polish ghettos, since it was still assumed that Jews were being slaughtered only when they became
useless through malnutrition, whereas healthy ones might be
allowed to live and work.

On November 25, 1942, Joseph Schwartz cabled the New York
office: "British government has authorized board of deputies of
British Jews send food packages Polish ghettos total not exceeding four tons per month at cost not exceeding three thousand
pounds per month. Packages will be sent through Polish Government Committee Lisbon. . . . Would suggest you attempt work
out similar arrangement for United States." He added that he
himself had agreed to be the agent in Lisbon of the Board of
Deputies of British Jews.

The United States Treasury Department agreed, and gave the
Joint a license to spend $12,000 a month for three months on
such parcels. Since the population of the major ghettos had by
this time been reduced to about 40 per cent of the population in
July, eight tons of food per month would not have been useless.
But of course it was too late. Young and old, fed and unfed, all
the Jews of Poland were on their way to the death camps. And
the post offices in the ghettos had mostly been closed.

The British, still ignorant of the true horror, went ahead with
their plan, sending such food as they could collect in Portugal.
The first 12,500 parcels contained nothing but figs, which are not
the best diet for starving people with dysentery. Another 7000
parcels included sardines and almonds. Only 88 personal ac-
knowledgments were received on behalf of more than 19,000

packages. By the time Mr. Schwartz had his first $12,000 from the Joint, in December, he knew it was too late and he refused to spend the money. Why send figs to the Gestapo? The Joint had a useful parcel service out of Switzerland and a superb service out of Teheran, but the Jews of Poland could no longer be saved. And by the end of 1942, of course, "the Jews of Poland" included the many thousand from every occupied country who were arriving each day at Auschwitz. Aside from France, the most important work in Europe was now centered in Switzerland, whence the Joint kept in touch with underground organizations throughout the enslaved lands.

7.

As soon as the Unoccupied Zone was decreed, the Joint opened an office in Marseille. French Jews, like other Frenchmen, had always been noted for their individualism. They had little of the close-knit community life of Eastern European Jewry. Yet when Hitler came to power in 1933 they had established the Comité d'Assistance aux Refugiés. Gaston Kahn was the director, Baron Robert de Rothschild the patron. M. Kahn thought that his Comité would merely have to care for the 4000 Jews who came to France in the first flight from the new Reich—"*le douloureux défilé,*" in his own words, "*des lamentables épaves de la sauvagerie hitlérienne.*" By 1939 he knew how wrong he had been. The *lamentables épaves* had become almost too numerous for France to contain. Like all refugees, they were disliked, and perhaps dislikable. Like most Jewish refugees, they had become charges of the Joint: when the Second War began, 80 per cent of the budget of the Comité d'Assistance came from New York.

Gaston Kahn's committee, however, had brought the Jews of France together in a work of mercy. When the coming of the Germans made cooperation the price of survival, they knew where to turn for help and whom to trust. New groups proliferated: for the hiding of children and their dispersal among Christian homes; for the smuggling of children into Switzerland; for the feeding and financing of the stateless Jews who had no rights, not even the right to eat; for the forging of birth certificates, certificates of baptism and of employment, identification cards, ration-books—all the pieces of paper without which no citizen of Hitler's Europe could survive. Whenever such a group was formed, the Joint could help immediately with money. In the early days of Occupied France, it helped with most of the money. Later, when the whole of France had been seized by Germany, it could only offer postwar payment without limit to anyone who would provide francs for the saving of Jews.

The first task of the Joint at Marseille, therefore, was to contrive a courier route across the demarcation line so that cash could be delivered to Paris. This was never a safe route. But the outwitting of Germans was a pleasing task. Christians as well as Jews volunteered for the service. Two splendid Christian women, Mme. Chevalley and Mlle. Trillat, made the trip countless times, not simply for the fun of Gestapo-baiting but from a religious sense of duty to save lives. They were also active in smuggling children to Switzerland. The Swiss, at first, were severe and legalistic about such smuggling. But as the death camps became more famous, the Swiss became more merciful. Then the Joint put more than a hundred million francs into this traffic. And the Joint also supported, by means of its courier route, canteens in Occupied France for those who did not even possess a forged food card.

In Vichy France—where the Marshal was prepared to expiate the "sins" of his nation with any required number of Jewish sacrifices—the Joint had three main tasks: to get the Jews out, to care for those who had been caught and put in concentration camps to await the pleasure of the Gestapo, and to hide the many who had not been arrested and who could not escape. In the first and most difficult job, a main contribution was to help finance the Hebrew

Sheltering and Immigrant Aid Society. During the two and a half years of Unoccupied France the Joint had a hand in clearing 10,000 French Jews through Lisbon and another 1200 through Casablanca. The latter included many Jewish members of the Foreign Legion who were demobilized on orders from Vichy and who made for the nearest office of the Joint—also Jews from the work battalions who had been building the trans-Sahara railway.

When the Germans took Paris in 1940, Gaston Kahn and his Comité d'Assistance moved south to Limoges, then to Bayonne, then to Marseille. The Comité was now financed entirely by the Joint, until the German take-over in the autumn of 1942. Thereafter it had to borrow against the Joint's promise of postwar repayment. Between 1942 and 1944 it raised 423,000,000 francs on this promise, and cared for 40,000 people who were mostly in hiding, and helped about 6000 children into Switzerland. ORT and OSE also had offices at Marseille and were also financed by the Joint.

The Jews in the Vichy concentration camps were desperate for food, clothes, and medicine. These the Joint could supply. The directors of the camps were given a per capita allowance for the care of their victims, which naturally insured a minimum of care: money not spent on Jews could be spent on the director. But the Joint, with the help of many French peasants, was lucky in its search for supplies. Its agents uncovered a variety and an abundance of food, which infuriated Vichy. The same farmers who gladly sold to the Joint would not disclose their hoardings to the agents of Laval, Darlan, and the Marshal. So the Jews in the camps—who were mostly stateless people, refugees who had fled before the German armies—were looked after not too badly until such time as the Germans collected them. A hundred and ninety-five thousand were sent from these camps into Germany. At the end of the war, 2000 were alive.

Darlan was the most persistent of the Jew-hunters at Vichy. He personally selected the officers who were to scour the South of

France. Yet during the unoccupied period the Joint and its collaborating agencies were successful in hiding and "Aryanizing" their clients. Since the United States had full diplomatic representation at Vichy, many powerful American groups kept committees in Marseille to help in the saving work: the Rockefeller Foundation, the YMCA, and the Quakers. As the day for the North African landings approached, the American consul-general at Marseille called a meeting of the heads of these agencies and warned them to disperse their staffs and to get out. But he could not tell them why. So they merely appointed a committee on liquidation and went about their several businesses. The committee, which was headed by the man in charge of the American Friends Service, contented itself with holding meetings and examining plans. Then the consul-general summoned the chairman and asked why nothing was happening. "I am afraid you do not understand us," was the answer. "Quakers do not move. They wait until the spirit moves them."

When the Germans crossed the demarcation line, however, the spirit did move them all, or almost all. The Joint went underground, with the guidance of Maurice Brener, who borrowed the money and kept the work going throughout the Occupation. "Where Brener is, there is the Joint," said the hidden, threatened Jews. And M. Brener was everywhere, with money, food, papers, and with new plans for concealment devised by himself and by the agents of the Comité d'Assistance. In regard to l'œuvre de secours aux enfants (the hiding and exporting of children), David Knout writes: "La presque totalité des fonds utilisée par les œuvres pour leur travail illégal provenait du Joint."

M. Brener survived the Germans, and on the day of the liberation he reopened the office of the Joint in Paris.

8.

In the ghettos of Eastern Europe, the Germans invariably set up a Judenrat, a council of Jews to transmit orders to the community and to be responsible for obedience. At first the members of the Judenrat believed they were serving their own people and hoped that certain privileges might appertain to their work. Later they found that the chief privilege was to select neighbors for the death trains and to remain alive until all friends were dead. Many committed suicide and most of them felt disgraced.

In France, which was proudly clean of ghettos, an analagous but respect-worthy organization was decreed by the occupying power and also by the government at Vichy: L'Union Générale des Israélites de France (UGIF). This committee was to represent all Jewish groups in their relations with the two governments. Was it a trap to catch the leaders of the communities and render them more amenable? Or might it be used, at least in Unoccupied France, to mitigate the harshness of Jewish life?

The members of UGIF were commissioners for Jewish affairs, with the handicap that they had no rights, no powers, and need not be consulted. Yet unlike the Judenrat of a ghetto they might sometimes be asked for their opinions and they might even hope to postpone some fatal decision. Should a Jewish leader lend himself to UGIF? French Jewry was rent asunder by the question; but, to its very great credit, when the war was over few enmities endured and few charges of treason and collaboration were exchanged. This could not be said of the French nation as a whole.

M. Jarblum discussed the problem of UGIF dispassionately with the author: to join or not to join? M. Jarblum and most of his friends abstained. Gaston Kahn supported UGIF. Yet M. Jarblum and M. Kahn both worked with the Joint at Marseille. Their Jewishness was more important than their French genius for finding fault. And the Joint's long-established habit of not taking sides in politics, of not getting dragged into other people's quarrels, paid abundant dividends.

Chapter Six

Saly Mayer was a retired manufacturer of lace who lived in Saint
Gallen, Switzerland. He was about sixty years old when the Second War began. He was of modest means and had given all his
time since 1937 to the protection of German refugees. He had
become well known to the Swiss government as a stubborn negotiator, and to the Joint as a friend deserving of all possible support. He was an Orthodox Jew, deeply religious, president of
the Jewish community of Switzerland. He was tall and robust,
and tireless.

When Morris Troper and Joseph Schwartz emerged from Hungary into Switzerland in June of 1940, they met with Saly Mayer
and arranged for closer relations between the Joint and Saint
Gallen. By the autumn of 1942 Switzerland had become a second
Lisbon, with refugees from France and Czechoslovakia, and even
a trickle from the Polish ghettos who had escaped on the Italian
trucks bought in Galicia. Saly Mayer had resigned as president

of his community and was giving all his time to the Joint. The refugees who had been lucky enough to reach Switzerland were now receiving money direct from New York, so most of Saly Mayer's life was devoted to helping the forlorn remnant in Occupied Europe. He was on good terms with the International Red Cross, whose agents could travel freely. He had friends in the Swiss and Swedish embassies, who helped him to keep in touch with the remaining Jews of Europe and to learn where money or medicine might still be useful. As a neutral, dealing in the most valuable of European neutral currencies, he could get money to any destination so long as the Joint had permission from the United States Treasury to buy Swiss francs. Sometimes he could even put his dangerous cash into a Swedish diplomatic pouch. And, best of all, Swiss medical-supply houses were allowed to send their representatives into Occupied Europe—another rich source for news and another route for smuggling. Thus Saint Gallen became a main clearing house for information coming in and for Swiss francs and medicine going out.

The Joint told the United States Treasury exactly what it was doing, and within reasonable limits was allowed to do whatever it could. The "reasonable limits," of course, were reached when private charitable aid could be suspected of helping the German economy. Washington was generous, and London niggardly, in appraising these limits; for the British had more faith than the Americans in the economic blockade. In 1943, for example, the Treasury Department made a ruling that private organizations such as the Joint might transfer funds to their agents in neutral countries for use in rescue operations, and that the agents might enter into communications with people in enemy or in occupied territory. The money might be Swiss francs bought for dollars, or it might be raised among the peoples under the German heel against the promise of repayment after the war.

The British government protested, but Washington replied that the saving of even a few lives outweighed the tiny financial aid which might accrue to the Germans, adding that no payment of ransom, direct or indirect, would ever be permitted. Thus the Joint's favorite system of raising money under the nose of the Gestapo, on its own postwar credit, was given official sanction. Thus also Saly Mayer was unleashed to do the most good possible. During eight months he managed to distribute 4,434,000 Swiss francs in France, Belgium, Holland, Bulgaria, Romania, and Slovakia—a small sum, to be sure, but the number of Jews in Europe was rapidly diminishing. Some of the ghostlike people who survived the camps may well have been kept alive by this money.

In May of 1944 Saly Mayer got 800,000 Swiss francs into Hungary, and another 200,000 into Bratislava, where the Jewish population was starving and where all other contacts had been cut for over a year. And by the end of 1944 he had moved 237,000,000 Chinese dollars into Shanghai.

Saly Mayer would telephone Lisbon that his spies told him some Jews were still alive and hiding in Krakow, but desperate for medical supplies. Joseph Schwartz would send the money; Saly Mayer would buy the medicine in Switzerland and smuggle it into Poland through one of his secret routes. Or he would learn that Austrian Jews had escaped to Budapest. If the Joint would send money he would promise delivery. Or Lisbon would telephone to him: could anything be done in Yugoslavia? Within a few days his multi-national spies would have the answer.

The Swiss were not entirely happy about these telephone conversations. Saly Mayer had devised a code—the usual substituted names, plus a confusion of Hebrew and Yiddish words. One day the censors asked him about this continuous telephoning, not only to Lisbon but to his agents (Jewish and non-Jewish) all over Europe. What did it mean? He asked the censors why they did not study Hebrew. "Don't worry," was the answer; "we are." Yet the telephoning and the money-smuggling were never seriously interrupted. The government put up a brave show of im-

partial neutrality, but, as the news from the death camps became increasingly hideous, few people could keep to the pretense
that the Germans were no better and no worse than their neighbors.

The Joint could never induce Saly Mayer to accept an expense
account, although his expenses must have been cripplingly high
for a man whose private fortune was on the scale of a hundred
thousand dollars. Mr. Schwartz begged him at least to allow the
Joint to pay for the telephone calls. "I have talked it over with
my wife," he answered, "and we decided that we could not live
with ourselves if we let the Joint reimburse us for anything we
do." His view on this was absolute: if people gave money for
charity, it must be spent on charity. If he was privileged to help
spend it, he must pay for the privilege. After the war, when his
work became even more burdensome, he permitted the Joint to
send him an American assistant—but he added, "Please, don't
send anybody who is brilliant."

On the wall over his desk at Saint Gallen was a large sign,
O. P. M., which meant "Other People's Money"—in English,
presumably, because the "Other People" spoke English. No one
has ever been more meticulous with O. P. M. After the war,
when accountants from the Joint visited Saint Gallen, hoping to
get a general notion of how the money had been spent, they
found an exact record of every transaction, aboveground and
underground, with every penny accounted for, and full reports
had also been given to the American legation at Bern on all the
money spent, and on the sometimes devious methods of spending
it. Since Saly Mayer was often disposing of a million dollars a
month, such accuracy is noteworthy.

This dedication of his, and this insistence upon detail, sometimes made trouble. The Joint, in its dealings with Occupied
Europe, was a conspiracy—a revolutionary conspiracy, from the
German point of view, since it sought to frustrate a major policy
of the Reich. Conspirators have to make use of rough human

material: adventurers who may not have a Swiss businessman's respect for money or an Orthodox Jew's devotion. Yet if Saly Mayer lost confidence in a man's integrity, or in his blind adherence to the cause of the Joint, nothing could induce him to deal with that man again. Not even Joseph Schwartz could break down this stubbornness, and, being a wise man, Mr. Schwartz did not try more than once.

2.

The most unlikely melodrama in which the Joint and Saly Mayer participated arose from the German offer to sell Hungarian Jews in return for war material. As early as 1943 this *Grand-Guignol* fantasy had suggested itself to Himmler. Joseph Schwartz first heard of it when on a flying visit to Istanbul, whence the Jewish Agency was in communication with the Underground in most of the occupied countries. Mr. Schwartz was told that Himmler wished to meet him, preferably in Spain, to discuss the liberation of a hundred thousand Hungarian Jews for Palestine (or for the West, if anybody wanted them) in return for some unspecified goods. Mr. Schwartz reported to the Joint in New York and asked for instructions. New York consulted Washington. The reply was that no American citizen could meet with Germans to discuss blackmail. The next question was whether Saly Mayer could accept Himmler's invitation. The Department of State said it had no control over Saly Mayer, but that funds from the Joint were not to be used without specific permission from the United States government. So the request went to Saint Gallen to open the negotiations.

By this time it was 1944 and the German offer had become even more astounding. The war was going badly for the Third Reich. The men in charge of the "final solution" were worried about their own necks. Suddenly the SS offered to export a million Jews in return for ten thousand trucks, which were to be used only against the Russians, plus two hundred tons of tea, eight hundred tons of coffee and two million cakes of soap.

The offer was made by SS Colonel Adolf Eichmann, Himmler's chief of staff for the killing of Jews. But not even Himmler could contradict the Führer on high policy. And throughout that disastrous summer of 1944 Hitler was depriving his army of precious rolling stock in order that the trains might run uninterruptedly to Auschwitz. The plan to sell living Jews, therefore, must have been a belated insurance policy for Eichmann and his friends. They may have hoped that Hitler was so busy with his war that he would not notice whether the gas chambers were filled to overflowing.

And who was Eichmann, this god who set himself to save or to condemn a million people? According to his friend, Baron von Wisliceny (who was also selling Jews on a retail basis in Slovakia), Eichmann "was in every respect a painstaking bureaucrat. . . . He always told me that the most important thing was to be covered at all times by one's superiors." Another version is that at the end of the war he boasted that he "would leap into his grave laughing because the feeling that he had five million people on his conscience would be for him a source of extraordinary satisfaction." Gerald Reitlinger described him, during the last days at Budapest, as "not the cautious, sly German bureaucrat, but a cynical drunkard and corrupt satrap of the SS displaying his smart mistress and his horses." On any showing, he does not sound like a reliable man with whom to conclude immense and fateful bargains.

In March of 1944 Hitler had forced the dissolution of the Hungarian government. He occupied the airports around Budapest and sent the SS to police the country under the command of Major General Winkelmann. The orders were "to perform tasks of the SS and police concerning Hungary, and especially political duties in connection with the Jewish problem." Eichmann moved to the Majestic Hotel in Budapest and began planning the greatest "resettlement" since the death of the Warsaw Ghetto: Action Hoess. He had almost a million new victims at his disposal.

Hoess himself, the commandant at Auschwitz, visited Budapest frequently—always complaining that he was swamped with too many Jews and that his five crematoria were overworked. In spite of the chaos of the German economy, he gained permission to build a new railway line which landed his passengers within a few hundred feet of the ovens. He built enormous new burning-pits to ease the pressure on his inadequate plant. And he dug a new shooting-trench in the woods—thirty feet deep, half a mile long—which he hoped would accommodate the bodies that could not be burned. His own estimate is that he consumed 400,000 Hungarian Jews in 46 days during the summer of 1944. Mr. Reitlinger thinks he was boasting and that the figure was not more than 300,000. In any case, this was the season when Auschwitz was at its highest point of efficiency. Yet the pressure was so great that at least 50,000 Hungarian Jewesses were always kept waiting.

Some of the males from Hungary were fit for work. Only the undernourished and the old men and the children were killed immediately. The rest were allowed to labor (and starve) at the I. G. Farben plant which had been built nearby, or on the construction of underground airplane factories—a tribute to the British-American-Russian bombing. This "Buna" plant of I. G. Farben, and also the factory-building, had a double purpose. The first was slow but useful extermination. Nobody was intended to survive, although a few abnormally robust Jews lasted until the arrival of the Russian armies. The second purpose was to camouflage the incessant massacre. The world was told, and tried its best to believe, that the Jews were being rounded up for war work rather than for the grave.

The young, strong females at Auschwitz were also worked to death, digging anti-tank trenches; but most women were destroyed as soon as possible. First they were shorn of all their hair, which was used for mattresses, felt rugs, and other necessities. Some women lived long enough for a second shearing.

People less careful than the Germans might have wasted that hair, to say nothing of the children's toys, the gold teeth, and the false arms and legs—all sorted and hoarded. One marvels at this diligent miserliness, which was undiscouraged by the noise of the approaching Russian guns. The camp attendants behaved like giant insects, conditioned from immemorial times to do one thing only, and unable to stop doing it even on the verge of death. Hoess, for example, complains in his autobiography at the necessity of killing the Jews who worked in the garden, because his children grew fond of them. When they asked where their friends were, Hoess felt as awkward as if he had put down a favorite puppy. Yet he did not spare a single gardener beyond the allotted time.

Strangely, in spite of this methodical preparation (new pits, new trenches, and a new railway line), Eichmann made his proposal to barter a million lives on the eve of the forty-six days during which Hoess claimed four hundred thousand victims. He made it to Joel Brand, a member of a Zionist rescue group in Hungary which had been bribing the local police with fair success and thus smuggling occasional Jews into Palestine. "I expect you know who I am," said Eichmann, according to Mr. Brand. "I was in charge of the 'Actions' in Germany and Poland and Czechoslovakia. Now it's Hungary's turn. . . . I am prepared to sell you one million Jews. . . . Blood for money, cash for blood. . . . Whom do you want to save? Men capable of procreation? Women who can bear children? Old people? Children? . . . We shall want goods, though, not money. . . . I want you to go abroad and get in direct touch with your people and with representatives of the Allied powers. Then come back to me with a concrete proposal."

The Saving Remnant

Since Joel Brand had been working in the Underground at Budapest, he knew that the last great concentration of Jews in Occupied Europe was about to be sacrificed. He was out of touch with the world and could not see the absurdity of expecting the Western Allies to give war material to the Germans for use against Russia. His own impoverished organization had succeeded in buying a few lives; why should not the rich West buy a multitude? So he accepted the mission and asked to be sent to Istanbul, where he could get in touch with the Jewish Agency and the Joint. The Germans flew him out in the company of a Hungarian called Bandi Grosz, a pure mercenary who was known to have been selling "information" to both sides. In British eyes the mission was thus discredited from the start. When Brand found that he could not raise the money (let alone the war material) through his friends in Istanbul, he and Grosz unwisely set out for Palestine. The British picked them both up in June 1944 and detained them at Cairo until the end of the war.

The news of the Eichmann plan reached the West in July. *The Times* of London called it "a monstrous 'offer'—a new level of fantasy and self-deception . . . an attempt to blackmail, deceive and split the Allies." The unhappy Joel Brand could never understand this point of view. He felt he had been given a chance to be the savior of his people. He pursued his dangerous mission bravely, knowing that if he failed, the whole of his family might perish. And today he still believes that the million Jews could have been rescued, had he only been eloquent enough to persuade an indifferent world that Eichmann meant what he said. This is a haunting thought, but it is not true. Whatever Eichmann meant, he could not possibly fulfil ten per cent of his promise. Hitler's main reason for seizing Hungary in March of 1944 was to kill nine hundred thousand Jews. Himmler and Eichmann and all the little sub-Eichmanns may have known that their days were numbered; they may have longed to buy themselves a Jew-saving reputation in order to escape the hangman's rope, but none of them had power to release more than a handful of the condemned.

"When Hitler learnt of one of these small releases," says Gerald Reitlinger, "he became so enraged that he gave orders that no living inmate of a concentration camp, whether Jew or gentile, was to fall into Allied hands." How, then, could Joel Brand believe that Eichmann, "a cynical drunkard and corrupt satrap," could cheat Hitler of a million corpses? The answer is that every one of us might believe it, if such a glorious prospect were spread before our eyes. Who could refrain from trying?

Descending from the false mountaintop where Satan (in the disguise of an SS officer) had been tempting his victim with impossible prizes, and re-entering the grim flatland of reality, we may take comfort from the fact that the Eichmann offer saved some lives. When the hope-intoxicated Joel Brand was defeated, the sober Saly Mayer took charge.

In January of 1944 President Roosevelt had created the War Refugee Board to help in rescuing "the victims of enemy oppression." The board was to work with such private agencies as the Joint, lending the support of government when possible, and keeping an eye on the enthusiastic citizens' groups to make sure that they did not overstep the bounds which were set by Washington. Between 1944 and 1946, the Joint spent more than fifteen million dollars on this cooperative work.

Roswell McClelland, a Quaker, was head of the board in Switzerland when Saly Mayer took over the negotiations with Eichmann—and with Kurt Becher, who met with Mayer as the representative of the SS. The relations between Mr. McClelland and Saly Mayer became increasingly cordial, and even affectionate, as the board learned that Mayer, like the JDC in New York, could be trusted not to ignore a directive. In time the Joint was even allowed to tantalize Eichmann by depositing $5,000,000, allegedly earmarked for Jew-buying, in the Swiss National Bank. The money was not to be used without permission from Roswell McClelland, but it gave Mayer a strong bargaining-point with the Germans. The dollars were at hand, just across the border. What would the SS do as a sign of good faith?

Since nobody in New York or Lisbon or Switzerland believed in the offer of a million Jews, and since ransom was out of the question, Saly Mayer's job was to keep the negotiations going at any cost, and to fool Eichmann and Becher into believing that if they would make some token concessions they might one day receive their huge reward. Mayer accomplished his task superbly. He has been cruelly attacked for not doing more. He has been described as a close-fisted Swiss businessman who could not bring himself to spend money freely even to save the lives of his fellow Jews. The criticism implies that he should have broken faith with the American government and destroyed the long reputation of the Joint for playing fair with the Department of State—not that he could have done it, even had he been a rogue, since no dollar could have left the Swiss National Bank without the permission of Mr. McClelland. The money, in fact, was false money, which the Germans were never to possess but with which Saly Mayer was to play a dangerous game of poker.

In view of these facts, the lives which were saved are a high tribute to a good, stubborn, and devoted man. According to a report from the War Refugee Board to the American Department of State, the results of the long-drawn-out wrangles between Mayer and Becher were as follows:

1. Sixteen hundred and seventy-three Jews were brought from Hungary to Switzerland, via Bergen-Belsen, as a sign of Eichmann's good faith.

2. The deportation of 200,000 Jews from Budapest to Auschwitz was canceled. (Many of these may have starved or been murdered in Budapest, but anything was better than Auschwitz.)

3. Another 17,000 Hungarian Jews who were headed for Auschwitz were diverted to a camp in Austria, where they had at least a chance of staying alive.

4. The SS gave a tacit agreement to allow the International Red Cross in Budapest to shelter 3000 Jewish children.

5. Permission was given to distribute food and clothing to 7000 Jews in labor camps in the region of Vienna.

6. In April 1945, 69 leaders of Jewish communities, from Slovakia and Hungary, were released into Switzerland.

7. Invaluable first-hand information was obtained as to what the Germans had done, and what they still planned to do, in regard to the "final solution."

And after all this, on May 23, 1945, Mr. McClelland and Saly Mayer asked the Swiss National Bank to return the $5,000,000 to the JDC in New York. The money which was not real, the chips which were only a bluff, had served a useful purpose.

Under the circumstances, neither Joseph Schwartz nor Saly Mayer nor the office in New York could have done more. Yet the circumstances were not imposed by nature; they were man-made and deserve examination. In the first place, the Western Allies had permitted (or encouraged) a conspiracy of silence in regard to the death camps. The facts about Treblinka reached London in 1942. The facts about Auschwitz reached the World Jewish Congress at Geneva in the same year. Had they been broadcast immediately, might not the British people have asked for a relaxation of the White Paper of 1939? Might not the American people have asked for a relaxation of the Immigration Act of 1924? In the second place, why did no government heed the pleas of the Jewish Agency and the World Jewish Congress to bomb the railway line from Eastern Europe into Auschwitz—a long, meandering line through scrub forest, easy to destroy, yet a death line for millions of our fellow men? In the third place, why did the West wait until after Hoess's abominable "forty-six days" before launching a psychological war against the SS? When at last President Roosevelt told the murderers that they would be held to strict account at the war's end, the death trains from Budapest were halted for several months.

Perhaps the answer in each case is that the West was fighting for its life and that our chosen rulers did not have time for such details. The world is a harsh place, admittedly; but must we regard 6,000,000 dead Jews as a detail? Might not the West have done better had it really tried? [1]

3.

When Joel Brand was sequestered by the British, the Hungarian-Jewish negotiations with Eichmann were taken over by Dr. Reszoe Kastner, Brand's superior officer in the Jewish rescue committee of Budapest. Kastner, therefore, became the liaison between Eichmann-Becher and Saly Mayer. This was unlucky, because Kastner did not share Mayer's view of "O.P.M." He had been a free-lance journalist and was unaccustomed to keeping accounts. Saly Mayer never trusted him, although Joseph Schwartz kept urging that this irresponsibility with money was unimportant in view of the fact that Kastner was a brave man who gambled his life each time he entered Eichmann's office—and for the sole purpose of saving his fellow Jews.

Since Kastner came to a tragic end, we record Mr. Schwartz's opinion that the worst which could be said about him is that he was a nuisance to accountants. He would never, for example, give a final list of the Hungarians who had advanced money against the postwar credit of the Joint. No matter how often he wrote that the enclosed list was the last one, a few weeks later

---

[1] "As I see it," wrote Gerald Reitlinger, "the blame of the Allies lies not in refusing to bargain with murderers, but in failing to use a clear, consistent and forthright language, broadcast in such a way that every German bureaucrat would understand and fear it. That way, I believe, hundreds of thousand of lives could have been saved."

he would send more names—troublesome, but surely a venial sin.

Suddenly, and against his will, Kastner was given a task which no man should be given but which no dedicated man could refuse. Eichmann told him to nominate the 1673 Jews (out of the 900,000) who were to be sent to Switzerland as a sign to Saly Mayer of the "good faith" of the SS. As Mr. Schwartz says, if Elijah himself were to make that selection he would be accused of favoring his friends. In any case, Kastner did not favor himself. He stayed behind, knowing that his usefulness to Eichmann was at an end and expecting each day to be shipped to Auschwitz.

Strangely, however, Kastner lived through the war. At the time of the Nuremberg trials, and without consulting his remaining co-workers of the rescue committee, he signed an affidavit saying that Becher had occasionally lived up to his promises and had thus been helpful in saving some Jewish lives. As a result of the affidavit, Becher is alive today but Kastner is dead. Yet we have seen that the Kastner-Becher-Mayer negotiations saved or prolonged many lives, in addition to the 1673. At some point during the endless bargaining, Kastner may well have offered, "Give me these extra Jews and if we both survive I shall say something good about you." Is it wicked to keep a promise made to an officer of the SS?

Ten years later this interesting question was argued in the District Court at Jerusalem. Kastner was living in Israel and had a post in the government. He was a saint to the few whom he had saved but not to the relatives of the many who had perished. A Mr. Greenwald accused him of collaborating, rather than bargaining, with the Germans. The affidavit which saved Becher was one main charge. Another was that, in order to extract from Eichmann the pitiful handful which reached Switzerland, Kastner had agreed to keep silent—not to warn the 900,000 of their impending fate, not to give them the chance to make a last revolt such as that of the Warsaw Ghetto.

The Saving Remnant

Mr. Greenwald was sued for criminal libel. The whole of Israel took sides passionately. The grateful survivors and their friends were aligned against the defenders of the ghosts. The court awarded Kastner only one pound in damages, thus in fact supporting the accuser. But the Supreme Court, on appeal, found against Mr. Greenwald on every count, except for the undisputed fact that Kastner had said a saving word for Becher. By the time he was thus exonerated, Kastner had been murdered, which is precisely what Mr. Greenwald suggested in his first attack: "Kastner should be liquidated."

One of the great leaders of the new Israel said to this author that he liked and respected Kastner, but that the unhappy man was probably not too sad at being killed. His life had been poisoned forever during the weeks when he had to select the few who were to live. Since this was the view of the representatives of the Joint who dealt with him—including those who found him unsympathetic—we repeat the posthumous tribute.

Joseph Schwartz sees the Kastner case as a symptom of a larger malady, of a guilt neurosis which afflicted all occupied countries but which was most virulent among the Jews. Many of the survivors felt that their neighbors were asking, "What crimes must you have committed in order to escape Auschwitz?" Collaboration is a meaningless word. It can mean selling your friends to the Gestapo, or it can mean formal politeness to a drunken German in order not to be shot on the spot. In the second sense, "collaboration" is in the eye of the beholder. And since the beholder is also scared and starved and half demoralized, his eye is frequently unkind. In the DP camps after the war, the Joint had often to deal with this nameless, incurable guilt: "Why did not I too 'follow where all is fled'?"

4.

An unassailable hero of the Hungarian massacre was a brave young Swede, Raoul Wallenberg, who for a change was murdered by the Russians instead of the Germans. We have seen how Sweden gave refuge to all Jews who could escape from her neighbor nations. In June of 1944, in the midst of the "forty-six days" of Eichmann and Hoess, when Auschwitz was functioning at its discreditable best, the King of Sweden asked the Hungarian "government" to send him some of the doomed men and women. All Western nations were in agreement that the Germans should stop killing Jews; but Sweden alone said, "Send them to us."

The magnificent gesture was impractical. The only transport available for Jews in 1944 ran straight to the gas chambers. Yet the Swedish *démarche* added strength to the psychological warfare which was at last being aimed at the crumbling Hungarian state.

The King's message was delivered to the so-called government by Wallenberg, a Swedish businessman, thirty-two years of age, who had been chosen by the War Refugee Board to do such rescue work as might still be possible in Budapest. He was exactly the man for the job, fearless, resourceful, and indomitable. His government gave him diplomatic status; the Joint gave him money to buy food on the black market and to bribe any Germans and Hungarians who had sense enough to know that the Russians would soon be at the gates. He bribed; he threatened; he coaxed the small, scared local officials with promises to save them from the hangman after the war. He issued thousands of Swedish passports, and by some private magic he induced the Gestapo and the civil officials to accept these fantasy-papers. When the Gestapo insisted that the "honorary Swedes" must at least work in labor camps until such time as they could set sail for their unvisited land, he organized his own camps in Budapest where he could keep an eye on his new fellow citizens.

Like all men who dare to snap their fingers at a tyrant, either Wallenberg had to be abolished immediately or he was bound to attract disciples: an absence of fear is almost as contagious as fear itself. He was not abolished. Before long, therefore, other legations began creating honorary citizens. Even some Hungarians offered Wallenberg buildings in which to house his Semitic Swedes. With these gifts, plus the quarters he rented in the name of his government, he soon had thirty-two houses under his flag and with extraterritorial rights—homes for some thousands of protégés. This plan also—simple, impudent, and unrebuked—was quickly copied. Soon the "international ghetto" of the diplomatic corps sheltered 13,000 Jews.

Occasionally these fugitives from the death trains could even strike back. Wallenberg, a born commander, knew that men should not merely wait passively and rot month after month, concerned only with whether the dread knock on the door came before dawn. Such was the fate of millions of Europeans for five years, but Wallenberg would not accept it. He organized a Jewish commando, in enemy uniform, to raid and to rescue, to kill and be killed, but chiefly to teach the ill-instructed that Jews are deadly fighters.

By the late autumn of 1944 the Kastner deal had been agreed on; most of Saly Mayer's poker hands with Eichmann and Becher had been played; the brief respite for the Hungarian Jews, following on President Roosevelt's threats, had come to an end; the Russians were besieging Budapest. Not only the Germans, but the crazed Hungarian members of the "Arrow Cross," proved once more that they would rather kill Jews than fight for their homelands. The mournful death camps of Poland were no longer useful. Their ovens were cold. Their ditches were replete with bodies. The order had been given to dynamite the installations, on the assumption that they could be obliterated and that nobody would ever know.

Eichmann was thus deprived of his best slaughterhouse by the end of October 1944. How was he to consume the remaining Hungarian Jews? His answer was the "death marches"—from Budapest to Vienna, endless columns of wasted, diseased people. Most of them died from exposure. Others, who sat down for a moment's rest, were shot in the back of the neck. But the last assuaging sight for many of them—suggesting that the world might not be totally, everlastingly evil—was Wallenberg riding along the columns, distributing food, bribing and abusing the SS, and demanding the release of his "Swedish" Jews.

Early in January 1945, the Russians took Budapest. The Red Cross and the foreign legations, who had done much to help and who were ready to do everything to save the remnant, were ordered to leave. This meant, among other disasters, that the money which had been sent by the Joint could not be distributed. So Wallenberg went to Marshal Malinovski to protest. Three days later he returned to his own office in the company of Russian soldiers. He left at once, telling his staff that he did not know whether he was a guest or a prisoner. He was never seen again. The Joint hired detectives, who could not enter Russia and who learned nothing in Budapest. The Joint asked the Department of State to seek information in Moscow. Finally, after the death of Stalin, the government of Sweden asked Khrushchev for a report. In 1958 the news came that Wallenberg had died of a heart attack two years after his imprisonment. Nobody bothered to explain why he had been put in jail.

5.

As a footnote to the whole dark Hungarian story—which has been confused by bitter charges, denials, and counter-attacks— we quote from a letter which was received in June of 1944 by the San Salvador consul in Geneva. The writer, Miklos Kraus, was head of the Palestine Office in Budapest. He has been described as the most reliable witness among all who have left a record. The letter is headed: Budapest, June 19, 1944.

The deportations from Hungary began on May 15. . . . As is shown in the attached reports, 335,000 Jews were deported up to June 7, and since that date a further 100,000. In the provinces there are only four towns where there are still some Jews, and after the deportations from these towns have been carried through, it will be the turn of Budapest. The number of Jews living in Budapest and the surroundings amounts to 350,000. . . . The whole Jewish race in Hungary is condemned to death. There are no exceptions, there is no escape, there is no possibility of getting away to a neighboring country. . . . There are only two possibilities left to us: suicide or acceptance of our fate.

This disposes of the notion that Eichmann might have been serious about his "offer" to Joel Brand. By the time Mr. Brand reached Istanbul, half the Jews of Hungary were dead. The letter also exposes the folly of accusing Kastner of conspiring to keep his fellow Jews in ignorance of their doom. And it suggests that the saving work accomplished by Saly Mayer and by Wallenberg was little less than a miracle.

6.

Since Auschwitz may gain permanent renown as the most hideous single item in Western history, its demise should be recorded. The first hint that the nightmare might be drawing to an end was given by Becher to Saly Mayer on August 21, 1944. Desperate to extract money from the Joint (and to save his own skin after the defeat), he offered to stop the deportations on that date. But he did not have the authority and he did not receive the money. Then Himmler intervened—also in the hope of buying postwar credit. So the last "selection" for the gas chambers took place on October 30. And on November 17 Himmler ordered: "The crematoria at Auschwitz are to be dismantled. The Jews working in the Reich are to get normal Eastern workers' rations. In the absence of Jewish hospitals they may be treated with Aryan patients." Thereafter the only people killed at Auschwitz were the *Sonderkommando:* the relatively healthy inmates who had been used to entice or force their fellow prisoners into the gas chambers and then to manhandle the bodies from the chambers to the crematoria.

As early as September 1944, the Germans were moving females from Auschwitz to Ravensbrück and Bergen-Belsen. Anne Frank was one of them. She died of typhus at Belsen. Toward the end of October, the evacuation of the males began, to Dachau, Buchenwald, and Sachsenhausen. By the middle of January 1945, when the Russian guns were pounding all day long, only 64,000 victims remained. Most of them were piled into open freight cars, dressed in their prison pajamas, for a slow train ride toward the West. The others set out for central Germany on foot. Very few survived from either group. Yet someone had blundered, or had disobeyed orders; for when the Russians arrived on January 26 they found 2819 living bodies—too weak to move, but at least not slaughtered when the last guards withdrew.

Auschwitz, during its heyday, had room for half a million people in an area of ten square miles. Hitler's plan, as late as the autumn of 1944, was to double the size of the camp, double the ovens and the gas chambers. Since the supply of Jews and gypsies was almost exhausted, the improved Auschwitz must have been intended for Poles and Ukrainians, in order that the Master Race might have *Lebensraum*. During its last days, therefore, Auschwitz surpassed itself in macabre grisliness. One group of Germans, under Himmler's command, was destroying the original installations. Another group was building permanent barracks for the bigger camp which the Führer had ordered. The Red Army, when it moved in, was puzzled to find these new buildings almost completed while the old crematoria had just been blown to bits.

On May 12, 1945, a Soviet commission reported as follows: "Using rectified coefficients for the part-time employment of the crematorium ovens and for the periods when they stood empty, the technical expert commission has ascertained that during the time that Auschwitz camp existed the German butchers exterminated in this camp not less than four million citizens of the USSR, Poland, France, Yugoslavia, Czechoslovakia, Romania, Hungary, Holland, Belgium, and other countries." Mr. Reitlinger says this was a gross exaggeration and that the camp was too inefficient to kill four million people. And Hoess himself, in a moment of humility, admits that "even Auschwitz had limits to its destructive possibilities." One can only add that it did its best.

Chapter Seven

"Action Reinhardt," says Hoess in his autobiography, "was the code name given to the collection, sorting, and utilization of all articles which were acquired as a result of the transports of Jews and their extermination." We have seen the care which was taken over such inexpensive items as hair, teeth, toys, and artificial limbs. But many Jews carried valuable property in the one suitcase they were allowed, and this proved a continual bother to Hoess and to the other camp commandants. The cases were left on the station platform while the Jews to be killed immediately were put on one side and those to be worked to death were sent to their barracks. In spite of Himmler's order that anyone who touched this precious luggage should be shot, Hoess complains that "an immense amount of property was stolen by members of the SS and by the police."

This was no small-scale operation. It involved "valuables worth many millions of pounds." Yet the Reich did not do badly, in spite of the pilfering. "Eichmann told me on one occasion," writes Hoess, "that the jewelry and currency were sold in Switzerland and that the entire Swiss jewelry market was dominated by these sales."

The Joint first learned of the magnitude of this trade in dead men's goods when the French and American armies captured the "Gold Train"—twenty-four freight cars packed with the most salable possessions of the vanished Hungarian Jews. The train was on its way toward Germany during the last days of the war. It was sidetracked at Salzburg, owing to a shortage of locomotives. The French seized eight of the freight cars, and the Americans took the rest. No detailed inventory has been found; but according to the Hungarians in charge of the transport the following items were included, to the value of at least $50,000,000:

> 50 crates of gold bullion
> 50 crates of gold coin
> 30 crates of jewelry
> 1560 boxes of silverware
> 100 valuable paintings
> 5000 valuable carpets

The Jewish Agency asked the new Hungarian government to renounce its claim on this loot so that the proceeds might be used for the rehabilitation of Jews. The government agreed. The Joint then approached the American Secretary of State, James Byrnes, requesting that "subject to restitution of identifiable items to owners or their heirs, this property should be made available for the purpose of relief and rehabilitation. . . ." Mr. Byrnes also agreed; yet the results were disappointing.

The contents of the Gold Train had been stored in a warehouse near Salzburg. The fighting troops of all armies take a negligent view of enemy property, especially when it is gathered conveniently under one roof as if it were asking to be "liberated." We have no information about the diligence of the French liberators, but we know that the Americans did not do badly. Several officers of high rank appeared before courts martial as a result of their efforts. When the best of the stolen goods had thus been stolen for a second time, the less portable remains were auctioned in New York for a little more than $2,000,000. Ten per cent was donated to non-Jewish relief, and the rest was shared between the Joint and the Jewish Agency.

2.

After the war of 1914-1918, the Joint had first to rescue its East European clients from disease and hunger, and then to help rebuild their lives on the spot. After the Second War there was no "spot." If the few remaining Jews of Eastern Europe stayed at home, they were met with pogroms as at Kielce. If they sought Palestine, they were met with the British White Paper. Elsewhere, as in the United States, they might hope one day to draw a lucky number in the quota—assuming that Belsen or Buchenwald or Sachsenhausen had left them sufficiently healthy to be accepted and sufficiently patient to endure the long wait. Many of them, therefore, fleeing from uncharitable fellow countrymen and repulsed by uncharitable foreigners, sought refuge in the DP camps: barbed wire again, and armed guards, and in many cases the old pajama-uniforms devised by the Germans. Before long, 250,000 Jews were in the camps, mostly in Germany and Austria.

When the Germans surrendered, the Western Allies found about six and a half million displaced persons in their areas. By the end of July more than four million had been repatriated; but Jews from the East had already begun to trickle into the camps. Then Earl Harrison, the American representative on the Intergovernmental Committee on Refugees, was sent to Europe to report on the American zone. Joseph Schwartz was asked to go with him. Their survey was handed to President Truman at the end of August: a gloomy document which was necessarily critical of the Army, although it pointed out that the Army should not have been expected to put its heart into this job. The generals and other high officials knew that they must live among the Germans for years to come; thus they sought to be lenient and conciliatory wherever possible—not weakness, not overt fraternization, but a sensible desire to get along with the people whom they were told to rule. The displaced persons, on the other hand, were a temporary nuisance and were treated as such.

Furthermore, after a great defeat the Germans have a talent for seeming meek, obsequious, and obedient. The displaced persons were angry, impatient, and disobedient—qualities which have never endeared themselves to the military mind. So the Army felt it had discharged its duty when it gave these unruly wards a food ration of 2000 calories a day (mostly bread, potatoes, and coffee), meanwhile policing them with sufficient rigor to keep them out of mischief. The hygiene and medical care were substandard, and the camps were overcrowded.

Mr. Harrison made two important recommendations which were accepted, and one which proved impracticable. The first was to set up separate camps for the Jews. The Joint warmly supported this—not because the Joint favors segregation but because the plight of the Jews in the large camps was heart-rending. Many had emerged as half-living skeletons from the care of the Germans and were in need of special medical aid and special diet. Others had fled their old homes because their old neighbors had become more anti-Semitic than ever under the tutelage of the Third Reich. And now they found themselves, still a minority, herded among Poles, Ukrainians, and others from the East, whose own experiences had made them more savage than ever toward the Jews. No one who had escaped from Auschwitz via Belsen should have been forced to live again in daily fear of his life. By the grace of Mr. Harrison's report, and with the help of strong pressure from the Joint, the separate camps were established.

The Saving Remnant

The second recommendation—also lifesaving—was that UNRRA should take the DP camps under its wing, thus improving the food and general relief program and perhaps even resulting in some rehabilitation. This too was accomplished, under the over-all authority of the Army. UNRRA, whose director, Herbert Lehman, had played an important part in JDC's relief and rehabilitation program after the First War, set up its own displaced-persons department, and the standards improved notably. Yet the field workers of UNRRA were puzzled by the Jews with their persistent demand for cultural and religious aid and their unwillingness to be content with food, clothes, and medicine.

Even more surprising, these Jews had apparently forgotten the gentle civilization of the shtetl, lost the submissiveness with which they had accepted centuries of persecution. The ovens at Auschwitz, it seemed, had smelted humility out of the mid-century Jewish soul, leaving a cold rancor in many hearts. The "new" Jew, who was soon to astonish the world in Israel (and who probably represents the majority of survivors from the ancient Pale of Settlement), was one of the least accommodating characters in history. His stored-up passions had been set free. At last he faced his utter homelessness in Europe east of the Rhine, where the Christians have never ceased torturing his people. Germans, Czechs, Poles, Hungarians, Russians, Austrians, Romanians, and Balts—at last he admitted to himself that he hated them all. He also hated the more innocent West, which preached the "rule of law" but which did not lift a finger to save a Jew. He hated the British Labour government, which had promised the Open Door in Palestine and whose promises were as dusty as all the promises of gentiles. And he did not spare America in his wide contempt, since the Americans had averted their eyes from Auschwitz and had refused refuge to the tiny remnant. He wanted to escape from the West with its sanctimony and its cruelty. His anti-goyism was a passion, maybe a disease—but if so, the disease had been inculcated by the goyim for at least seventeen centuries. Slow to take hold, it became a raging fever when it finally struck.

Richard Crossman, Member of Parliament, was astonished to see a Polish Jew tear up his emigration papers for America, saying that he could never trust a Christian again. In the first of the little mimeographed newspapers produced in the camps, another Jew from Poland wrote: "No! I cannot return. The shades of my nearest and dearest will constantly stalk before my eyes and demand of me, 'Why, why did you come back to perform your wedding ceremony on our graves?' . . . No, let the men from Mars go there, but I? Never!" And the last issue of one of the newspapers, when the camps were almost empty, took leave of its public with these words: "We have given the world the will and testament of those who perished: 'Do not put your faith into European civilization. In the Stygian chambers of inhuman persecution we signed the divorce. We are handing the divorce papers over to you. Return to the sources of Jewish morality!'" Out of this rage and scorn came the passion which built Israel.

Thus the Jewish DP camps, more and more incomprehensible to UNRRA, more and more repugnant to the Army, became increasingly dependent upon the Joint, not only for necessities, but for books and articles of religion, help in organizing committees, and schools for the children from the forest refuges and from the captured murder camps—the first uninstructed children in European Jewish history.

As we shall see, the Joint itself had no easy time with these camps, especially with the morally broken members, a few of whom took the human but unwise view that they should be looked after by other people indefinitely. Meanwhile, Mr. Harrison's third recommendation was that the President should ask Great Britain to help clear the camps by allowing 100,000 Jews into Palestine immediately, and that the United States should make an equivalent gesture. This might have solved the problem once and for all, but it was not to be. The request to the British government was subsequently made, and rejected. The American "gesture" was limited to the Truman directive of December 1945. In the light of American history, and coming from the President of a nation whose inhabitants are all by origin either immigrants or redskins, this was a disappointing document. Mr. Truman clearly believed that if he asked the Congress for anything worth having he might provoke a chauvinism that would undo even the existing laws.

In a statement preceding his directive, the President told Congress that he had no thought of expanding the quotas which had been established in 1924. All he asked was that they should not be diminished: "This period of unspeakable human distress is not the time for us to close or to narrow our gates. I wish to emphasize, however, that any effort to bring relief to these displaced persons and refugees must and will be strictly within the limits of the present quotas as imposed by law."

Mr. Truman pointed out that "very few persons from Europe have migrated to the United States during the war years. In the fiscal year 1942, only 10 per cent of the immigration quotas was used; in 1943, 5 per cent; in 1944, 6 per cent; and in 1945, 7 per cent. . . . These unused quotas, however, do not accumulate through the years, and I do not intend to ask the Congress to change this rule." Had he dared to demand legislation permitting these unused quotas to be fulfilled, the world might have felt that the United States was at least trying to be helpful. But Mr. Truman had long experience in the Senate; presumably he knew that 1945 was not the time to press for an overtly humanitarian act.

He did demand, on his own executive authority, that "the Secretary of State [should] establish with the utmost dispatch consular facilities at or near displaced-persons and refugee-assembly areas in the American zones of occupation. It shall be the responsibility of these consular officers, in conjunction with the immigration inspectors, to determine as quickly as possible the

174

eligibility of the applicants for visas and admission to the United States." He added that "visas should be distributed fairly among persons of all faiths, creeds, and nationalities. I desire that special attention be devoted to orphaned children." And the President directed the Secretary of State to make arrangements with welfare organizations whereby they could offer a corporate affidavit of support, instead of having to find a man or woman to make an individual affidavit in respect of each immigrant.

In the course of his statement explaining and defending the directive, Mr. Truman had said: "This is the opportunity for America to set an example for the world in cooperation toward alleviating human misery." Had America seriously chosen to set such an example, to do her fair share in emptying the DP camps of the homeless and the stateless, she should have admitted some four hundred thousand immigrants. In fact, she never even admitted the annual quota which the old law allowed. Mr. Truman announced that he was dissatisfied. Even he, with his long experience in government, had underestimated the power of an unwilling bureaucracy to thwart his small but generous effort. And so, to some extent, had the Joint.[1]

Moses A. Leavitt (Secretary of the JDC since 1940 and Executive Vice-Chairman since 1947) sat in New York at the center of the world-wide information which poured into the offices of the Joint. He had seen too much suffering, too many grievous disappointments, to be easily hopeful. He knew that the directive ignored the major problem, yet he was thankful for small favors. He wrote to a friend in Canada: "Although it is true that the prospective immigrants to the United States would all come un-

---

[1] In 1946, 16,000 Jews reached the United States; in 1947, 25,000; in 1948, 16,000. This 57,000 in three years was scarcely the American equivalent to 100,000 in one lump into Palestine. During the twenty-one years after Hitler's rise to power, 317,000 Jews were admitted to the United States, averaging about 15,000 per year. This may or may not have been generous; but it bore no relation to the problem created by Germany.

der existing legal quotas, the fact is that these quotas were never filled and administrative regulations have made it almost impossible to fill even a percentage of them. The directive, however, cuts through all the red tape, and secondly and most important, permits private agencies to give a corporate guarantee of maintenance."

Both the President and the experienced Mr. Leavitt hoped that at last "the administrative regulations and all the red tape" had been circumvented. The figures just quoted suggest that neither the consular nor the immigration services agreed. The President could give orders; he could make sure that the machinery existed for sorting applicants and awarding visas; but he could not travel the DP camps and insist that the machinery be used. Clearly he was wise in not asking for new legislation, since he could not even enforce his executive order.

Since we have mentioned the "world-wide information" which reached Mr. Leavitt in New York, this is the time to scotch an old libel—propounded first by the Germans and then by the Russians—that the Joint served as an international spy service. The files of the New York office, and statements volunteered by officers of the Department of State, make it clear that the Joint kept the government of the United States wholly informed as to its own operations and as to the conditions of the Jews in various lands. It never collected information outside the sphere of its restricted work. If such information, or rumors of such possible information, came its way, it turned a deaf ear.

Although the Germans sometimes accused the Joint of spying, they were never spy-maddened as were the Russians and the satellite governments. The first of the Joint's American workers to become a victim of this mania was Israel Jacobson, who had been sent to Italy in 1944. After serving in Greece and Czechoslovakia, he became the Joint's Hungarian director in 1947. Two years later, when returning to his post after a visit to the United States, he was arrested on crossing the border and taken to the prison where Cardinal Mindszenty was being "softened" for his trial. He was threatened with lynching and was not allowed to wash, shave, or move about. After twelve days of such incarceration, Mr. Jacobson was released, charged with espionage, and expelled from the country. The Joint was not directly implicated, perhaps because it was spending more money in Hungary than in any other country except Israel. And the Joint was eager not to lose this foothold behind the Iron Curtain, since this was the last satellite country where it was permitted to work. Thus, although rich offers were made for Mr. Jacobson's story, the Joint induced him to keep quiet. One strong blast about the "life in a Hungarian prison," and the remaining Hungarian Jews would have been left helpless and friendless. To survive Eichmann, and then to be destroyed by a press release from an agent of the Joint, would have been an ironic fate. But Mr. Jacobson kept quiet; the Joint pretended nothing had happened; and the good work went forward—to the tune of more than $52,000,000 between 1946 and 1952: $18,000,000 on cash relief and canteens, $9,500,000 on relief in kind, nearly $5,000,000 on child care, $3,000,000 on the aged, $5,500,000 on medical and dental care, more than $5,000,000 on religious and cultural life and education, etc. The most revealing figure is the meager $645,000 spent on emigration. After the first postwar years, hardly anyone got out; so the Joint was desperate to stay in, and would accept larger insults than the arrest of Israel Jacobson. In 1949 the Hungarian government promised Joseph Schwartz to allow 3000 Jews to emigrate. By 1953, 2800 had left. Since then, emigration has been on the scale of 100 a year, or less. Yet more than half the Jews are registered at the Israeli Embassy, for going home—although this means that they are treated as spies, lose all privacy and most chances for holding a job.

In 1914 the Jewish population of Hungary was about 933,000. In 1939, it was about 800,000. And when the bloodthirsty Eichmann arrived in 1944, it was still about 600,000. We have seen that some Hungarian Jews were saved by ingenious measures and heroic men. A little more than 100,000 survived. These were the remnant to which the Joint gave its $52,000,000—and under the most awkward circumstances. Mr. Charles Jordan, who had represented the Joint in Hungary, reported in 1952 that here

> JDC violates one of its most fundamental principles; i.e., not to carry on, or give money to, an operation which it is unable to directly supervise, control, or at least audit through a *personal* representative. The tense diplomatic relations between Hungary and the United States have not allowed us to send anyone into Hungary since I left there in May 1951. But, JDC is so deeply concerned with what it knows to be the real and acute danger of death from starvation to thousands of aged Jewish men and women in Hungary who are without any other source of support that it takes upon itself the calculated risk of continuing to send substantial sums of money.

The Joint, in the days when it could act freely in Hungary, had created the Welfare Department of the Union of Jewish Communities. This department now administered the Joint's money, reporting by letter and telephone to headquarters in Paris. But since the letters were opened and the telephone calls were monitored, Mr. Jordan in Paris could never be certain that the Hungarian government allowed the truth to be told. Yet the gamble had to be taken. "Please do not think for a moment," said Mr. Jordan in his report,

> that we carry on this operation with any real sense of satisfaction. As a matter of fact, we feel that we are caught and we do not see an easy way of extricating ourselves. . . . The [Hungarian] Government states, whenever the question arises, that they have neither concern nor responsibility for the indigent Jews owing to the fact that they belong to the former bourgeoisie who have no claims on a People's State. For the same reason most of these people are ineligible for social benefits. . . . And yet, oddly enough—they and they **alone of all the satellite countries at least let us help some**

of their people. They permit it to be known that money from "American Imperialists" is permitted in to help their nationals. . . . Nobody really knows why.

Mr. Jordan hoped that this irrational situation might continue, and might even improve; but the end had come. The curtain fell in January of 1953, as a result of the "doctors' plot" in Moscow. The Hungarians followed the Russian line and even exaggerated *Tass*'s attacks on the Joint. All relations ceased. The leading Jews who had been responsible for administering the Joint's money in Hungary were arrested, as usual with no charge. The end of this grudging relationship with "American Imperialists" was as mysterious as the relationship itself.

Russia, after the Second War, had of course refused to allow her Jews to have dealings with the Joint. So Russia, unlike Hungary, could suffer no loss by accusing the Joint of spying and plotting on an impressive scale. This she did on January 13, 1953, when Moscow announced that "terrorist Jewish doctors" had killed two Russian leaders and were planning to kill many more. *Tass* added that the doctors were "connected with the international Jewish bourgeois-nationalist organization 'Joint' set up by the American Intelligence Service. . . . [The Joint] conducts broad-scale espionage, terroristic, and other subversive activities." This confused language was largely a repetition of what had been said two months earlier in Prague, when fourteen Czech Communist leaders—including Slansky, the head of the party—were tried for treason. The Joint had been accused of instigating all the strange, elaborate crimes—of thought as well as of action and inaction—for which these unhappy men were put away. Then, when *Tass* made the attack respectable, the little servile press followed: first Hungary; then Warsaw, where the Joint was described as the instrument of American warmongers engaged in "criminal, murderous work." And in Paris, *Ce Soir* ran a series of "Revelations" about the Joint, none of them complimentary.

The Saving Remnant

The "doctors' plot" was somehow connected with the bewildering struggle for power inside the Kremlin. Stalin died two months later, and the "plot" was dismissed as a fraud. Temporarily the violent anti-Semitism and anti-Zionism of Stalin's last days were set aside.

The Russians were unbalanced on the subject of espionage. If they learned that an organization had world-wide ramifications, they were almost bound to assume that it was a world-wide haunt of spies. Perhaps the Joint should be flattered that its ubiquity was thus recognized. Yet one must lament the vulgarity, inseparable from a dictator's control over mass communications, which leads people to read the following phrase without laughing: ". . . the international Jewish bourgeois-nationalist organization set up by the American Intelligence Service."

3.

We said that the Army and UNRRA found the Jews in American DP camps unruly wards, and that the Joint had its own troubles in seeking to help them. In part, the troubles were owing to that "divorce" from European civilization which so many Jews had signed in the shadow of the gas chambers, and in part to the admirable effort to run their own affairs (to become at least the shadows of free men) which developed as soon as the segregated camps were permitted. Yet they could not run their own affairs, even within the limits decreed by the Army, without money from the Joint. And the Joint (except for the extraordinary case of Hungary) did not give money unless it retained a measure of control. Crossed purposes were inevitable.

As early as June and July of 1945, the Jews in the camps formed working committees and adopted a constitution: a federation of the committees to represent their people before the Army, UNRRA, the Joint, and the Jewish Agency. This federation became the Central Committee of Liberated Jews, overwhelmingly

The Saving Remnant

Zionist in aspiration. They were the men and women who had returned by a miracle from the edge of hell and they recognized no homelands in Europe. They longed for Israel, but the doors were closed except for a derisory crack. They called themselves the *Sheerith Hapletah*, which we have translated as the "Saving Remnant." At their first meeting Dr. Zalman Grinberg told them, "We have been robbed of family and fortune, but not of fortitude. The landmarks of a thousand years have disappeared. New ones must be built, alongside those of the pioneers who preceded us, on our own soil. This and no less must be the goal of the representative body we have assembled to organize." The meeting was then addressed by Major Kaspi of the Jewish Brigade in the British Eighth Army—one of the most successful revolutionary groups in the history of Israel. The mere name of the brigade brought fresh hopes to the long-incarcerated Jews, who did not know that such a thing existed.

Major Kaspi said that, during the war across Egypt, North Africa, and Italy, the Brigade had had one thought in mind: the rescue of all fellow countrymen who had survived the Germans. The Saving Remnant and the Yishuv (the Jewish community of Palestine) were thenceforth inseparable. "You are bone of our bone, flesh of our flesh. Our families are overjoyed to know you have survived, and are waiting to welcome you with open and loving arms. . . . Unite! Be organized and disciplined!" The meeting then adopted a resolution: "We demand the immediate annulment of the 1939 White Paper, the opening of the gates of Palestine to all Jews who want to emigrate there, and the creation of the groundwork for the proclamation and establishment of a Jewish State in Palestine."

Everyone knew that the resolution was a polite way of declaring war on the British—an astonishing war of illegal immigration which quickly caused a great power to retreat. The Central Committee, therefore, was committed to three large tasks: the wresting of home rule from the American Army; the rebuilding of com-

munity and cultural life in the camps, with help from the Joint;
and the planning of a vast conspiracy against the British government, with help from the Brigade.

The first task proved unexpectedly difficult, since it brought
the committee hard against General Patton. The general, who
was in charge at Bad Tölz, could not understand the official
policy toward Germany. He took little interest in the death
camps. Denazification seemed to him an absurdity; the loss of
the war had seen to all that. The displaced persons, he admitted,
were victims of a mistaken policy on the part of the Germans,
who now confessed the mistake—so what was the fuss about?
Send the DPs home, forget the displeasing sight, and refrain from
heavy criticism of the Germans, who were, after all, first-class
soldiers.

Patton, with his obdurate folly, was a blessing to the DPs who
still had nations to receive them and homes to rebuild. In his
zeal to tidy up Germany and hide the ugly past, and with his
customary energy, the general repatriated millions of Europeans
within a few months. But the Jews, who insisted that they had
no country except Palestine, angered him. He did not want them
hanging about, looking miserable, and thus reminding the world
that the Germans had ill-treated them. In spite of General Eisenhower's order to set up special camps for the stateless victims of
the SS, Patton sought to treat them as citizens of the countries
of their prewar residence. When they resisted he lost patience
and ordered that all liberated persons in the Munich area should
be transferred at once to repatriation centers (July 10, 1945).
This would mean that Patton would no longer have to look at
them or think about them. It would also mean that the Jews
who had escaped from Poland (although the Poles forbade them
to leave) and who had crossed Czechoslovakia (although the
Czechs forbade them to enter) would now be shipped back to
the land of ghosts and pogroms.

The deportations were canceled. Early in October of 1945

The Saving Remnant

(after another outburst against denazification) Eisenhower relieved Patton of his command, transferring him to the Fifteenth Army, which existed only on paper.

Yet the Central Committee was as far as ever from its first objective. The Army still refused recognition, insisting that the only governing body was itself, with advice from UNRRA and help from the Joint. In November, General Eisenhower was succeeded by General McNarney, who found himself in command of a disappearing army. He had a million troops when he took over, but five months later he had three hundred thousand. Refugees from Eastern Europe were still making their devious ways to the American Zone. The doors of Palestine were still scarcely ajar. So the problem grew larger each week, as the army personnel became more sparse. In August of 1946 General McNarney opened his zone officially to the Jews from Poland and Czechoslovakia, welcoming them into his enclave of freedom. Having thus made the problem insoluble according to the old terms, he changed all the rules on September 7 by accepting the Central Committee as a little government for the Jews—still subject to the Army's laws but free within the confines of those laws to run their own affairs as best they could in the shadow of the harsh postwar shortages. "It is my earnest wish," he said, "that by extending the Army's recognition to the Central Committee greater mutual aid and understanding will result in the attainment of the maximum that present political and economic conditions will permit."

Broadcasting over the Armed Forces Network, an elated Jew explained what the recognition meant to him and to his fellow sufferers: "This act of General McNarney's writes a new page in our history. He has recognized the existence of a little democracy . . . liberated in the heart of Germany. The Central Committee of Liberated Jews is now a government without a flag."

Ceaselessly, by all means peaceful and revolutionary, that "government" was to seek its flag in the only corner of the earth where it could ever fly. The Central Committee joined hands with the Jews in the British and French Zones for the unwavering purpose of breaking the British mandate. David Ben Gurion visited the camps and brought the message of unrelenting war:

> Nothing will ever deter or frighten us. Immigration will not be cut off while there is a single Jew living [in Palestine]. . . . We have created our life there; we are self-reliant, and that is the most important message which Palestine sends you; rely on yourselves! . . . You are the living witnesses to the crime committed against humanity. Your dignified existence is a living protest against the immorality of civilization. . . .
>
> We must forge the new unity which was born in the ghetto fires and the struggles of the partisans. Even after the White Paper will have been abolished we shall have to stand united for a long time. A homeland is not created with applause.

This seems a far cry from the learned and submissive rabbis of the little wooden towns in the Pale of Settlement. Europe had taught the Jews that saintliness and scholarship were not enough. Gentleness and charity and kindness led to torture and gas and burning. Toughness was what the goyim respected. So the Saving Remnant faced the truth: they could sit quietly rotting in the camps, since nobody wanted them; or they could fight their way out, against dismaying odds, with an implacable will and an indifference to rules, laws, orders, and all the apparatus of power. Before describing this exodus, which was completed during three years, we must turn to the relations between the Jewish DP camps and the Joint. The Central Committee had won its home rule. It was deep in plots with the Bricha—the escape group, manned chiefly by members of the Brigade and under the orders of Mossad le Aliyah Beth (the Committee for Illegal Immigration). But meanwhile the camps had to organize their economic, religious, cultural, and social life. And for this they needed the

Joint, which provided 58 per cent of the committee's income during the formative days.

The relationship was never wholly easy. For one thing, the committee was hostile toward the German-born Jews who had returned to their homes—from the camps or from some lucky, undiscovered hiding-place. It thought all Jews should stay together and work together until they forced their way into Palestine. Jews who chose to go "outside" and live in Germany deserved no help. But the Joint, as usual, said that Jews who were in need deserved all possible help so that they might live where they chose. If they wished to move, and had found a country to accept them, the Joint would give aid. If they wished to stay, the Joint would not abandon them.

Then the question arose, who was to handle the food and clothing which the Joint brought from abroad? Steadily the Joint's contributions grew heavier. As the fugitives from the East increased in number, the Joint built a large supply department, with trucks and warehouses, which dwarfed the similar department of the Central Committee. The committee asked, as part of its struggle for home rule, that all distribution be left in its hands. This was impossible. The committee lacked the facilities, and in any case UNRRA had decreed that the work of voluntary agencies must be coordinated with its own work and with that of the Army. The committee accepted the inevitable and made a friendly agreement with the Joint on the understanding that they would be equal partners in the work of rehabilitation and relief—including medical and legal care, child welfare and cultural activities, in addition to food and clothing. The work went forward smoothly throughout the summer of 1946.

In the autumn, however, jealousy revived. UNRRA was preparing to go out of business during the first half of 1947. This might provide the committee's long-awaited chance for genuine home rule—but not if the Joint increased its own activities, under its own aegis, as the activities of UNRRA diminished. And this the Joint was doing. In fact, it could do no other. Leaving aside the conspiracies against the British, and the plans which were being perfected to evade their laws and humiliate their Foreign Secretary, the success of the committee's program within the camps depended upon goods, money, and social services supplied by the Joint. Tension was inevitable, in view of the large ambitions of the committee; but a visit from Joseph Schwartz relieved some of the bad feelings. He praised the committee for creating "a miniature government directing the lives of the people," and for helping to transform the hopeless wrecks who emerged from the torture camps into the dynamic, pushful DPs of 1946. But he reminded them that the commitments of the Joint were worldwide and that the responsibility for the use of other people's money was absolute. The Joint could never be as generous to any one group as it wished, nor could it escape the duty of accounting exactly for the use of its goods and services.

The Central Committee had asked the Joint to provide funds for an employment program in the camps. The plan was to build a little industry within the "miniature government" which would supply its own needs and some of the Army's. The Army gave its blessing and promised machinery, farm lands, and raw materials. The ORT promised to help in the training of craftsmen. Then the Joint was petitioned for money, so that the workers and farmers might receive real wages. Mr. Schwartz welcomed the idea; but he could promise only that he would ask New York to be sympathetic and to do as much as possible. The committee was never satisfied with New York's response; it felt misunderstood until the very end, when the Joint helped the last of the DP Jews on their route to Israel.

Perhaps we can see why the Joint's best efforts were disappointing to the "government without a flag" if we list some of the major works which the JDC in New York had to authorize during these years. For example, in 1947 the Joint spent $75,000,000. Mr.

The Saving Remnant

Leavitt pointed out that the Joint was running six businesses with this money:

First, a material-aid business, on the scale of a large department store. Twenty millions were spent on food, clothes, medical supplies, religious and cultural articles.

Second, a warehouse business, with 68 large warehouses in Europe and ten in the United States.

Third, a transport business, with 565 motor vehicles in Europe, and many service stations and garages. (Some of these "non-political" motor cars proved unexpectedly useful to illegal transients.)

Fourth, a travel business which cost $5,000,000. Thirty thousand people were moved during 1947 and were cared for in transit.

Fifth, a banking business of unusual complications. The Joint could not operate on the black market. Yet if it bought foreign exchange at the official rate, it was wasting other people's money. Sometimes it was given favored treatment by a foreign government. More often, having secured the proper licenses, it bought and sold scarce goods in bulk—large quantities of coffee, bought in Brazil for dollars, were sold in Hungary for forints (and for a huge profit). Shortly after the war, according to Mr. Leavitt, every cup of coffee made in Hungary was provided by the Joint. Similarly, the Joint bought sugar in Cuba with dollars and sold it in Morocco for francs. And the Joint would buy American securities in dollars, for a Frenchman who was not allowed to export capital, receiving payment plus a premium in francs.

Sixth, a hospital and social welfare business: in Europe alone, 326 children's and orphans' homes, nurseries and day schools; 53 homes for the aged; 380 hospitals, clinics, and sanatoria. (By 1947-1948, the center of spending for the Joint was shifting from Europe to Palestine-Israel, Cyprus, and North Africa.)

The Jewish community of Libya, for example, was time-honored and had felt safe in its venerable age. A compact community in the midst of the Arab world, it enjoyed the legal status

The Saving Remnant

of an ancient Hellenistic Jewry: communal taxes, and self-rule in education and religion. Also these thirty-five thousand Jews contributed much to the prosperity of Libya. They felt themselves indispensable. After the rise of Mussolini, the Italians confirmed them in their status; after the advent of the Wehrmacht, the Afrika-Korps was too busy to murder them. Their troubles began in the autumn of 1945.

Two-thirds of the Libyan Jews lived in Tripoli, and the rest in small inland towns. Some of the latter were artisans; but in Tripoli the Jews were merchants and traders, attracting the inevitable jealousy but adding to the economy an expertise which few Moslems could equal. Yet in November of 1945 an unheralded pogrom swept the country. Just as a passing herd of cattle can infect the earth with foot-and-mouth disease, so the German armies would seem to have poisoned the desert sands with the germ of Jew-killing.

The pogrom lasted only two days because the British troops were diligent in suppression. Thirty children and 100 adults perished; 7 synagogues, 500 shops, and 350 private houses were destroyed—a small affair compared to Ukrainian or Polish efforts, but the results were startling. This pogrom marked the end of creative Jewish life in Libya. Perhaps the unexpectedness of the attack broke the nerves of the victims; perhaps the two-year drought which followed added to the sense of spiritual exhaustion. In any case, the Jews abandoned hope. World-wide, the usual Jewish practice after a pogrom is to clean up, rebuild, and start again—like the peasants and villagers whose homes are shattered by earthquakes or volcanoes. But not this time. The Libyan Jews were cowed; they saw no future on Libyan soil. And since they were not allowed to leave, they turned increasingly to the Joint and to its relief rolls. In 1945, 350 were receiving aid, and in 1948 more than 12,000.

This new, disconsolate timidity was made all too clear in 1948, when the state of Israel sprang suddenly to life: the Libyan Jews were silent; they dared not celebrate. Like trembling hares, they hoped that if they made no sound or movement nobody would see them. But they lacked the hare's protective coloring, so in 1948 another pogrom occurred—less harmful than the first because it was half expected and the Jews were half ready for self-defense.

The only possible answer, for Libya as for the DP camps, was Israel. By the time of the second pogrom, no Jewish schools and no synagogues were open. The once-prosperous Jews of Tripoli were ruined. Eighty per cent of those from the small towns suffered from trachoma. The Joint, of course, had been expanding its Libyan program ever since the end of the war and was ready with medical aid, with emergency relief, and with help for all who were waiting to emigrate. A few Jews had escaped illegally, to make ready for the coming war against the Arabs. Then, in February 1947, the government of Libya opened the gates to all who chose to leave. Fifteen thousand went within eight months. Meanwhile the Joint brought the eye-infected Jews from the interior and nursed them until they too could escape. By 1952 some 32,000 had emigrated. The Joint closed its office in Tripoli. By 1954 only 3000 remained, and the Joint retired from a country which was becoming almost Hitlerianly *Judenrein*.

4.

In spite of the repeated jealousies which bubbled and flared within the Central Committee of Liberated Jews, the European staff of the Joint was proud of these stubborn, intransigent clients. Jews who were ready to fight everyone—including General Patton, the British Empire, and their fellow Jews—were a reassuring sight. Less reassuring were those who wished to live off everyone, or anyone, for the rest of time. This was the tiny group of morally defeated people—the miracle being that the German camps had not defeated many thousands more.

The Saving Remnant

At the Föhrenwald camp, near Munich in the American Zone, were gathered the most troublesome cases: the incurables, the aged, and the natural unemployables, who had small hope of gaining a visa to any Western country and who had no wish to plunge into the stern, adventurous life of Israel. What they wanted was to be cared for like children and never to be asked a troublesome question. These slack, unnerved people were often accompanied by their families, many of whom were not slack at all and made their perilous way to Israel. But the very young and the very sick were left behind, as well as a few healthy adults who were infected by the moral lethargy of their elders.

One by one the DP camps emptied—but not Föhrenwald. By 1951 all other Jewish refugees had been absorbed; but 2500 still clung to Föhrenwald. The Joint was now solely responsible for such amenities as they received—cultural, medical, and economic. Since the last official Americans had been withdrawn, the government of the camps devolved upon the Germans. The inmates were furious at this indignity, and refused to register. The Germans were firm and sent in the police accompanied by the dogs which had played such a sinister role in the old days at Auschwitz.

Yet the Bavarian government was as gentle as it could be in the face of such obstreperous people. It tried to help. It gave generous relief grants and set up a school and a hospital; but what it wanted most earnestly was to close the camp and disperse the unamiable squatters. And the Joint wanted the same—not only because the camp was a burden but because it contradicted the Joint's lifelong policy of rehabilitation. These Jews had no interest in rehabilitation. They refused to make new homes in Germany. They refused Israel. And the rich countries of the West, into which they might have been willing to emigrate, refused them. Meanwhile children were living, and forming their characters, in this village of morose valetudinarians.

The Saving Remnant

The Joint was "caught," as Charles Jordan confessed it had been caught in Hungary. It could not get the people out of the Föhrenwald. It could not keep them there indefinitely. And it could not desert them. Year after year, at the annual meeting of the Joint's European directors, the problem was re-examined with increasing acrimony but with no increasing hope. Someone whose patience had worn thin might suggest that the Joint should pull out; but the sense of the meeting always was that Jews must not be abandoned.

The Joint sought to create a gentle pressure by threatening to diminish its benefactions. This only led the inmates to make larger and more astounding requests. Then the problem was complicated by the return to Föhrenwald of some ex-members who had tried Israel and who did not like it. Far from emptying, the camp began to refill. In December 1952 the Germans closed the gates and said that not another person could return. Some two hundred managed to slip through; they were arrested by the Bavarian police, and the Joint had to provide them with legal aid, although in this case it was on the side of the Germans.

Still hoping to empty the camp within finite time, the Germans offered a grant of DM 1500 per adult, and DM 500 per child, to any family which would resettle in Germany or move elsewhere. Nothing happened. The conditions at the camp were too good, said Charles Jordan: free rent and utilities from the Germans, and cultural and physical amenities from the Joint. Why move?

Instead of moving, their next step was to make a new, inordinate demand. The Joint had just received from the Claims Conference[2] the sum of $6,500,000, which was to be used to help the survivors of the death camps. The inmates of Föhrenwald claimed that $5,000,000 should go to them, since they were the only remaining victims who had not been resettled. This was ingenious. Having refused resettlement, they now demanded ran-

[2] See pages 241-44.

som as a reward for their stubbornness. The Joint refused with
some vigor, pointing out that it had a duty to Jews who were
rebuilding their world and not merely to those who refused to do
anything. Thenceforth open recrimination was the rule between
Föhrenwald and the Joint. The camp leaders organized a protest
march on Munich. The Joint appealed to the German police, who
responded with a moderate display of their old talent for beating
Jews.

The Föhrenwald committee then appealed to the Jews of America against the hard-hearted Joint. They claimed to be forgotten,
piteous people, neglected by the Germans and misunderstood by
the Joint. In El Paso and Chicago committees were formed to
help them with clothes and money. The Joint could only testify
that this was wasted charity.

When nine years had passed since the end of the war, neither
the Germans nor the Joint had made any headway. Föhrenwald
seemed to have become an incurable abscess in the Bavarian
body politic. The Joint had closed its office in the camp and was
planning to move out of Munich. It had made final offers to each
inmate who would emigrate or resettle in Germany: a year's sub-
sistence in any country of refuge. This was in addition to the
grant made by Germany. The Joint also arranged for the admission of 200 tubercular patients to Norway and Sweden,
and it guaranteed care for the aged and the genuinely ill if they
moved to Israel.

Still nothing happened—until the Germans finally lost patience
and announced that the camp would be closed in 1955, with or
without inhabitants. Even this was over-optimistic, for the inmates of Föhrenwald had become the world's most expert lim-
pets. But they did begin to move (with renewed help from the
Joint), to Israel and to South America. The Germans—on this
occasion long-suffering—pried loose the last 700 in February
of 1957.

The Saving Remnant

Föhrenwald had definitely shown that Jews can be tenacious. A few thousand people, many of them invalids, had frustrated and bewildered the Germans and the Joint throughout twelve years. Meanwhile, Jews by the hundreds of thousands had been proving their tenacity in a braver cause against far greater odds.

Chapter Eight

The map on page 195 shows some of the secret Jewish routes from Europe to the Mediterranean and the Black Sea—the goal being Palestine. They were not much use during the war. Even Constantsa was abandoned after the sinking of *Struma*. But many exiled Jews lived in the Middle East and North Africa. Here the Mossad turned its attention while waiting for the war to end and praying that a Saving Remnant might survive the Germans and be ready for rescue.

The underground Jewish Defense Force (Haganah) had set up the Committee for Illegal Immigration (Mossad le Aliyah Beth) as early as 1937. In 1938 it sent emissaries throughout the Levant to kindle young Jews with hopes of Palestine. Within a few years 150 to 400 Syrian and Lebanese Jews were smuggled each month across the northern border. Others came from Iraq via Damascus, in spite of prison terms and death sentences imposed by the Iraqi government on those who helped the Mossad.

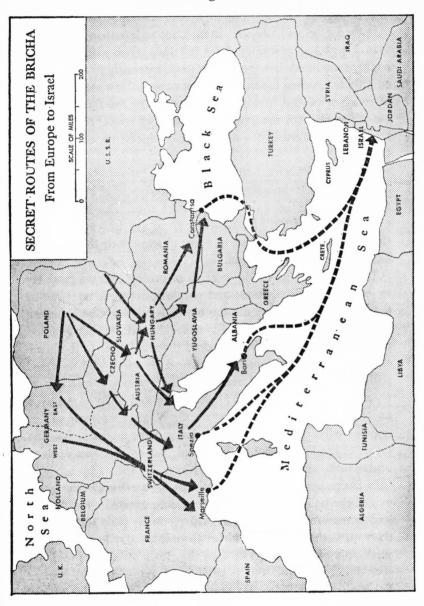

SECRET·ROUTES OF THE BRICHA
From Europe to Israel

SCALE OF MILES

The Saving Remnant

The smuggling was so well organized that the cost per head (mostly for bribes) dropped from £200 to less than £60.

In Egypt the well-to-do Jews felt themselves safe and thoroughly integrated. But the poorer Jews, especially in Alexandria, contributed money for the illegal work and also a steady trickle of young men. And from North Africa, during the war, the Mossad lured about a thousand immigrants who reached Palestine by ship—the British Navy still being chiefly concerned with Germans.

All this was little more than practice: the gathering of weapons, the learning of techniques, and the establishment of bases. When the war ended, the training days were over. The Bricha—the escape section of the Mossad—sent its agents into every camp; ships of a sort were readied in every obscure port; the most unlikely battle in history began.

The results of the battle were so surprising that we must try to understand the divisions and perplexities which undermined the British morale. Why did the troops leave Palestine, rejecting the mandate and abandoning a long-sought and carefully guarded position? How could a few hundred thousand Jews in the home country, plus a few hundred thousand penniless and unarmed refugees, compel such a retreat? This was not a question of power, since the British held all the power and could have stayed in Palestine indefinitely if they chose. What broke their will so unexpectedly? We must look for the answer in the hearts and minds of the British, not in the pitiful "battles" between ancient, unseaworthy ships and the Royal Navy.

In December of 1944—six months before an overwhelming victory at the polls—the Labour Party Conference adopted the following resolution: ". . . the Arabs have many wide territories of their own; they must not claim to exclude the Jews from the small area of Palestine, less than the size of Wales. Indeed, we should examine also the possibility of extending the present Palestinian boundaries, by agreement with Egypt, Syria, and

Transjordan." This was not put forward by Zionist enthusiasts or by a few constituencies which happened to have many Jewish voters; it was drafted by the Executive Committee of the Labour Party.

At another conference on the eve of the election of 1945, Mr. Hugh Dalton made a more cautious statement which might have warned the over-hopeful Jews that all need not be plain sailing in the event of a Labour victory: "We consider Jewish immigration into Palestine should be permitted without the present limitations which obstruct it, and we have also stated very clearly that this is not a matter which should be regarded as one for which the British government alone should take responsibility." And he added that "steps should be taken in consultation with the American and Soviet governments to see whether we cannot get common support for a policy which will give us a happy, a free, and a prosperous Jewish state in Palestine." Someone must have reminded Mr. Dalton about the Arabs, who also wanted to be happy, and whose friendship was also a British interest in the Middle East. The rank and file of the party, however, merely felt that traditional Labour policy had been reaffirmed, though they had no notion of the complications this might involve.

When the new cabinet met, after victory at the polls, it was immediately faced with a new set of facts—or rather with the old facts reinterpreted. Every memorandum insisted that Britain dare not antagonize the Arabs by abruptly canceling the White Paper of 1939. This was a harsh awakening for the men who had dreamed, when out of power, that the Jews could easily be made "happy, free, and prosperous," and that only Tory stupidity had inspired the White Paper.

We have one clear example of the advice to which the new government was subjected. The Cairo Study Group of the Royal Institute of International Affairs prepared a paper for distribution to the Commonwealth Conference of 1945. Among other things the paper said that "neither her [i.e., Britain's] military nor her economic position can be assured unless the Arab countries . . . are subject to stable governments which are either themselves under British control or are friendly and willing to conform their policy to hers." With regard to Palestine the paper says:

> The British government is trying to find a compromise . . . but in reality *it has already found the only possible compromise.* . . . The Zionists would never accept the White Paper officially but many of them would acquiesce if it were carried out firmly. The Arabs would certainly revolt with the assistance of the Arab states if a Jewish state were established but if the White Paper were carried out they would lose their fear both of Zionism and of the British government's intentions. . . . Were Great Britain to permit the French to maintain their military or political power in Syria, or to establish a Jewish state in Palestine or any part of it, the Arabs, not only of the Fertile Crescent but of other countries as well, would write off the possibility of friendship and alliance with Great Britain.

We are back in the First World War, with one difference: in 1917 the experts said that the Arabs would accept the Balfour Declaration "if it were carried out firmly"; in 1945 they said the same thing about the Zionists and the White Paper. The constant factors were that the French must leave Syria and that the experts were wrong. Nevertheless the Institute of International Affairs had stated the British dilemma. And incidentally it had answered Chaim Weizmann's question: Why was it a completely invariable rule that politicians who were enthusiastically for the Jewish homeland during election forgot about it completely if they were returned to office? The answer is in Webster's definition of a dilemma: "an argument which presents an antagonist with two or more alternatives . . . equally conclusive against him."

Neither the new Prime Minister nor the new Foreign Secretary was equipped to argue with the "experts." So the government played for time. In October of 1945 it announced that the restrictions of 1939 must be preserved, at least for the present. Nobody was happy about this somersault. Events were to prove that the Labour Party as a whole was most unhappy, and therefore in the crisis undecided; but temporarily it was committed to the views of its advisers; namely, that the forty million Arabs had a military strength and a political unity which did not exist but which sounded formidable on paper. And behind this myth of solidarity lay a further myth of potential Arab friendship, which meant abundant oil, if only the British were considerate.

The party which had been emotionally pro-Zionist was now officially pro-Arab, but most uneasily and with a divided soul. Then came the appointment of an Anglo-American committee to report on Palestine—a device to gain time and to evade decisions. But in April 1946 the committee recommended, most inconveniently, that 100,000 Jews should be allowed into Palestine at once. Since the Americans offered no commensurate gesture of their own, and since the Arabs threatened violence, the British did nothing and the White Paper still ruled. Ernest Bevin, the Foreign Secretary, grew more and more stubborn as the American Jews abused the British and the American government took no serious responsibility for the emptying of the Jewish DP camps. The next event, as is usual in such deadlocks, was the outbreak of terrorism in Palestine: the dynamiting of strategic bridges, the blowing up of the King David Hotel, and finally (in July 1947) the hanging of two British sergeants.

These acts were deplored by the Mossad and the Bricha, who believed that their own deeds were legally "illegal." They were bringing the tortured remnant from Europe to the Jewish home, and they were confident that in time the humane British would relent. But terror would merely stiffen the back of Ernest Bevin and postpone indefinitely a happy ending. Astonishingly enough, terror had the opposite effect. Instead of saying, "We shall now show these ruffians, who have appealed to force, exactly what force means," the British public cried out for the abandonment of Palestine. And to the stupefaction of the nations, the British government agreed.

The same government which had allowed itself to believe that the Middle East was a vital interest and that the Arabs must (and could) be wooed into friendship, now sent its Colonial Minister to drop the whole unseemly bungle into the lap of the United Nations. And by way of comic relief the British added that they could not take part in any future plans for Palestine unless the Jews and the Arabs had freely agreed to the proposal.

Meanwhile the Mossad had maintained the steady pressure of illegal immigration. Had the British been undivided in their aims, the galantry of the Mossad would have gone for nothing. But how could the British help being at cross-purposes with themselves? Their civil servants told them that the Arabs were strong and potentially friendly. Their common sense told them that the Arabs were weak and hostile. Their experts on the Middle East told them that the Jews were interlopers in Palestine and that it was an act of justice to thrust them into detention camps on Cyprus while awaiting a solution which no man could foresee. Their hearts told them that this was cruel nonsense and that "the meteor flag of England" did not burn with its accustomed zeal when a cruiser and six destroyers were sent to arrest a foundering tubful of Jews. On the other hand, we must remember that although the Mossad would have been helpless before a resolute government, Ernest Bevin would surely have enforced the White Paper of 1939 had it not been for the Mossad.[1]

2.

The return of the Saving Remnant to their Holy Land was an operation in three stages. First, the Jews had to be helped from Eastern Europe to one of the occupation zones in Germany, or to

[1] For a brilliant discussion of the British dilemma at this time, see Jon Kimche's *Seven Fallen Pillars*, Chapters 13, 14, 15.

Austria or Italy, where they could be cared for temporarily in camps. This was the work of the Bricha (the name means "running"). The Joint helped with finances as inconspicuously as possible. It also provided food, medicine, and sometimes motor vehicles all along the line.

Daring and ingenuity were the hallmarks of the Bricha, most of whose members had served in the British Army and had learned the uses of precise planning. They hunted out and rescued the surviving Jews of Poland, Romania, and Hungary. They bribed and smuggled them across closed borders, inventing new devious routes as fast as the old ones were blocked.

The Joint's decision to subsidize the Bricha was the most difficult in its career. Bricha, in connivance with local authorities, was making nonsense of the laws of half a dozen countries and of the edicts of great armies. The Joint was already accused of spying against the "People's Democracies" and of other sinister bourgeois deeds. And what might the American Department of State say when it found that the Joint was helping to undo the policy of an ally? Paul Baerwald took the lead in urging that, come what may, the Joint must save these last available Jews among the ten million who had inhabited Eastern Europe when the work began in 1914. So the Joint gave Bricha about twenty-five million dollars. And it induced friendly army commanders to turn their backs at the appropriate time. And it developed a blind eye in regard to the Bricha's trucks which carried the JDC shield—as useful a badge of immunity as could be found in Europe. And we have seen that the Joint was a chief provider for the Jews whom Bricha delivered into the DP camps.[2]

The American Army, of course, could have put a stop to this flow of illegal persons whenever it chose. At one point the Army became dangerously impatient, pointing out that, no matter how many Jews were "cleared," the population of the camps never

[2] The Jewish Agency was an ever-alert and invaluable aid to the Mossad and the Bricha. That story has not been fully told.

The Saving Remnant

diminished. Mr. Leavitt was called to Washington and confronted with Dean Acheson plus three colonels. The burden of the ever-replenished camps, he was told, had become intolerable. The borders of the American Zone in Germany must be closed. Mr. Leavitt answered that the only way to close the borders was to kill all Jews as they crossed. Nothing would keep them in Eastern Europe. And if the Americans shot only 90 per cent of them, the remaining 10 per cent would push forward. The borders remained open.

The second stage of the Return—far more difficult, and also in charge of the Bricha—involved moving the Jews from the camps to the ports and the beaches where the illegal ships were waiting: Marseille, Port-de-Bouc, Spezia, Venice, Bari, etc. The refugees pushed onward as if by instinct, like a locust-swarm or like an ancient folk-migration, from every camp in Europe—a ghostly army whose hope had been renewed by these quiet, imperturbable young leaders inured to hardship and danger.

Leo Schwarz has reconstructed the story of one contingent which set out from the French Zone in Germany at the end of April 1947: 521 Jews, including old people, children, and 8 pregnant women.[3] They started their journey in "liberated" Army trucks—groups from three camps who were to assemble near the Austrian frontier for the dangerous trip across the border. At dawn they reached Achensee, whence two night marches would take them to the Brenner Pass. On the morning of the second day they made camp in a lonely upland meadow where the Austrian police found them and informed the French military government. The chief of the French DP section interviewed them, accompanied by the Joint's director for that zone, Jean Bernstein, who persuaded the French not to send them back into Germany but to move them to a camp in the French Austrian Zone. Thence

[3] *The Redeemers* (New York: Farrar, Straus and Cudahy, 1953), pages 236ff.

they were transferred—by force, and after the maximum of resistance—to the American Zone of Austria.

It was now the seventeenth of May. On the twenty-fourth the
refugees escaped camp for the second time and made again for
the Brenner. The pregnant women and the youngest children
crossed the pass in Italian trucks labeled "Rhine Wine." The rest
took a long walk across the Alps and the Dolomites—a difficult
hill-climb, but safe, because the patrols were few and friendly,
whereas in Austria the British put pressure on the natives and
on the occupying powers to arrest all Jewish fugitives.

On May 28 the foot-sloggers and the "Rhine Wine" reassembled
at Fortezzo. The rest was easy. Civilians and soldiers alike, the
Italians took pleasure in helping the Jews and in thwarting authority. A long night run in Army trucks landed them on the
coast north of Bari. During the evening of June 4 they were
ferried (along with eight other groups which had been waiting
for weeks) to a forbidden ship which made the forbidden run
toward Palestine. They were shadowed all the way by the British
Navy, arrested at the appropriate distance offshore, and deposited behind barbed wire on Cyprus. Here, too, they found the
Joint awaiting them.

That sea journey, in a decrepit, overcrowded ship, was the
third stage in the Return. Whether, by some rare miracle, the
ship landed on a lonely beach in Palestine, or whether as usual
the end was Cyprus, the Mossad claimed victory. Their aim was
to show the world the adamantine will which backed this ingathering of exiles. The British could not forever halt them
within the three-mile limit and dump them on a convenient
island. Cyprus would soon be filled to overflowing, and then
what? Somehow the British must prevent the ships from sailing.
Somehow they must persuade the French and Italian governments, and they in turn must coerce their citizens into withhold-
ing aid from the Jews. This would have been difficult at best. It

became impossible because of the ruthless disregard for laws and for life itself displayed by the Mossad and by the graduates from the German death camps. These men had nothing left to fear. Their collective disdain for the world which had betrayed them is symbolized in one heroic figure: Yehuda Arazi.

Arazi, "the Man with Seven Faces," was the son of Reb Avraham Tenenbaum of Lodz. The whole family moved to Palestine in 1924. Yehuda, who was seventeen, joined the Haganah and was trained as an underground soldier. Thenceforward life among the Tenenbaums was colored with melodrama. A visitor tells of putting his teaspoon into a sugar bowl one day: "I felt it strike something hard. It was a hand grenade which Yehuda had hidden there. His mother knew about it but had forgotten."

In 1926 the boy was ordered to join the Palestine police force in order to keep an eye on the British. He was soon an officer, in charge of the Political Department. Ten years later the Haganah told him to leave the police and to become a salesman for a citrus-fruit company. In this peaceful guise he was sent to Poland to buy arms. He found the supply unlimited—except by his own sparse funds—if he could promise that the arms would be moved in secrecy. So he bought a small workshop where he built steamrollers. In the hollowed-out rollers he sent 2250 rifles and 250 machine guns to the Haganah. He left Poland for home a few days before the Germans arrived in 1939, and became head of Intelligence for the Haganah and also a British agent. The ex-fruit-salesman and ex-officer of the Palestine police was sent to sabotage Romanian oil fields. While in the German-occupied Balkans he continued buying arms and stealing arms and hiding them against possible postwar needs.

Arazi's final effort as a servant of the British was his most insolent: he persuaded Naval Intelligence to buy a Greek ship and give it to the Mossad for illegal immigration. After a few round-trips from Constantsa to Haifa, he argued, the Romanians and the German agents would ignore the ship, since she was

clearly an anti-British vessel. Then she could be fitted with tor-
pedo tubes and used as a secret weapon in the Black Sea. But
when SS *Doron* on her first "cover" voyage landed 800 Jews
openly in Palestine, the mandatory government was not amused.
Naval Intelligence blamed Arazi for the publicity, and *Doron*
sailed no more.

The British were at last suspicious of Arazi. They soon uncovered his double identity and sentenced him to prison; but they
could not find him, in spite of a heavy price on his head. In 1945
he turned up in Cairo with false papers and in the uniform of a
British sergeant-major from the Palestine Brigade. He was
promptly flown to Milan, as his papers requested. Nobody took
much interest in this redundant NCO so he settled comfortably
to his real task, which was to command the Mossad and all the
agents of the Haganah in Italy.

A quiet, soft-spoken man, Arazi used the method of *toujours
de l'audace;* yet he never thought of himself as audacious. Perhaps the secret of his calm effrontery was his lifelong experience
with armies. In Poland and the Balkans, as well as in Palestine,
he had learned contempt for military organization and military
paper-work. They were too elaborate. Boldness and impudence
could make nonsense of them both—especially in postwar Italy,
in the slack, unbuttoned atmosphere of an army in occupation.
The black market was the key to Italian life, and military supplies
were the key to the black market. So Arazi taught the Palestinian units of the British Army to "borrow" vehicles, to requisition
farms and remote country houses for the use of the troops (i.e.,
for the hiding of refugees), to forge papers for the "military
convoys" which delivered Jews to the beaches, to manufacture
coupons for gasoline, orders for Diesel oil and for lifebelts and
for the requisition of ever larger farms and more luxurious es-
tates.

In an amateurish way, similar corruption was infesting all the
Allied armies in ex-enemy countries. But here the work was done

by pure professionals with a lifetime training in the defeat of authority, with an altruistic purpose, and with the backing of one of the most cool-minded gamblers of modern times. No stakes, however alarming, could give pause to Arazi. He gambled his own life daily as a matter of course. But we shall see that when the enemy challenged he thought nothing of throwing another thousand lives, like chips, onto the green baize table. Then he watched, seemingly imperturbable, while the little ball rattled, and finally settled, and all the lives were saved.

Aside from under-the-counter help from the Joint, Arazi had few funds when he began his bizarre work. But why should he need money for soothing Italians, when he had the British Army's liquor at his disposal? Each Palestinian soldier gave two bottles a week into the "liquor bank," and when the forging factory was in full swing the medical demands for whisky increased notably. Drink was more quickly negotiable than gold. According to Jon and David Kimche, "Arazi traded a case of whisky for a complete map of the minefields round Italy from the Italian Admiralty at Taranto; without it, illegal immigration would have become a much more hazardous adventure." [4]

The first little boat, carrying only 35 Jews, sailed for Palestine in August 1945. A diminutive ship made seven round-trips during the summer, delivering 1200 immigrants in all. But this was paltry stuff. Scores of refugees reached Italy for every one who sailed toward the homeland. The Mossad could never swamp Cyprus or impress the world with such cautious work. Arazi grew steadily more daring: the ships grew larger, the department of forgery proliferated, and the costs mounted swiftly as the British Navy became more alert and fewer and fewer vessels returned. Chartering was almost out of the question. This was becoming a one-way passage, and for the most part the ships had to be

[4] *The Secret Roads* (New York: Farrar, Straus and Cudahy, 1955), Chapters 8, 9, 10.

bought. The Joint advanced money and helped to care for the waiting multitude; but it did not buy illegal transport in its own name.

At the end of 1945 half the Palestine Brigade in Italy was ordered to North Africa for demobilization, and the rest was disbanded early in 1946; yet the work could not go forward without a military unit as cover. So Arazi invented a unit, forging the necessary papers and requisitioning a large garage in Milan. Demobilized soldiers made their way back from Palestine to staff this phantom group. The Mossad trucks were busier than ever, carrying refugees and food and Diesel fuel the length of Italy, passing and repassing the British check-points without a hitch. Arazi had proved his theory that military methods were too complicated, that nobody knew what anybody else was doing, or why, and that a bold face and an expert knowledge of procedure could make babies of the high command.

Many thousand Italians, of course, knew what was happening. Arazi counted on their friendliness, their love of whisky, and their aversion to authority—any one of which might keep them quiet.

The traffic was still too small to please Arazi. Midnight sailings from desolate beaches, however romantic, would never break the will of the British. So he decided to sail big ships from real harbors with the help of bribed Italians and ever more outrageous forgeries. In April of 1946 he chartered the *Fede* with a license to carry salt from Spezia to Sardinia. The harbor authorities were bought, or seduced by Arazi's honeyed speech, and a thousand "illegals" were loaded into twenty trucks, mostly at Brescia and Magenta. But the Italian police—not the tame local authorities—thwarted the plan in all innocence. They thought the *Fede* was running fascist refugees into Spain. By the time this tangle was unwound, the British had been alerted; so the refugees went on board ship as prisoners rather than as passengers. The trucks (by Heaven's grace and the Devil's effrontery) escaped back to Milan—otherwise the phantom unit would have been exposed and all future operations frustrated.

Arazi joined the refugees on board the *Fede*, calling himself "Dr. De Paz." The British took charge of the harbor, at first to the annoyance and later to the delight of the Italians. Arazi refused to disembark his immigrants. The British threatened to send troops on board. Arazi answered that the moment a British soldier laid hands upon a Jew the ship would be blown up, Jews and soldiers together. He added, mildly, that his passengers had a distaste for Europe and would rather die than revisit its inhospitable soil.

During the subsequent lull, Dr. De Paz gave his story to the news agencies, with special messages to the heads of government in Britain, the United States, and Russia. The *Fede* was now newsworthy. The world's press gave her abundant space. As the deadlock continued, Arazi's descriptions of the refugees' plight grew more and more sensational. The British case was muffled in the corridors of the Foreign Office. Choosing his own time, Arazi increased the tension by declaring a hunger strike: the thousand refugees would fast until they died or until they were released. Given such masterly leadership, the men and women of the *Fede* became almost as melodramatic as Arazi. Within a few days scores of them had conveniently fainted. They were displayed on deck for the comfort of the photographers— but still nobody would touch food. On the fourth day of the fast Harold Laski, Chairman of the British Labour Party, was begging Arazi to order his fellow passengers to desist. This provoked the great adventurer, who now played his last and fearful card.

He was the leader of these brave Jews, he said, and he would never ask them to do anything unworthy. On the contrary, he and his people were determined to take their own lives unless the British set them free. (The Italians, by this time, were wholly on the side of the Jews.) Each day thereafter, said Arazi, ten refugees would commit suicide in public, until no one was left alive. If soldiers tried to intervene, the ship would go up in a blast of flame. On the other hand, as soon as everyone on board had either starved or killed himself, the British could assume command.

Horrified, but with no authority to act, Laski promised to report at once to Mr. Attlee and to Ernest Bevin. Arazi agreed to postpone action—deaths and hunger strike alike—until Laski had presented the Jewish terms. The first British offer was to issue 679 certificates to the *Fede*, the rest of the passengers to be released for Palestine the following month. Arazi refused; the British capitulated; the ship was allowed to sail with all hands. The number of the immigrants would be deducted from future allocations, said the British. This was nonsense, said Arazi. The whole idea of allocations was "illegal." The British were wasting their time by subtracting 1000 from a nonexistent figure.

Once *Fede* was well clear of harbor, Arazi returned by rowboat to Italy, where his work was just beginning. The Italians were now his friends and would never again mistake him for a fascist agent. In June and July he shipped more than 5200 immigrants. Meanwhile the Black Sea ports were reopened by the Mossad. Arazi's plan to crush the White Paper, and the mandate itself, under the weight of illegal immigrants was beginning to seem practicable. The British blockade of the coast of Palestine was now very nearly impregnable, but this did not bother Arazi. Already his immigrants had swamped out the prison camp in Palestine. In August 1946 the British announced that all future "illegals" would be taken to Cyprus. Arazi believed he could fill these new camps to bursting within a year (he still had a quarter of a million clients in Europe); then what would the British do? The answer to that question, as Arazi had foreseen, was given in the summer of 1947, when Cyprus was almost full and the patience of the British government was broken by SS *Exodus*, "the ship that launched the state of Israel."

The Saving Remnant

By this time Arazi had returned to gun-running—from the United States. He sensed that the war on the mandate was as good as won. The next step was to be ready for the Arabs. His timing was perfect: eight months after the sorry end of the *Exodus* affair, the British had left Palestine and the War of Liberation had begun.[5]

3.

The *President Warfield*, of 4000 tons displacement, had been an excursion ship on Chesapeake Bay and adjacent waters. High-shouldered and with the long funnel of an old-fashioned wood-burner, she needed only paddle wheels to recall Mark Twain's adventurers on the Mississippi. In spite of her looks she was under twenty years of age and had seen ocean service during the war. The Mossad found her at Baltimore, where she was waiting to be translated into scrap iron. With the help of quiet subsidies from the Joint, the Mossad bought her and renamed her *Yeziat Eiropa 1947* ("Exodus from Europe 1947"). She sailed for France in March with a crew of American volunteers plus half a dozen graduates from the Jewish Brigade of the British Eighth Army. Her first port of call was Marseille, whence she made for Spezia. A conspicuous vessel—capable, on Mossad standards of comfort, of carrying 4500 refugees—she had been watched by British Intelligence ever since refueling at the Azores. Spezia was by this time too notorious and too well covered, so on the Fourth of July *Exodus* made for the French port of Sète on the Gulf of Lions. Here, on a relatively unfashionable and inconspicuous coast between Aigues-Mortes and the Spanish border, the Mossad had "borrowed" five large villas from ex-collaborators. From these villas, and from camps as far away as Germany, refugees gathered at the harbor on July 10—all with Colombian visas issued by the Mossad in Paris. The British Foreign Office,

[5] Arazi died in Israel early in 1959. He was fifty-two years of age.

however, had been putting pressure on the Quai d'Orsay, and five minutes before sailing time the order came to hold the ship. She sailed anyway, without a pilot and without clearance papers. She went aground once, freed herself, and made the open sea. The troubles of her 4530 passengers (including 8 children) had just begun.

Exodus was given an impressive escort: the cruiser *Ajax* (of *Graf Spee* fame), six destroyers, and a flight of Lancasters overhead. Off the coast of Palestine, *Exodus* refused to surrender. She was rammed by the destroyers (gently, but firmly enough to show how easily she could be sunk); then she was towed into the port of Haifa. The passengers were loaded onto three British transports which made for Port-de-Bouc, sixty miles east of Sète and near Marseille. This was the policy for which Arazi and the Mossad had been praying. Cyprus would no longer serve as a hiding-place for the intercepted immigrants—a hiding-place where they could quietly disappear from the world's view. So where would the British put them? And how much publicity, how much anti-British feeling, could they engender en route?

Colombia repudiated the *Exodus* passengers, saying quite truthfully that their visas were forged. The French agreed to accept anybody who went ashore of his own free will, but refused to allow the British to dump people forcibly upon French soil. This gave the Jews their chance. A few who were seriously ill were taken ashore. Nobody else would budge. The British had announced that their sole responsibility was to return these Jews to French territorial waters, whence they had sailed. Now they found themselves in charge of 4500 men, women, and children who were living in squalor on prison ships and attracting the keen attention of the world's press.

For three hot summer weeks the ships lay off Port-de-Bouc. The Jews' health deteriorated. The reports of French journalists and French officials who visited the ships were uncomplimentary toward the British. And still the refugees would not move. The

The Saving Remnant

Joint sent Laura Margolis to the rescue. She was allowed to provide 150 tons of food, clothing, medicine, and school supplies. But nothing could make the crowded, unsanitary holds habitable. And nothing could break the stubbornness of the human cargo.

The kindly British sailors and officers who were on the spot, and the faraway policy-makers in the Foreign Office, could not understand these people—any more than they had understood Arazi's anarchic death-volunteering Jews at Spezia. "What is all the excitement about?" said the British in their civilized ignorance. "The Russians lost twice as many lives as the Jews, during the war. The Poles and Czechs and even the Germans had a rough time. And what about us? If these Jews want to trade troubles, we had plenty of our own. But no one else is so utterly impossible, so wholly, self-centeredly nihilistic." The argument is appealing; but it lacks merit because it ignores history.

These men and women on their filthy transports were the remnant of East European Jewry. Some had walked from the Asian borders of Persia (where the Joint had sent them packages) across Russia, Poland, and Czechoslovakia; but all the time they had been walking toward Israel. Since they lacked wings to fly over the Arab countries, and dollars to buy Romanians, this was the shortest route. Once free of Russia, they discovered the young men of the Bricha; they heard about the Mossad. Their own people, who clearly held their own lives as nothing, had come among the camps of the enemy to find them and to take them home. When the Foreign Secretary of Great Britain said, "This is illegal," they were not impressed.

For seventeen hundred years they and their fathers had been treated like dogs, and on suitable occasions killed like rats, by Christians. And now the Germans had pushed them beyond endurance—the Germans and all the other relentless enemies from the Rhine to the Urals. Not only their personal, but their corporate and historic patience had been broken. At long last they had become a wholly recalcitrant people. No rules, no laws, no scruples of the goyim could stand between them and Israel—only force. And to force they had a simple answer: death.

> So shalt thou feed on Death, that feeds on men,
> And Death once dead, there's no more dying then.

Power melts from armies and navies and air forces when they are sent against men who sincerely mean those lines—the prisoners must all be killed, or they will blackmail their captors. When the Jews at Port-de-Bouc chose unanimously to die in the holds of their floating ovens (the temperature on deck was often 110) rather than return to Europe, the British were trapped. Unwisely, but almost inevitably, they decided to take the whole cargo back to Germany.

An effort was made to stop the ships at Gibraltar with a writ of habeas corpus. This failed, and on September 8 and 9 the three transports docked at Hamburg. The first day saw only a token struggle before the passengers were pushed ashore. But on September 9 came bloodshed and rioting. Troops armed with truncheons, ax-handles, and fire hoses had to wound more than a score of Jews before they could quiet the 1485 passengers of the third ship and carry them struggling and screaming to the hated German soil. They were sent to a camp near Lübeck, whence many escaped within a few months and restarted the long walk. By the spring of 1948 more than half the passengers from *Exodus* had reached Palestine or Cyprus. Three hundred of them fought in the Negev during the War of Liberation. By 1949 every survivor of *Exodus* was a citizen of Israel.

The British, as many of their own journalists and politicians admitted, had been exacerbated into an act of folly. The world had been half sympathetic toward the problems of a mandate power seeking to maintain a truce between Jews and Arabs; but the re-export of Jews into Germany was not approved. The British were troubled and divided by their government's lack of imagination. Questions were asked in Parliament. A nascent sense of esteem for the Jews might have led to a relaxation of the terms of the White Paper. At that point the terrorists in Palestine hanged two British sergeants. The world was shocked; the British were infuriated; the Mossad was in despair, fearful lest all its work had been undone by murderers. The struggle between the mandate and the Mossad had been an honest fight. Arazi, with his gentle manner and his almost insane daring, had been a worthy foe. But the revengeful killing of innocent men is disgusting at all times everywhere.

We have seen, however, that the fears of the Mossad were exaggerated. The terrorists destroyed all hope of kindlier feelings, but they did not goad the British into retaliation. On the contrary, they set alight an anti-Zionism so extreme that it turned against the mandate and all its attendant woes. Watching this unforeseen response, the Mossad decided that one more super-*Exodus*, one more proof that Cyprus could never hold the boiling tide of immigrants, and the British would be glad to depart.

The culminating blow of the Mossad was the deadliest. This was no straw to break a camel's back. This was an elephant piled on top of all the other luggage: 15,169 "illegals," in two ships, intercepted by the Royal Navy and landed on Cyprus between January 1 and January 5, 1948.

Once again, with subsidies from the Joint, the Mossad had bought two ships in the United States, seaworthy ships for a change, of 4500 tons apiece: the *Pan York* and the *Pan Crescent*. After many adventures and much false-trail laying in the Mediterranean, they made for Constantsa. No operation on the intended scale could succeed without the helpful "neutrality" of a government—hence Romania, which had received an unwelcome influx of Jews when her eastern territories were annexed by Russia. Unlike Italy and France, Romania was not a friendly ally of the British. But this time Russia protested, for Constantsa was used by the Red Navy. So the ships were moved to Burgas in Bulgaria, on the understanding that each refugee would pay a transit fee in dollars.

When all was ready, the British made their final effort—through the American government and the United Nations. The Jewish Agency, which was in charge of legal immigration, was told that if it valued American support at Lake Success the ships must not sail. Even Chaim Weizmann urged caution, and at the last moment a reluctant Ben Gurion ordered the Mossad to hold the two *Pans* at Burgas. The order was ignored, and the ships sailed on Christmas Day. When Turkey refused to intervene they passed the straits and entered the Mediterranean. The Royal Navy could now arrest them at its leisure; but what would it do with the passengers? Warships could not enter the Black Sea on a belligerent mission, so the British could not return the immigrants to their port of departure. Neither could they conduct them to Germany; *Exodus* had closed that door forever. Yet if the fifteen thousand Jews were off-loaded at Cyprus, the long-sought "flooding" would have been accomplished and the mandate made to look ridiculous. But to Cyprus they went. The homeless, illegal immigrant, guided along the secret routes by the Bricha, exploited on the world stage by the Mossad, subsidized by the Joint and other agencies, had won the battle of will-power.

(At the height of the American depression during the thirties, a pamphlet appeared with a beguiling title: *How to Lose Your Money Prudently*. The answer was to seek all the best advice and follow it with care. You could never blame yourself, thereafter, for your poverty; but you would still be poor. The same applied to the unborn Jewish state on Christmas Day of 1947. The friendliest of the great powers, and the wisest advisers, urged that the mandate should be upheld and that *Pan York* and *Pan Crescent* should not sail. Israel would thus have lost her birthday most prudently: no blame, no angry Arabs, but also no baby. The philosophy of Danton and Arazi triumphed—*toujours de l'audace*.)

4.

The first of the many immigrants who had failed to run the blockade were moved from Palestine to Cyprus in August of 1946. Ten days later Charles Passman arrived on behalf of the Joint. The British were not pleased. The advent of the Joint would attract publicity, whereas Cyprus was meant to be a quiet spot where Jews could be sequestered inconspicuously until such time as they might trickle into Palestine without annoying the Arabs or interfering with the flow of oil. The mandatory government, in other words, had been reduced to waiting forlornly for the Greek Kalends—an undignified policy which anyone would prefer to carry out in the dark.

Mr. Passman was not allowed to inspect the camps, so he held a press conference at Famagusta where he asked the obvious question: "What are the British hiding?" Within a fortnight he was given carte blanche. Early in September the cooperation of the Joint was welcomed officially. Doctors, nurses, teachers, dietitians, and social workers were quickly imported into Cyprus, chiefly from Palestine. The Joint sent Morris Laub from New York to administer the program, and he found may qualified workers among the refugees.

On the seashore near Famagusta were five "summer camps," consisting of army tents to hold about twelve thousand people. Twenty kilometers away, in the hills, were the "winter camps," made of Nissen huts, which could house about fourteen thousand people. The Joint persuaded the British to add two special camps: one for married couples with newborn infants, where the Joint built a well-equipped nursery; and one for two thousand orphans, who were taught to run their own affairs. Between August of 1946 and February of 1947, 53,000 refugees passed through these camps, the highest number at any one time being

31,400—the population of a small town. Twenty-two hundred babies were born on Cyprus, and 150 people died.

The minimum needs for these refugees, or prisoners, were supplied by the British; but everything which made life faintly bearable was added by the Joint.

First, special food for sick people, pregnant women, and children up to the age of fifteen—also large supplementary rations of bread for everybody. Hundreds of tons of flour were shipped from America. Three bakeries in Famagusta worked exclusively for the Joint.

Second, medical and dental care, including hospitalization. (The British military hospital at Nicosia, with three hundred beds, was turned over to the Joint.)

Third, education and recreation, which included education in self-government for the orphans' village.

Fourth, religious and cultural requirements: books, Torahs, kosher food, etc.

Fifth, a parcel service which was reminiscent of the old days at Teheran. The Joint distributed parcels from friends and relatives in every corner of the world. It also delivered tens of thousands of pounds sterling, which were sent through its office in Cyprus. And in order to give this money some tangible value, the Joint opened canteens where the inmates might buy minor luxuries.

Officially, 750 Jews were allowed to leave Cyprus for Palestine each month—less than half of the famous "quota" of 1939. With the help of the Cypriots a small illegal emigration also took place —about 1500 in five months. Sometimes the British arrested a boatload in Palestine after the passengers had landed and had been issued with new clothes and false papers. Then chaos ensued. All the refugees said they were natives and all the natives said they were refugees. Whenever the British were thus enticed into taking a few hundred sabras (native Palestinians) to Cyprus, months of weary investigation would follow before the facts and the true identities could be unraveled.

The Army in Cyprus was eager to see the last of the Jews; yet even after the state of Israel had been born, Whitehall insisted on holding these unruly charges. In June of 1948, 20,000 refugees were still on the island. The last of them did not leave until February 1949.

The one bright spot for the Cyprus Jews, during the weary months of waiting, was the arrival of *Pan York* and *Pan Crescent*. The camps became overcrowded, uncomfortable, and very happy. More clearly even than the British, the refugees knew that so far as their island prison was concerned the game was won. If faraway friends could buy and equip such ships as these, and if the Mossad could sail them in spite of threats from London and grumblings from Lake Success, Operation Cyprus had failed. The willingness to die at each stage of the homeward journey had blackmailed a great power which would not kill its obstreperous wards and which could not otherwise prevent this mass migration.

Chapter Nine

1.

The map on page 221 tells all we need to know about the War of Liberation: the lines of Arab invasion, the Israel of today, and the partition of Palestine which had been approved by the Assembly of the United Nations in November 1947. When the news of the vote at Lake Success reached Palestine, the Jews rejoiced wholeheartedly. The Arabs declared a three-day strike and made ready for war. The map makes clear the extra territory, beyond that allotted to the Jews by the United Nations, which the Arabs lost during their war. One of La Fontaine's worldly and cynical animals could draw the moral to this tale.

The British, as their troops withdrew, had been friendly and helpful toward the Arabs, assuming that they must win their war and wishing to be on good terms with the future lords of Palestine. If the Foreign Office was as badly informed as the world's press, the British policy must have seemed not only wise to those who adopted it, but inevitable. The Chief of the Imperial General Staff, Lord Montgomery, put the common sense of the matter during a lecture to the Imperial Defence College: "The Jews have bought it."

The war began on May 15, 1948, after the United States had given *de facto* recognition to Israel. Reuters announced that the Egyptian Army was almost two hundred thousand strong. According to the Associated Press, the Premier of Iraq declared that two or three million of his "tribesmen" were ready to overwhelm Palestine. The Syrians blustered on the same Münchhausen scale. And even in the realm of sober truth the Arab Legion of Transjordan—British-trained and British-equipped—was more numerous than the little Jewish force, which still depended upon smuggled arms. On the seventeenth the *Daily Telegraph* reported: "Lydda airfield taken. Fall of Beersheba. Armies of five Arab States are advancing into Palestine on three fronts; the Iraqis have crossed the Jordan; the Lebanese are pushing south on the coastal road; the Syrians are advancing on Lake Tiberias; the Egyptians are driving inland."

The triumphs might have seemed less formidable if readers had been told that Lydda and Beersheba were in Arab hands before the war began and that the Syrians were merely "advancing" toward their own frontier when they made for Lake Tiberias. Presumably Lord Montgomery knew his geography; but he also knew that the Jewish case was almost as hopeless in hard fact as in Arab fantasy. Egypt had ten thousand troops, Iraq five, Syria three, and Lebanon one. In addition, the Arab Legion from Transjordan had five thousand genuine troops, men who had been trained to fight when necessary. These twenty-four thousand soldiers, under five commands, had airplanes which were unopposed in the skies. And the Arab Legion had heavy armor.

The Jews began the war with five thousand trained men: the Palmach, or shock companies of the Haganah. They had no artillery, since Arazi's steamrollers could not contain even the smallest field guns. Conscripts were of course mobilized during

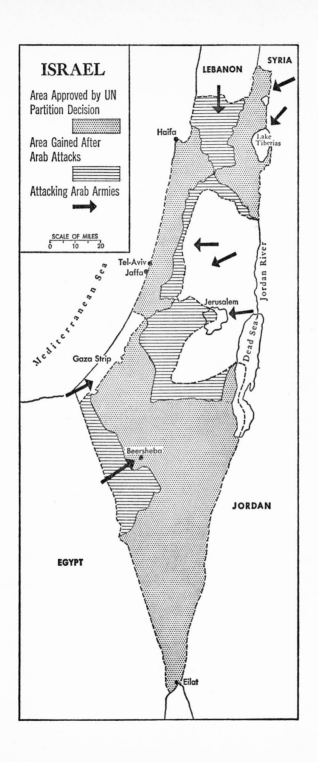

ISRAEL

Area Approved by UN
Partition Decision

Area Gained After
Arab Attacks

Attacking Arab Armies

SCALE OF MILES
0   10   20

LEBANON

SYRIA

Haifa

Lake
Tiberias

Mediterranean Sea

Tel-Aviv
Jaffa

Jerusalem

Jordan River

Gaza Strip

Dead Sea

Beersheba

JORDAN

EGYPT

Eilat

the war, and volunteers came from abroad—including the three hundred angry men who had reached Palestine a second time after their long round-trip on the *Exodus*. Nevertheless, during the first and decisive phase Israel never put more than ten thousand badly armed troops into the field.

In terms of reality Lord Montgomery should have been right: the Jews had "bought it." On the first day of the war the Arab League announced that it would now create a civil administration for the whole of Palestine. No military explanation for the subsequent failure is plausible. Unlike the British, who did not care to kill Jews in sufficient numbers to impose a policy, the Arabs were eager to finish what Hitler had begun. Either they were very bad troops (which seems unlikely in the case of the Arab Legion), or their distaste for one another dwarfed their hostility toward the Jews. Against all hope, the little nation survived.

After the first truce, on June 11, 1948, the Arab cause was lost. The Jews had won a breathing-space in which to search for arms and money: machine-guns and rifles from Czechoslovakia, Flying Fortresses from the United States, tanks and half-tracks and uniforms which the British had not yet evacuated. The Security Council imposed an embargo, but the men who had flooded Cyprus and broken the British mandate were not impressed. When the Arabs began their second war in July, and their third war in the Negev in October, they were quickly defeated. Thirty-eight days of fighting, in between truces and wrangles at the United Nations, had established the state of Israel. The fact was recognized at Lake Success on December 10. Fourteen months later Great Britain gave *de jure* recognition to Israel and to the kingdom of Jordan with its present slice of Palestine. The United States and France joined in the acceptance and the stabilization of the new borders.

The Saving Remnant

Between 1914 and 1947 the Joint spent about eleven million dollars in Palestine. Since the birth of Israel the Joint has spent a hundred million dollars within the country and a great deal more in supporting the immigration which raised the population from eight hundred and fifty thousand to two million within ten years. In 1949, for example, the Joint appropriated $54,000,000. The map on page 225 shows the result in terms of emigration: 235,000 Jews were moved from Europe, North Africa, and the Middle East, and 4300 from Shanghai and India. Two hundred and ten thousand went to Israel. By the end of the year the Jewish DP camps in Europe—except for Föhrenwald—were almost empty: 71,000 had been evacuated from Germany, Austria, and Italy. The camps on Cyprus were at last closed, and so was the Joint's office in Bulgaria, whence almost 49,000 Jews had been taken to Israel.

The Joint hoped for an easier time in 1950; but Iraq, Romania, and Poland all chose to open their gates for a brief period: the Jews must leave "now or never." So the Joint had to cut its welfare work and use most of its resources for this emergency flight. During the year 174,500 Jews were rescued—162,000 landing in Israel. Twenty-three thousand were flown from Baghdad and 10,000 from Teheran. Fifty thousand sailed from Constantsa and 1085 from Shanghai. The exodus from Yugoslavia was completed during the year, and so was the famous Operation Magic Carpet, which we discuss later.

All this was magnificent; yet it was somewhat discouraging to the American Jews who had to foot the bill and who had hoped that their long task might be drawing to a close with the War of Liberation. Already in 1948 Mr. Edward M. M. Warburg had told a conference of the Joint's directors from many lands, "Three years ago we went to the community [i.e., the Jews of the

United States] and said this was a special emergency that required one-time giving on an all-out basis. I was assured that that was a fact and told everybody this was one-time and that they would never be asked again. I sincerely believed it. The next year we found we had to get seventy per cent more, and that was not easy. We didn't get it but we raised somewhere between a hundred and twenty and a hundred and twenty-five million dollars. This year we are struggling to raise two hundred and fifty millions." (The money was for the United Jewish Appeal, the Joint receiving about 40 per cent.)

Two emergencies explain this need for vast new funds just when the Joint, as usual, thought it might be going out of business. First, the American community found to its chagrin that nine hundred thousand Jews in the Moslem world were threatened with starvation because their neighbors hated them with a new virulence since the failure of the Arab war on Israel. Second, the little Jewish state was too poor to provide for the unproductive, handicapped thousands who came from the death camps of Europe and the *mellahs* (or ghettos) of the Arab world. Someone had to take care of these people, and the task fell to the Joint.

The first problem, the nine hundred thousand Jews who had not previously impinged upon the American mind, proved most difficult for the money-raisers of the United Jewish Appeal. Ever since 1914 the woes of the East European Jews had been known and had been assuaged within the bounds of possibility. Ever since Kristall Nacht in Germany the need to rescue Jews from that ever-expanding inferno, and to force the gates of Palestine, had been known and had been met in whatever ways proved feasible. Now the European remnant had been saved and the homeland had been created. Suddenly a million new Jews were unearthed, demanding succor. And the worst of these new Jews was that they were black, or dark brown, which did not help the money-raisers in Texas. Was there never to be an end? Some of the discouraged donors—who had to pile the burden of the UJA

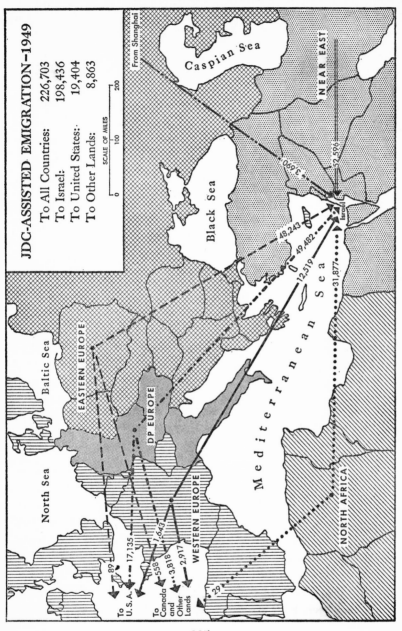

JDC-ASSISTED EMIGRATION—1949

To All Countries:	226,703
To Israel:	198,436
To United States:	19,404
To Other Lands:	8,863

SCALE OF MILES

0   100   200

From Shanghai

Caspian Sea

NEAR EAST

Black Sea

Israel

3,690

52,596

48,243

49,482

12,519

31,877

Baltic Sea

North Sea

EASTERN EUROPE

DP EUROPE

WESTERN EUROPE

Mediterranean Sea

NORTH AFRICA

89

17,135

558

1,643

3,818

2,917

29

To U.S.A.

To Canada and Other Lands

on top of their generosity to every local charity—wondered whether the Joint was not inventing business for itself.

Nobody who visited the Moslem world had such thoughts. From Morocco to the deserts of Arabia, and in mountain villages beyond, Jews lived in a squalor which made the worst DP camps look like sanatoria. Tuberculosis, trachoma, and malaria were the prevalent diseases. In one city of North Africa only half of those who survived infancy lived into their thirtieth year. In 1947 the Joint's director for Morocco and Algeria reported on an unusually comfortable Jewish village twenty miles from Marrakech: "Out of two hundred persons we found a hundred and ninety-nine with trachoma. Only one one-month-old baby did not have trachoma in that village. That does not mean that they are not healthy, because we have discovered that trachoma can be dealt with quickly."

What it did mean, of course, was that the Joint could not transport these people immediately into Israel, even assuming that they were allowed to leave. The first step was to cure their threatened blindness, just as the first step in most of the mellahs was to find milk and hot meals for half-starved children, and to provide clinics, hospitals, dispensaries, nurses, doctors, and medicine—also courses of training for their future life in Israel. And meanwhile, at the other end of Islam, the Joint learned that 80 per cent of all Jewish children in many regions of Iran died before the age of five.

This was ancient history. Ever since the decline of the high Moslem civilization Jews had been the undernourished and the underdogs in a diminishing and quarrelsome society. Hence, when Joseph Schwartz went to America and told his fellow Jews that they must rescue these long-oppressed people, he received a dusty answer. "Why don't you leave us alone for a while? And leave those Jews alone. They have been on the brink of destruction for hundreds of years, yet they have not bothered us. Let sleeping dogs lie." "Or die?" asked Mr. Schwartz. With the in-

The Saving Remnant

creased enmity, following on the war in Palestine, the Jews were no longer tolerated in their traditional submerged position. They must now be rescued or they would perish—not necessarily in pogroms, but by the slow withdrawal of every means for making a living.

Mr. Schwartz was persuasive. The American Jews found the money. Doctors and social workers began the rehabilitation of people whose hopes and whose economic status had touched bottom. By the end of 1949 the Joint had helped more than a hundred and thirteen thousand to reach Israel from the Moslem lands and was in charge of twice as many who were not yet able to move. For the most part the act of emigration meant, in addition to the terrestrial journey, a journey of at least a thousand years through the fourth dimension of time. And in the best-known case of all the time-change was two thousand years.

The prehistory of Arabia is an unsolved riddle. Nobody knows who, or whence, were the Arabs. And nobody knows when Jews first settled in Yemen, north of Aden on the southwestern Arabian coast, although tradition places them there in the sixth century B.C. during the final days of the First Temple. The Greeks called Yemen εὐδαίμων ("the blessed"), and the Romans named it Arabia Felix. This was kind of the Romans, since their knowledge of Yemen derived from an expedition under Aelius Gallus which marched through Arabia in 24 B.C. and died of exhaustion and disease on reaching its goal. Yet the name bears out the legend that Yemen was once the fairest of the realms of the Queen of Sheba, with a flourishing agriculture and a rich export trade in frankincense and spices—by sea to India and Africa, by caravan to Syria. In the third or fourth century B.C. the Yemenites crossed the Gulf of Aden and founded the kingdom of Ethiopia. Could this be the origin of the community of Falashas, the Ethiopian Jews whose existence had been rumored throughout the centuries, who were discovered by the West in 1790 and who were aided by the Joint after the First World War?

227

The Saving Remnant

In the second century A.D. the Jewish community of Yemen was reinforced from Palestine. It was still only three thousand strong but it made many converts and Judaism became a force in the country during the centuries before Mohammed. These were the "heroic" days of Arabia, celebrated in verse which depicts the bedouin as the romantic Westerner still sees him: proud, hospitable, generous, loyal, freedom-loving, and addicted to blood-feuds which somehow seem more charming in Arabia than in Sicily or the mountains of Kentucky. The Koran takes a different view of these pre-Mohammedan Arabs, stressing their faithlessness, gambling, drunkenness, contempt for women, anarchy, sodomy, and the practice of burying female babies alive.

After the rise of Islam the Yemenite Jews were at first lucky. The Prophet offered them protection and freedom for their religion, whereas the Jews of the neighboring Hejaz had been expelled or massacred. Then in 901 the dissenting Shiite Mohammedans seized Yemen. The new sectarian rulers proved more oppressive than the orthodox Moslems of North Africa and Spain. The laws against unbelievers were rigidly enforced. Jews were forbidden to ride on animals or to build a house more than two stories high, lest they look down upon a Moslem. They were forbidden to wear the conventional clothes of the neighborhood, lest they appear to be aping their betters. They were not allowed to hold property and they were systematically mistreated on high religious grounds—the assumption being that the law of God required heretics to be disgraced and abused. On the same principle of piety every Jewish orphan became the property of the state and was forcibly converted to Islam.

In our times the plight of this ancient people became yet more severe. To the old oppression and poverty was added the new danger of pogroms. By the time of the Second World War many of the most expert Jewish craftsmen had made their way from Yemen to the relative safety of the British protectorate at Aden. During the war, when legal emigration from German-occupied

The Saving Remnant

Europe was impossible, the British allocated some of the White Paper certificates to the refugees at Aden: 2500 moved to Palestine in 1943, 1800 in 1944, and 190 in 1945. Then the mandatory government closed the door: every certificate was needed ten times over for the remnant from the death camps.

Thousands who had fled Yemen were still in Aden when emigration stopped. Another fifty thousand remained unwillingly behind. In 1945 the Imam adhered to the covenant of the Arab League. Quickly he absorbed the headstrong Arab nationalism, and with each step toward autonomous pride his treatment of his Jews became more harsh. Thus the will to escape hardened steadily, in spite of the death penalty imposed by the Imam. Yet the population of Aden (including Perim) was only eighty thousand. The British could not welcome refugees. They allowed five thousand to live in the port, and they put the rest as they arrived into a desert camp at El Hashid—a primitive camp for backward people who knew nothing about the need for hygiene in such conglomerate quarters. In 1946 the Joint was invited to help and sent the small alleviation of a doctor and nurses and medicine.

At the end of 1947, when the United Nations decreed the partition of Palestine, a pogrom broke out in Aden: seventy-six dead, hundreds wounded, and all Jewish property destroyed. The British brought troops and destroyers from the canal zone. Order was restored by Christmastime. The Joint sent food, medicine, money for repairs, and more money for loans to help the ruined to restart their little businesses.

In Yemen, during 1948, the danger and the threats mounted with each Israeli victory in the War of Liberation. More and more Jews made the reckless trip across the desert. The camp at El Hashid became crowded and disease-ridden. The Joint could no longer hope to maintain a tolerable standard of life. Yet the inmates could not be evacuated by sea since no nation wanted them except Israel, and the Suez Canal threatened that route. Daringly, the Joint decided to fly them to their newborn home—

1450 miles from Aden to the airport at Lydda. By March of 1949 the camp was empty. But by this time the old Imam had been assassinated, and the new one told his Jews that they could leave if they could find anybody to accept them—another case of "now or never." The British said they might all come to El Hashid if the Joint would promise to move them out.

Civil war in Yemen, Arab war upon the children of Israel; the oldest Jewish community on earth, outside the Holy Land, had at last become uninhabitable. Like the Jews of Poland after the Kielce pogrom, the Yemenites had had enough. Unanimously they took the route toward Aden, two hundred miles south across lonely sands. And like the Jews of Poland they ended in a camp where they were cared for by the Joint. They had been forced to abandon their household goods and to pay a head-tax for the privilege of escaping, plus another tax if they took with them their Torah scrolls, plus further taxes (if they had anything left) to the chivalrous bedouins en route.

Nevertheless, by September 1950, 48,813 refugees from Yemen had been delivered by air to Israel. Operation Magic Carpet was complete.

Since these Jews had lived in penury and had not been allowed to ride a mule, the air crews were startled at how readily they took to flying—without panic and without surprise. They were reassured by the Biblical prophecy that they would return to the Promised Land "on the wings of eagles." They felt so much at home in an airplane that they had to be restrained from lighting fires on the floor of the fuselage. Yet they were terror-struck at Lydda when asked to enter a motor-bus. At first the whole life of Israel puzzled and troubled them. They would have been at home in the Jerusalem of the prophets; but Tel Aviv was distant by thousands of years from anything they could imagine.

Yet the American donors who were persuaded by Joseph Schwartz to accept responsibility for coffee-colored Jews must be glad of their generosity if they visit Israel today and see the

Yemenites. These are charming people, gentle and delicate, and with their learning and dignity intact. After living for centuries among half-illiterate Arabs, they still knew their Bible in Hebrew and Aramaic. Their scrolls were works of art. They had long been celebrated as craftsmen. Either as artisans, therefore, or as fruit-farmers, or as skilled workers in the most modern factories, they quickly found a place in the life of Israel and added something exotic and precious of their own.

3.

The Yemenites, when they descended from their magic-carpet airplanes, went to a reception camp near Tel Aviv. The young and the healthy began preparing for their new life. The old and the decrepit moved to one of the homes for the handicapped which thenceforth became the chief responsibility of the Joint in Israel.

In 1949 the Joint was asked to join with the Israeli government and the Jewish Agency to help care for the sick and the aged among the new immigrants, and for those who had been partially or wholly crippled while in the hands of the Germans. The result was Malben, a word made from the Hebrew initials of "Organization for the Care of Handicapped Immigrants." In 1951 the other partners withdrew and the Joint took full charge of Malben, appropriating $9,500,000 for the first year and over $12,000,000 in 1953. Charles Passman directed this many-sided institution until 1958, when he was succeeded by Louis Horwitz.

The official policy was that all Jews everywhere were welcome to Israel, irrespective of their health or their poverty. In fact, as we have seen, "all Jews" meant such Jews as could be helped by the Joint or by other agencies to escape from their domestic plight and to accomplish the long, expensive journey. Very few active and self-supporting Jews left the free West. The immigrants came from countries where their living conditions had been debased, or from death camps where their bodies had been starved and their souls distorted. Israel received a "selective immigration" in reverse: whole communities sent their problem cases in advance, the young and the healthy staying behind until the Joint could afford another transport. The proportion of the "handicapped" was unique in the history of migrations. Israel could barely afford to house the healthy and to find work for them; only about one-third could be gainfully employed during the first year of residence.

From May of 1946 until May of 1948, 78 per cent of the immigrants were between fifteen and forty-four years of age, and only 9 per cent were over forty-five. For the two years after the birth of Israel, 29 per cent of the newcomers were under fourteen, and 22 per cent over forty-five, leaving less than 50 per cent for the most productive age group. And half of this intake came from the Middle East, Asia, and North Africa, where most of the Jews were destitute and many were chronically diseased. Malben was a necessity if the country was to keep its bold promise to the exiles; the fact that it was also a triumph of intelligence and ingenuity was owing to the long experience of the Joint.

When Mr. Passman recruited his first staff of doctors and nurses and social workers, in December of 1949, the Joint alone had brought more than two hundred thousand Jews to Israel during the previous twelve months. There was no time for careful planning. Nevertheless, just as in its early days in Eastern Europe, the Joint refused to think merely in terms of relief but insisted upon rehabilitation, so with Malben the major effort was directed toward preparing the old and the broken for a normal life in the community. And where this was impossible, as in the case of the hopelessly crippled, Malben sought to create the semblance of a normal life within its own communities. And just as the Joint has always sought to finish its task and go out of business, Malben has tried to build its private social services in such a way that one by one they may be integrated into the social services of the state. Already this has begun to happen. But during the first eight years the main job was experiment and invention and the building of a physical plant.

The conviction which animates Malben is that few people are so old or so wounded that they cannot be fitted for some type of work, and that once they have found work most of them need not live in institutions. For those who can be cured outright (such as many of the tuberculous cases and the cases of trachoma), and for the semi-crippled, Malben provides loans so they may start again to earn a living. It seeks out locations for one-man businesses and secures licenses from the government. For example, most of the telephone-boxes in the streets of the big cities are attached to stands where newspapers, trinkets, and stamps are sold. Everyone must go first to the stand in order to buy a slug with which to use the telephone. And each stand is served by a crippled man or woman who came to Israel feeling that usefulness and independence were ended. (More than 80 per cent of these "constructive loans" are repaid.)

During the first eight years 120,000 immigrants were served by Malben. Four hospitals for chronic diseases were built (or converted from old army camps), also a tuberculosis hospital with 525 beds. Malben founded a school for nurses and a rehabilitation center for mentally retarded boys and girls. For the aged (especially the aged whose entire families had been put down by the Germans and for whom a new environment must be conjured from the air) Malben built twelve homes and four infirmaries and two whole villages. It also created a village for the blind: Kfar Uriel ("The Light of God"). The villagers make mattresses, wicker furniture, raffia matting, and other goods for which the demand is constant. The head of every family is sightless but permanently employed. The non-blind farm garden-plots, growing food for themselves, selling a surplus to the market, and tending the goat and chickens with which Malben endowed each house.

Since Israel's housing problem grew worse with every year and every hundred thousand new inhabitants, few buildings could be requisitioned and converted for the old people's homes or for the villages. Malben had usually to start from the beginning. Charming rural sites were chosen. Many of the communities are models of landscape gardening. Even the relicts of the "final solution" need not feel totally bereft in these surroundings.

One result of such farsighted spending was that the older settlers who were not eligible for Malben's care were provoked to jealousy. On June 24, 1958, the *Jerusalem Post* wrote as follows:

> Conditions in Malben homes are good and sometimes even ideal. The inmates live well, are excellently cared for and have opportunities to work, to read, to attend shows; but the entire system is an artificial one. It is not natural that old people should live by themselves: they belong to families just as children do. If they have no family, or if the children's quarters are crowded, there may be no choice but to confine them to a home; but generally speaking, in care for the old as in many other fields, it is more natural and often no more expensive to help the family than to set up costly institutions. . . . There is a sharp difference between the standard of service available to the aged, the chronically ill and the handicapped who have sought help when they had been in the country for eighteen months or less, thus meeting Malben's eligibility requirements, and that available to all other Israelis, many of whom simply have nowhere to turn. This difference is enhanced by the first-rate standard of the Malben institutions, which often stand in glaring contrast to the parallel ones for the rest of the population. . . . One must admire such achievements but one wonders at the same time whether we are really putting first things first.

This was a cheering complaint for the Joint, which had struggled for so many years, with mounting but ever-inadequate funds, to do so much more than was possible. Yet the charge of extravagance might have been just, but for two points. First, Malben was building a pilot scheme to set a standard for the future—a standard which should not be lowered because the state was temporarily overburdened. Second, as soon as the government of Israel could accept the responsibility the Joint would hand over the whole of Malben: staff, buildings, experience, and plans. So before long all the hardship cases in the country would benefit. Meanwhile, the duty of Malben was to prove what could be done with much imagination and sufficient money until Israel could take full charge of her citizens, including those whom the Germans had brought to the edge of ruin.

The *Jerusalem Post* admitted that "non-selective immigration has overburdened our services to such an extent that they would have broken down entirely without outside agencies and outside help"; but it asked for "better integration of the services and shifting some of the burden to local agencies." This was the task for the second phase of Malben, which had worked closely from the beginning with the Ministries of Welfare, Labor and Health, and with the municipalities.

The first hand-over, the first bowing-out of Malben, came in the field of tuberculosis, which had been the most common disease both among the North Africans and among the survivors of the camps. Lucikly the birth of Israel coincided with the discovery of new drugs which have taken much of the curse from what was once "the white man's plague." Ten years after building its hospital for chest diseases and its institute for the tuberculous aged, Malben was able to transfer its work, its workers, and its plant to the Tuberculosis Division of the Ministry of Health. And today the ministry is taking over the care of the mentally ill.

Next came a redoubled effort to get every possible client out of the hospital or other protective institution and into the creative life of Israel. Aside from the homes for the aged—especially the aged who have no living relatives—the average stay in a Malben hospital has been only forty days. More and more Malben sees its main task as inventing ways to give its clients that extra push, that vitalizing new hope, which helps to set them free through the use of their own energy and imagination. Founded as the last refuge for the handicapped, Malben has proved that very few people belong of necessity to that mournful class. In 1958 the new director, Louis Horwitz, reported to the Joint: "The turning over of our direct-care programs to Israeli organizations will take place only as quickly as the necessary skills and financial resources are developed within the country. It would be folly to bind ourselves with dates. Yet we must work toward a future when more and more Malben activities will become integrated with the country, a part of the social-welfare-health-rehabilitation fabric of Israel itself."

Even with the aged, the seemingly most intractable problems, Malben has found that all who are not chronically ill have a longing to take part in the life of the new state. By 1960 so many inmates had been moved to homes of their own that a hundred places for the infirm aged were offered to the government for the use of those not eligible for Malben aid.

This is where the Joint started during the First World War. Always it has seen itself as a temporary helper, a catalyzer, an agency to give physical and spiritual stimulus so that its clients may once more live their own lives fruitfully according to their own desires and not according to a plan devised in New York. No people have ever tried more persistently to work themselves out of a job. The Germans frustrated them in 1932. The Arabs are frustrating them today. In 1960, for example, the Joint is spending more than three million dollars in Morocco alone, on relief and education for about two hundred thousand Jews. The Moroccans do not want the Jews but will not let them emigrate.

The world is too cruel and too stupid for the Joint to go out of business.

Chapter Ten

1.

"A man's nature and way of life are his fate," wrote Menander in the fourth century B.C., "and that which he calls his fate is but his disposition." The fate of the Joint is to continue offering help in any corner of the world where Jews are refused the privilege of living orderly and useful lives, serving their own God while obeying their parochial Caesar. This is an expensive "disposition."

We have given samples of the Joint's work since the Second War in promoting the birth and fostering the childhood of Israel, in lending hope to the inaccessible Jews behind the Iron Curtain, and in protecting the victims of a new political anti-Semitism which has swept the Moslem world. Meanwhile the surviving remnant of occupied Europe had not only to rekindle its moral purpose after years of degradation but to rebuild its physical plant from the smoke and rubble which the Germans left behind.

Synagogues and schools and colleges, hospitals and sanatoria,

help for the orphans and the decrepit—all these are requisites for
a community life. They cannot be improvised by bankrupt Jews
—and neither can books, the archives and the life-ennobling
poems and prophecies. The libraries of a people are its memory,
its consciousness, almost its soul. If the Germans could have killed
all the books they might have spared themselves the trouble of
cremating the bodies. Being well instructed, they knew this fact.
Their war against the books was ferocious and methodical. Since
books are easier to burn than men and women, the results of this
Kulturkampf put Rudolph Hoess to shame.

Here, then, was another field for the Joint's beneficence—350,-
000 Jews in France, 32,000 in Italy, 35,000 in Belgium, 26,000 in
Holland, 6000 in Denmark, and perhaps 30,000 in Germany itself.
None of these countries was affluent at the war's end. If the Jews
needed extra help, beyond all the other stricken citizens, that help
had to come from abroad. The whole world contributed; the Jews
of Canada, especially, gave consistent and substantial support.
But since America was the chief reservoir of unpersecuted and
unbroken Jews, the Joint contributed most, both in money and in
technical and professional manpower. The time has come to say a
word about how these multifarious obligations could be met. A
study of American Jewish money-raising might be a book in itself.

We have seen that in the first days of the Joint, when the
work was on the scale of a few million dollars a year, the money
came largely through individual exhortation, as in the case of
Judah Magnes, and through the generosity of a few rich men,
among whom we have mentioned Felix Warburg and Julius
Rosenwald. As the figures mounted, the old methods became
obsolete. Between 1939 and 1959 the United Jewish Appeal raised
$1,242,000,000—mainly for the Joint and the Jewish Agency, with
a small residue for welcoming immigrants to the United States. If
we add the funds for domestic Jewish charity we find that since
1945 the American community has contributed $2,000,000,000.
This is big business and cannot be conducted merely by good will

and good speeches. "A homeland," as Ben Gurion said, "is not created with applause."

At the time of the First World War the 1,500,000 Jews of New York City supported 3637 charities. This was the model throughout the country: a confusion of local, independent causes and agencies in aid of hospitals, schools, synagogues, loan associations, and homes for the aged. Overlapping was inevitable, and needless competition, and occasional bitter rivalry. The tradition of charity was binding upon all Jews; but it led to much uncharitableness within communities, each group going its own way and jealous lest the neighbor group receive an undue share from the rich families who dominated the world of philanthropy. The response to the calamities in Europe, beginning with the First War, broke this amateurish pattern and produced the united professional appeals of today. A by-product was the welding together of the national Jewish community: assimilated Jews have found through this burdensome and time-absorbing work a link with their own heritage.

While welcoming to the Holy City the twentieth-anniversary conference of the United Jewish Appeal, the *Jerusalem Post* wrote: "Before World War II there were famous and authoritative Jewish sociologists who predicted, with a mass of very persuasive data to back their assertion, that the American Jewish community would have disappeared by attrition and assimilation within three generations. No one would make such an assertion today." Reflecting upon this unplanned result of "the final solution," one is reminded of the Pharaoh Menephta, who announced in the thirteenth century B.C. that "the seed of Israel is rooted out forever."

The essence of the new money-raising system is that all the little groups merge into a federation which makes a single appeal throughout a city, a region, or the whole country. No one has an excuse to say, "I have already given to the limit of my resources to such-and-such a fund." In fact no one has an excuse to say anything except that he will do as well as last year if not better. And no one has much chance to escape. Misplaced letters, trips abroad, illnesses, and business worries are of small avail.

The first step is to group the contributors according to trade, profession or industry, synagogue or temple affiliation, social club or place of residence. Each man or woman is then solicited in private, in preparation for a "Big Gifts" dinner. This is organized in honor of a well-known member. Names of those who attend are checked at the door, and the "voluntary contributor" who fails to appear will not be forgotten. At the dinner every guest will state the size of his gift, and he is lucky if the "card-caller" has not already told the audience what he gave last year and how much the committee thinks he should add in view of this year's emergency. The Germans and the Arabs between them can be counted upon for an annual emergency of any required size or shape. And if perchance they flag in their trouble-making zeal, some country behind the Iron Curtain will issue a "now-or-never" exit order to a portion of its Jews. Romania recently played this cat-and-mouse game. At such moments all other projects take second place, and world Jewry gathers for the rescue of one more tiny remnant.

We should remember that the men and women who give to these nation-wide appeals, whether for domestic charities or for work overseas, have already given to the nonsectarian "community chests" which flourish in every American town and which are copied from the Jewish federations. Hence the need for the punitive rites of the United Jewish Appeal, for the professional money-extracting interviews, drives, and dinners, to make sure that each man's conscience is harrowed to the utmost and each man's bank account diminished accordingly. Since charity to the limit of the need, not of the donor's convenience, is deep in Jewish culture, many Americans who had almost forgotten they were Jews have submitted themselves to this costly public appearance each year since the end of the First War. And the more acute the demand for "welfare funds"—i.e., money for the rescue work abroad—the smaller the slice but the larger the actual sum which can be left at home for local charity. Giving has become a habit-forming task. A million men and women contribute annually. This represents almost every family among the five million American Jews.

In 1960 the United Jewish Appeal has tried a daring approach. The annual "crisis," the latest blood-curdling headline, has been ignored. The implied hope that the burden may one day be lifted has been abandoned. Silently, after forty-six years, the Joint has accepted its fate. This year's campaign assumes that emergencies are a permanent feature of Jewish life. The temptation was strong to exploit the swastika-daubings, the neo-Nazis of Germany, the unearthing of such anomalies as Oswald Mosley. But a long-term slogan was chosen: "Rescue a people and build a land." A lifetime of dedication was thus demanded. Yet at the end of the first eight weeks the returns were 12 per cent above those of 1959.

2.

In spite of such money-raising the Joint could not have faced the rehabilitation of postwar European Jewry without funds from the Claims Conference (the Conference on Jewish Material Claims against Germany). Israel and the consequent Moslem crises must have come first, and the healing of Europe must have been postponed, had not Germany made some small restitution. First, the Allies allocated $22,500,000 out of German reparations, for the succor of Jews, on the grounds that most Jewish survivors were stateless persons and were thus without a government through which to seek redress. This was useful for relief but not for rebuilding. Far more important were the agreements of 1952 between Germany, Israel, and the Claims Conference.

The Saving Remnant

In 1951 Mr. Adenauer announced to the West German Parliament: "Unspeakable crimes against Jews were perpetrated in the Third Reich and they make it obligatory to extend moral and material reparation for injuries and damages suffered by individuals. The German government will concern itself with the early enactment of legislation in this sphere. . . ." In 1952 a German delegation met at Wasenaar, near The Hague, with representatives of Israel, who spoke for the Jews who had reached home, and of the Claims Conference, who spoke for the German Jews and for all the stateless refugees elsewhere. Moses Leavitt of the Joint was the chief negotiator for twenty-three Jewish organizations. The first purpose was to get money to resettle survivors and to rebuild a cultural and community life. Second, the conference asked compensation for wounds and diseases, and the return of stolen property.

Germany agreed to pay Israel $714,000,000 over a period of twelve to fourteen years, and to pay the Claims Conference $107,-000,000 simultaneously. Israel gave $16,000,000 to the Claims Conference out of her own reparations for use overseas and set aside $130,000,000 for use at home on behalf of newcomers and refugees. In a protocol the Germans promised laws for the compensation of individuals and for the return of property. Many Germans feel this was an act of needless generosity. Many non-Germans feel that whether you pay ten cents or ten thousand dollars for each murdered neighbor the books do not balance. Israel accepted the blood-money with a divided heart. Bernard Goldstein and his few Bundist (socialist) friends who survived the Warsaw Ghetto refused to take crumbs from their tormentors.

One pleasing cultural project was aided by Germany without her knowledge or permission. During the bleak winter of 1945, when the Battle of the Bulge had just been won, a Lithuanian rabbi dreamed of a new edition of the Talmud, printed in the land of book-burning in memory of Sheerith Hapletah, the Saving Remnant. This would be the fifty-second edition, in nineteen folio volumes. In 1947 the United States Military Governor of Germany, General McNarney, approved the plan—and so did his successor, General Clay. The Army supplied paper and sufficient German funds to print fifty sets. The Joint gave the money for an additional six hundred and fifty sets and sent two copies of a famous Vilna edition of the Talmud so that the plates might be as beautiful as possible. The work was done in Stuttgart. The first volumes were bound in 1949 and the last in 1951: seven hundred sets dedicated to the United States Army and presented to the great libraries of Europe, Canada, the United States, South America, South Africa, North Africa, Australia, and Israel.

By the end of 1959 the Claims Conference had received $60,-000,000, the Joint's share being about $41,000,000. Seven and a half millions have been spent on schools, libraries, archives, synagogues, publications, and related aspects of cultural and educational reconstruction. Two million six hundred and fifty-seven thousand have been given to institutes for research and historiography so that the work begun so valiantly by Emmanuel Ringelblum in the Warsaw Ghetto may be concluded. The rest has gone for the same forms of rehabilitation which we saw in Poland at the end of the First War—but no longer in the old Pale of Settlement and no longer with the confident hopes of those innocent days.

German reparations in goods and services have been paid on time; but compensation for ruined bodies and stolen property is another story. The promised law was passed in 1953 and was amended for clarity and accuracy in 1956 and 1957. By that time nobody could find fault with the wording; but laws have to be administered by people and in this case the people were wholly unsympathetic. More than two and a half million claims have been entered. A million have been settled, after lethargic years of delay. Time is running out. The victims are dying, and the terminal date for the whole program is 1963—and for the return of property, 1962.

The Saving Remnant

With the help of money from the Claims Conference the Joint has done one of its proudest jobs in the reconstruction of Western European Jewry. The communities have not only been rebuilt and re-enlivened; they have been made increasingly self-sufficient. They have been taught the alien notion that if you want something you should be willing to pay for it. This doctrine was the basis of the Joint's work in Eastern Europe; but in the West, and especially in France, the habit was to send the bill to a Rothschild.

The French have never been insistent on paying taxes. Here the French Jews were thoroughly assimilated with their neighbors. They respected the tradition of Jewish communal life, but they added their own tradition that millionaires should pay for it. After liberation, when all was in ruins, the Joint was the millionaire and was unaccustomed to helping people who did not take over at the earliest moment and do the job themselves. The result of this clash was startling and agreeable. The *mystique* of the Joint throughout the war had been so powerful that that the influence of the Joint was now decisive.

French Jews were soon attempting their own United Jewish Appeal, abandoning their nerveless dependence upon a few rich men. The community became adult. France became a model and an inspiration for Belgium and Italy. The Joint now hopes to withdraw gradually over the years. As in the old days in Poland it will offer technical assistance and advice, or money to encourage a new project; but the major fund-raising for local needs will become the responsibility of the local people. This is the hope and the intention, although so far the Joint still pays at least half the bills.

In so far as the Joint dares to imagine a future pattern for its

The Saving Remnant

work, this withdrawal from direct social welfare is the plan for
Western Europe and the Moslem world. As ever, the hope abides
that the day will come when the communities may be largely self-
supporting, calling upon the Joint for emergency funds or expert
advice, or for men and women with special skills. And Charles
Jordan, Director-General of Overseas Operations, foretells a
growing cooperation between the Joint and the international civil
service of the United Nations. The fiery nationalism of today
makes many infant governments unwilling to ask for help from
an American agency such as the Joint, or even the Quakers. An
appeal to charity would seem undignified—but not an appeal to
the United Nations, which each young country regards as its own
club and which only the most highly disgruntled accuses of
"American imperialism." Then the servants of the United Nations
feel free to turn for help to the private groups who can work
fruitfully and trustfully with people of their own faith or race
or tradition and whose experience is world-wide and rooted in
time.

If this book proves anything, however, it proves that peering
into the future is a waste of time for the Joint. Somewhere on
the globe each new year brings new calamities to Jews. Whatever
happens, the Joint must try to help. This is its "nature and way
of life" and thus its fate: offering aid during every unpredicted
crisis, and between crises striving doggedly to build a viable
Jewish life on foundations which are repeatedly swept away. And
this fate determines the character of the men and women who
work for the Joint. Governments wonder at its skill in finding the
best nominee for Shanghai or Warsaw or the mellahs of North
Africa, for nations deadened by occupation or made frantic by the
wine of independence, and even for the nimble minds of France
and Israel, where the mildest criticism is the beginning of the
largest possible argument. The reason for this success is that the
servants of the Joint are moved by compassion and love and are

the heirs to the oldest human tradition of charity. Thus they are fulfilling themselves in a fashion which few members of the foreign services of great nations can hope to emulate.

Yet a pattern has emerged among the workers overseas; a special form of training has proved generally most useful. The makers of the JDC in 1914 were an assortment of born leaders who came from every background, and the same is true of the men who have presided over the headquarters in New York; but the harassed men-on-the-spot, without whom every effort must be vain, have been increasingly enlisted from the ranks of professional social workers.

In 1948, therefore, as part of its time-honored effort to bow itself out and to leave the local communities in charge, the Joint gave a quarter of a million dollars for a school of social work at Versailles. The school opened in the autumn of 1949 with thirty-two students from Europe and North Africa, plus a few Israelis. Fittingly, it was named in honor of Paul Baerwald, one of the founders of the JDC, who had served as chairman during the Second War and who for thirty-five years had been a benign and self-effacing influence in keeping the work under wise direction.

"The school," said the official announcement, "will offer a one-year course of study in the most recent methods and techniques of welfare assistance. It is planned as a sort of legacy, an institution which will train local Jewish social-service personnel to carry out the work of helping their fellow Jews to a better life." The Joint paid for board and lodging, tuition and books, asking only that the student promise to return home at the end of the year and carry on in his own community. Teaching was in French, German, and Yiddish.

Always the emphasis upon a "legacy," upon something which the Joint may leave behind when it retires from the field. But it can never retire unless the day comes when the mysterious fever of anti-Semitism has subsided. This particular legacy, however, quickly proved its value. After a few years of experiment at Versailles the Joint gave half a million dollars, plus technical assistance in setting up the curriculum, for a permanent school of social work at the Hebrew University in Jerusalem. This too was named in honor of Paul Baerwald.

4.

Some readers may feel we have been unkind to the Germans by recalling so many of the Third Reich's atrocities. Over the centuries the Poles and the Ukrainians have been as anti-Semitic as the Germans; but they have never been as logical, so their hatred was expressed in sporadic massacres which stopped short of annihilation. The same might be said of the Romans and the Babylonians, and indeed of the West as a whole. We are all stained with this ancient crime against the Jews; but the Germans are more stained than most of us.

In our hours of moral idleness we all like to flatter ourselves with the Hegelian dream that we belong to a "historic" nation which is fated "to play a historic role" and which therefore has a right to dominate the "submerged" people, the lesser tribes whose lot it is to bow to our might and wisdom. "Manifest Destiny," of which Americans boasted when they conquered Mexico and took an empire of land, is only a vulgar form of Hegelianism. But again, the Germans are more Hegelian than most of us.

For those who enjoy looking down upon their neighbors, the Jews have long been a convenience. They have been present in small numbers and therefore unable to retaliate. They have been easily identifiable, by religious customs or by appearance. So they have offered the maximum of temptation, and no Christian or Moslem people can boast of being sinless. Will the rebirth of Israel cause us to mend our ways? Will the faith of Moses Hess and Theodor Herzl and the other prophets of Zionism be justified? Or will the Joint discover that once again it has helped to preserve a concentration of Jews for the convenience of their murderers?

No great historian in the West has tried to explain anti-Semitism. Sometimes it is described; more often it is taken for granted, like other occasional poisons which infect the air we breathe or the water we drink. Since we cannot diagnose it we can neither cure it nor predict its next virulent recurrence. Like medieval doctors after the Black Death, we can only pray that the future may be less somber than the past.

But let us remember that the Arabs take a long view of history. "Have patience," they say, "and the body of your enemy will be carried past your door." They intend to destroy Israel—a fool's dream, if the West showed a spark of determination. Since the First War we have not lacked knowledge, or even foresight— only determination. For example, during the Peace Conference of 1918-1919, Colonel Meinertzhagen was transferred from General Allenby's army to be a junior member of the British delegation in Paris. He was as adventurous as his friend T. E. Lawrence; he was a better soldier and a far more careful prophet. At Lloyd George's request he wrote down his recommendations in a letter of startling clairvoyance:

25.III.1919. Paris.

My dear Prime Minister:

. . . This Peace Conference has laid two eggs—Jewish Nationalism and Arab Nationalism; these are going to grow up into two troublesome chickens; the Jew virile, brave, determined and intelligent. The Arab decadent, stupid, dishonest and producing little beyond eccentrics influenced by the romance and silence of the desert. . . .

In fifty years' time both Jew and Arab will be obsessed with nationalism, the natural outcome of the President's self-determination. . . .

A National Home for the Jews must develop sooner or later into sovereignty; I understand that this natural evolution is envisaged by some members of H.M.G. Arab nationalism will also develop into sovereignty from Mesopotamia to Morocco. . . .

The British position in the Middle East today is paramount; the force of nationalism will challenge our position. My proposal is based on befriending the people who are more likely to be loyal friends—the Jews. . . .

With Jewish and Arab nationalism developing into sovereignty and with the loss of the Canal in 1966 (only 47 years hence) we stand a good chance of losing our position in the Middle East. . . .

General Allenby with British forces, unaided by the Egyptian army, conquered and occupied Turkish Sinai which, by right of conquest, is at Britain's disposal. . . .

If Britain annexes Turkish Sinai, the following advantages accrue:

1. It establishes a buffer between Egypt and Palestine.

2. It gives Britain a strong foothold in the Middle East with access to both the Mediterranean and the Red Sea.

3. It gives us room for a strategic base and, with Jewish consent, the best harbor in the Eastern Mediterranean.

4. It not only places us in a position whence we can frustrate any Egyptian move to close the Canal to British shipping, but it enables us to build a dual canal connecting the Mediterranean and the Red Sea.

5. No question of nationalism can arise in Sinai, as its nomad inhabitants are but a few thousand.

Signed, R. M.[1]

Thus the facts had been stated and the future defined with accuracy; but nothing was done. We have seen the constant pattern over the subsequent forty-one years: first a small concession to the Jews, then a strong reaction in favor of oil and the Arabs. Had all of this backing-and-filling served the interest of any single nation, its lamentable by-products might be justified. But

---

[1] *Middle East Diary, 1917-1956*, by Colonel R. Meinertzhagen, C.B.E., D.S.O. (London: Cresset Press, 1960), pages 17-19. Colonel Meinertzhagen adds: "Philip Kerr acknowledged this letter, asking if I had any objection to it being sent to Curzon and Balfour for their comments. I replied that I had no objection. But I heard no more about it."

as we said before, the French are out; the British are out; the oil supplies of the West are repeatedly threatened; the Jews are precariously established, and the Arabs have declared a state of perpetual war. The only beneficiaries have been those "two troublesome chickens": Jewish and Arab nationalism. For a world which shows signs of destroying itself in the name of nationalism, this is a mixed blessing.

We are too close to the scene to find reasons for such bewildering failure. Oil? Sentimentality toward the "noble Arab"? Anti-Semitism? They may have played a part, or the whole debacle may stem from total incompetence. Yet in view of Colonel Meinertzhagen's diagnosis, one doubts the incompetence. The latest historian of the Palestine mandate takes refuge in fatalistic despair. "One of the hills on which Jerusalem is built," writes John Marlowe, "is called the Mount of Evil Counsel. The spirit of this hill seems to have brooded over the British adventure in Palestine. At the beginning the attempt to use Zionism as an instrument of British policy was prompted by evil counsel. At the end the attempt to use Arab nationalism as an instrument of British policy was equally prompted by evil counsel. But always this evil counsel, whispered to Balfour in 1917 and to Bevin in 1947, seemed invested with the irresistible cogency conferred by the unconscious obsessions of the men who uttered it." [2]

5.

What, then, of Israel? "Watchman, what of the night? . . . The morning cometh, but also the night; if ye will inquire, inquire again; come ye, return." While waiting to "inquire again," we may suggest on the evidence of this book that the "new Jew" will be difficult to dislodge from Israel. If the West persists in its indecision and the Arabs postpone their family hatreds long enough for a united effort, the Jews will not be removed alive.

[2] *The Seat of Pilate*, pages 252-53.

The Saving Remnant

They have had their fill of wandering. This time they will abide till the end, like the Spartans on the sea-wet rock, consulting only

> What reinforcement we may gain from hope,
> If not what resolution from despair.

Another safe prediction is that whatever happens, for good or ill, the Joint will be present.

APPENDIX

BIBLIOGRAPHY

INDEX

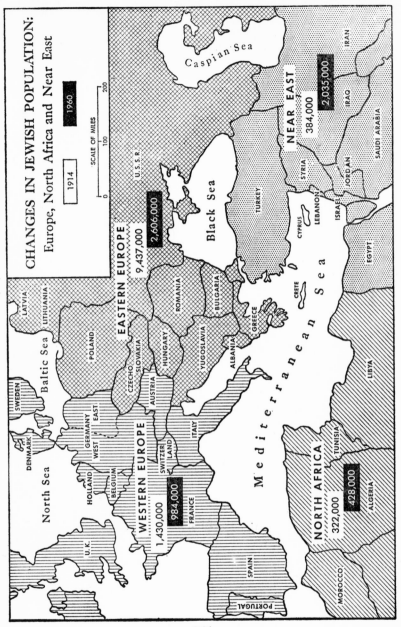

CHANGES IN JEWISH POPULATION:
Europe, North Africa and Near East

1914 | 1960

SCALE OF MILES
0   100   200

North Sea

SWEDEN

DENMARK

Baltic Sea

LATVIA

LITHUANIA

U.K.

HOLLAND

BELGIUM

GERMANY WEST | EAST

POLAND

U.S.S.R.

Caspian Sea

WESTERN EUROPE
1,430,000 | 984,000

FRANCE

SWITZER-LAND

AUSTRIA

CZECHO-SLOVAKIA

HUNGARY

EASTERN EUROPE
9,437,000 | 2,606,000

ROMANIA

Black Sea

ITALY

YUGOSLAVIA

BULGARIA

ALBANIA

GREECE

TURKEY

CRETE

PORTUGAL

SPAIN

M e d i t e r r a n e a n   S e a

CYPRUS

LEBANON

SYRIA

ISRAEL

JORDAN

IRAN

IRAQ

SAUDI ARABIA

NEAR EAST
384,000 | 2,035,000

MOROCCO

ALGERIA

TUNISIA

LIBYA

EGYPT

NORTH AFRICA
322,000 | 428,000

255

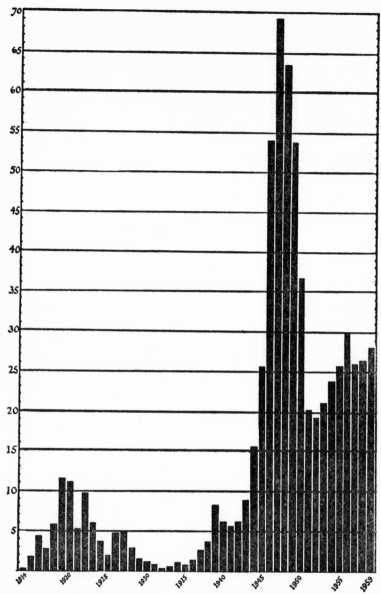

The American Jewish Joint Distribution Committee
Expenditures from October 1914 through December 31, 1959
(*Figures at left represent millions of dollars*)

Bibliography

Adler, Cyrus. *Jacob Schiff.* 2 vols., New York, 1959.
American Jewish Committee. *American Jewish Year Book.* New York: Jewish Publication Society, annually, 1957-1959.
American Jewish Joint Distribution Committee. *Annual Reports.* New York, 1914-1916, 1931, 1933-1958.
————. *Maladie de Famine: Recherches clinique sur la famine executées dans le ghetto de Varsovie en 1942.* Warsaw, 1946.
————. *Minutes of Conference on Jewish Relief and Rehabilitation.* Paris, 1948.
————. *Minutes of Country Directors' Annual Conferences.* Paris, 1949-1957; Geneva, 1958-1960.
————. Published reports and unpublished records, 1914-1960, in the files of the American Jewish Joint Distribution Committee.
Arnoult, P., Billig, Jr., Boudot, F., et al. *La France sous l'Occupation.* Preface by Daniel Mayer. Paris, 1959.
Baron, Salo W. *A Social and Religious History of the Jews.* 8 vols., New York: Columbia University Press, 1952-1958.
Bentwich, Norman. *They Found Refuge: An Account of British Jewry's Work for Victims of Nazi Oppression.* London: Cresset Press, 1956.

The Saving Remnant

————. *For Zion's Sake: A Biography of Judah L. Magnes.* New York: Jewish Publication Society, 1954.

Berlin, Isaiah. "The Life and Opinions of Moses Hess." Lecture delivered in London, 1959.

Bernstein, Herman. *The History of American Jewish Relief, 1914-1928.* Unpublished manuscript in the files of the American Jewish Joint Distribution Committee.

Bernstein, Philip S. *What the Jews Believe.* New York: Farrar, Straus, and Cudahy, 1951.

Bogen, Boris D. *Report of Joint Distribution Committee Activities in Poland.* New York, 1920.

————, and Segal, Alfred. *Born a Jew.* New York: Macmillan, 1930.

Conference on Jewish Material Claims against Germany. *Annual Reports.* New York, 1954-1958.

Dubnov, S.M. *History of the Jews of Russia and Poland.* 3 vols., Philadelphia: Jewish Publication Society, 1946.

Eban, Abba. *Voice of Israel.* New York: Horizon Press, 1957.

Elath, Eliahu. *Israel and Her Neighbors.* New York: World, 1957.

Eliot, C. (pseud., Odysseus). *Turkey in Europe.* London, 1900.

Eytan, Walter. *The First Ten Years, A Diplomatic History of Israel.* New York: Simon and Schuster, 1958.

Finkelstein, Louis, ed. *The Jews: Their History, Culture and Religion.* 4 vols., New York: Harper, 1949.

Fisher, H.H. *The Famine in Soviet Russia, 1919-1923.* Stanford: Stanford University Press, 1927.

Frank, Anne. *Anne Frank: The Diary of a Young Girl.* New York: Doubleday, 1952.

Friedlaender, Israel. *The Jews of Russia and Poland.* New York: Hebrew Publishing Co., 1920.

Friedman, Philip. *Their Brothers' Keepers.* New York: Crown, 1957.

Frumkin, Grzegorz. *Population Changes in Europe since 1939.* New York: Augustus M. Kelley, 1951.

George, Antonius. *The Arab Awakening: The Story of the Arab National Movement.* London, 1938.

Ginzberg, Eli. *Report to American Jews on Overseas Relief, Palestine, and Refugees in the United States.* New York: Harper, 1942.

Glazer, Nathan. *American Judaism.* Chicago: University of Chicago Press, 1957.

Glueck, Nelson. *Rivers in the Desert, A History of the Negev.* New York: Farrar, Straus and Cudahy, 1959.

The Saving Remnant

Goldstein, Bernard. *The Stars Bear Witness*. New York: Viking, 1949.

Gordon, Charles, and Rosenfield, Henry N. *Immigration Law and Procedure*. Albany, N.Y.: Banks and Co., 1959.

Graves, R.M. *Experiment in Anarchy*. London: Victor Gollancz, 1949.

Grayzel, Solomon. *A History of the Jews from the Babylonian Exile to the Establishment of Israel*. Philadelphia: Jewish Publication Society, 1959.

Harris, Whitney R. *Tyranny on Trial*. Dallas, Tex.: Southern Methodist University, 1954.

Heller, Abraham M. *Israel's Odyssey*. New York: Farrar, Straus, and Cudahy, 1959.

Herzl, Theodor. *The Diaries of Theodor Herzl*. Edited and translated by Marvin Lowenthal. New York: Dial, 1956.

Heschel, Abraham J. *The Earth Is the Lord's. The Inner World of the Jew in Eastern Europe*. New York: Abelard-Schuman, 1949.

Hoess, Rudolph. *Commandant of Auschwitz*. New York: World, 1960.

Hyman, Joseph C. *Twenty-five Years of American Aid to Jews Overseas*. New York: American Jewish Joint Distribution Committee, 1939.

Janowsky, Oscar and Fagen, Melvin M. *International Aspects of German Racial Policies*. New York: Oxford University Press, 1937.

Jung, Leo, ed. *Israel of Tomorrow*. 2 vols., New York: Herald Square Press, 1949.

———. *Jewish Leaders* (*1750-1940*). New York: Bloch Publishing Co., 1953.

Kaplan, Mordecai M. *Judaism as a Civilization*. New York: Thomas Yoseloff, 1957.

Kastner, Rezsö. *Der Bericht des jüdischen Rettungs-Komitees aus Budapest, 1942-1945*. Mimeographed typescript, copyright by the author.

Kimche, Jon. *Seven Fallen Pillars, The Middle East, 1915-1950*. New York: British Book Centre, 1952.

———, and Kimche, David. *The Secret Roads, The "Illegal" Migration of a People, 1938-1948*. New York: Farrar, Straus and Cudahy, 1955.

Knout, David. *Contribution à l'Histoire de la Résistance Juive en France, 1940-1944*. Paris, 1947.

Leavitt, Moses A. *The JDC Story, 1914-1952*. New York, 1953.

Levin, Shmarya. *Childhood in Exile*. Translated by Maurice Samuel. New York: Harcourt, Brace, 1929.

The Saving Remnant

Lowenthal, Marvin. *The Jews of Germany, A Story of Sixteen Centuries*. Philadelphia: Jewish Publication Society, 1944.

Lurie, Harry L. "Jewish Communal Organization." Unpublished MS.

Manvell, Roger, and Fraenkel, Heinrich. *Doctor Goebbels, His Life and Death*. New York: Simon and Schuster, 1960.

Margolis, Laura L. "Race Against Time in Shanghai." *"Survey Graphic*, March 1944.

Mark, Bernard. *Der Aufstand im Warschauer Ghetto*. Berlin, 1957.

Marlowe, John. *The Seat of Pilate. An Account of the Palestine Mandate*. London: Cresset Press, 1959.

McDonald, James G. *My Mission to Israel*. New York: Simon and Schuster, 1951.

Meinertzhagen, R. *Middle East Diary, 1917-1956*. London: Cresset Press, 1960.

Morrissey, Evelyn. *Jewish Workers and Farmers in the Crimea and Ukraine*. New York, 1937.

Nadich, Judah. *Eisenhower and the Jews*. New York: Twayne Publishers, 1953.

Néher, André. *Moses and the Vocation of the Jewish People*. Translated by Irene Marinoff. New York: Harper, 1959.

OSE. *Mélanges Dédiés au Dr. B. A. Tschlenoff a l'Occasion de son 80ᵉ Anniversaire*. Geneva, 1946.

Pearlman, Maurice. *Adventure in the Sun*. London: Victor Gollancz, 1948.

Pinson, Koppel S., ed. *Essays on Anti-Semitism*. New York: Conference on Jewish Relations, 1942.

Reitlinger, Gerald. *The S.S.: Alibi of a Nation*. New York: Viking, 1957.

———. *The Final Solution*. New York: Thomas Yoseloff, 1953.

Reznikoff, Charles, ed. *Louis Marshall, Champion of Liberty. Selected Papers and Addresses*. 2 vols., Philadelphia: Jewish Publication Society, 1957.

Ringelblum, Emmanuel. *Notes from the Warsaw Ghetto*. The Journal of Emmanuel Ringelblum, edited and translated by Jacob Sloan. New York: McGraw-Hill, 1958.

Rosenberg, James N. *On the Steppes, A Russian Diary*. New York: Knopf, 1927.

Russell (Lord Russell of Liverpool). *The Scourge of the Swastika*. New York: Philosophical Library, 1954.

The Saving Remnant

Schnabel, Ernst. *Anne Frank, a Portrait in Courage*. New York: Harcourt, Brace, 1958.

Schwarz, Leo W. *The Redeemers, A Saga of the Years 1945-1952*. New York: Farrar, Straus and Cudahy, 1953.

———, ed. *Great Ages and Ideas of the Jewish People*. New York: Random House, 1956.

———, ed. *The Root and the Bough, The Epic of an Enduring People*. New York: Rinehart, 1949.

Segal, Simon. *The New Poland and the Jews*. New York: Lee Furman, 1938.

Smith, Wilfred C. *Islam in Modern History*. Princeton: Princeton University Press, 1957.

Sperber, Manes. *The Achilles Heel*. London: André Deutsch, 1959.

SS im Einsatz, eine Dokumentation über die Verbrechen der SS. East Berlin, 1957.

St. John, Robert. *Ben Gurion*. New York: Doubleday, 1959.

Stern, Geraldine. *Daughters from Afar, Profiles of Israeli Women*. New York: Abelard-Schuman, 1958.

Stroop, Jurgen. *The Report of Jurgen Stroop Concerning the Uprising in the Ghetto of Warsaw and the Liquidation of the Jewish Residential Area*. Warsaw, 1958.

Talmon, J.L. "The Nature of Jewish History—Its Universal Significance." Lecture delivered in London, 1957.

Tartakower, Arieh, and Grossman, Kurt R. *The Jewish Refugee*. New York: Institute of Jewish Affairs, 1944.

Waxman, Meyer. *A Handbook of Judaism*. Chicago: L. M. Stein, 1953.

Weissberg, Alex. *Desperate Mission: Joel Brand's Story*. New York: Criterion Books, 1958.

Weizmann, Chaim. *Trial and Error*. New York: Harper, 1954.

White, Lyman C. *300,000 New Americans*. New York: Harper, 1957.

Williams, L.F.R. *The State of Israel*. New York: Macmillan, 1957.

Wilson, Francesca M. *They Came as Strangers, the Story of Refugees to Great Britain*. London, 1959.

Wischnitzer, Mark. *To Dwell in Safety, The Story of Jewish Migration Since 1800*. Philadelphia: Jewish Publication Society, 1948.

Wouk, Herman. *This Is My God*. New York: Doubleday, 1959.

Wulf, Josef. *Raoul Wallenberg*. Berlin, 1958.

Yad Washem. *Studies on the European Jewish Catastrophe and Resistance*. Vol. I, edited by Benzion Dinur and Shaul Esh,

Jerusalem, 1957; Vol. II, edited by Shaul Esh, Jerusalem, 1958; Vol. III, edited by Shaul Esh, Jerusalem, 1959.

Zborowski, Mark, and Herzog, Elizabeth. *Life Is with People. The Jewish Little-Town of Eastern Europe.* New York: International Universities Press, 1955.

Index

Abyssinia, 60
Acheson, Dean, 202
Aden, 228-30
Adenauer, Konrad, 242
Agro-Joint, *see* American Jewish Joint Agricultural Corporation
Alexander I, 47
Alexander II, 47
Allenby, Edmund, General, 57, 58, 248, 249
"America First," 90
American Jewish Joint Agricultural Corporation (Agro-Joint), 48-51, 52, 82
American Jewish Relief Committee, 17
American Joint Reconstruction Foundation, 43-44
American President Line, 118, 119
American Relief Administration, 31, 32, 39, 47, 58
American Society for Jewish Farm Settlements in Russia, 50
Anenkov, General, 64
Antiochus III, 34
Arab League, 222, 229
Arab Legion, 220, 222
Arabia, 227-228
Arabs, 56, 95, 196-200, 210, 219, 220, 222, 227, 228, 236, 248
Arazi, Yehuda, 204-12, 214, 215, 220
Ashkenazim, 12, 13, 17
Attlee, Clement, 209

Auschwitz, 4, 10, 99, 125, 128, 129, 142, 152, 153, 157, 158, 160, 162, 165-67, 171, 172
Australia, 82
Austria, 26, 39, 72, 96, 158, 170, 203

Baerwald, Paul, 77, 92, 246, 247
Badoglio, Pietro, 130
Balfour, Arthur, 53, 54-55, 76, 249 *fn.*
Balfour Declaration, 33, 47, 52-56, 58, 59, 95
Balkans, 39, 204
Bearsted, Lord, 92, 101
Becher, Kurt, 156, 157, 159, 160, 161, 163, 165
Beckelman, Moses, 115
Belgium, 85, 128, 244
Belsen, 108-109, 166, 170, 171
Ben Gurion, David, 184, 215, 239
Benedetti, Padre, *see* Marie-Bênoit, Father
Bentwich, Norman, 58, 92, 96
Bernstein, Herman, 61
Bernstein, Jean, 202
Bernstein, Rabbi Philip S., quoted, 68
Bessarabia, 44
Bevin, Ernest, 199, 200, 209
Bismarck, Prince Otto von, 130
Blum, Léon, 76
Bogen, Boris, 31, 32, 39
Brand, Joel, 154-56, 159, 165
Bratislava, 149

Index

Brener, Maurice, 145
Bricha, 195, 196, 199, 201, 202, 212
British White Paper, 95, 124, 158, 170, 181, 197, 199, 200, 214
British Zionist Commission, 58
Buchenwald, 166, 170
Bukovina, 26, 27, 62
Bunche, Ralph, 119
Bundist movement, 11
Byrnes, James, 169

Canada, 82, 238
Cantor, Rabbi Bernard, 36
Cardozo, Benjamin, quoted on Louis Marshall, 76 *fn.*
Catherine II, 22
Catroux, Georges, General, 56
Céline, 132
Central British Fund for German Jewry, 91, 92, 96
Central Committee of Liberated Jews, 180-89
Chevalley, Mme., 143
Children's Movement, 97-98
Christian, King, 129
Churchill, Sir Winston, 114
Claims Conference, 241-42, 243, 244
Clay, General Lucius, 243
Committee for Illegal Immigration (Mossad le Aliyah Beth), 184, 194, 196, 199, 200, 203-206, 209, 210, 212, 214, 218
Committee for the Settlement of Jews on the Land (Komzet), 48, 49
Constantsa, 194
Cooperatives, credit, 43-44
Council for German Jewry, 92, 96
Crimea, 48-52
Crossman, Richard, 173
Cuba, 83-84, 139

Cyprus, 200, 203, 206, 209, 211, 214-18
Czechoslovakia, 97

Dachau, 94, 166
Dalton, Hugh, 197
Danton, Georges, 6, 215
Danzig, 36
Darlan, Jean, 144
de Gaulle, Charles, 131
Denikin, Anton, 46
Denmark, 129
"Doctors' plot," 179-80
Dominican Republic, 82
Doron (ship), 205
Dreyfus case, 18

Earth Is the Lord's, The (Heschel), 14 *fn.*
Eichmann, Adolf, 152-57, 159, 160, 162, 163, 165, 169, 177
Einstein, Albert, 77
Eisenhower, Dwight D., 182, 183
Ekaterinburg, 63-64
El Hashid, 229, 230
England, 91, 95-98, 196-200
Exodus (ship), 209, 210-13, 215

Fascism, 130
Fede (ship), 207-209
Finland, 128-29
Föhrenwald camp, 190-93
France, 85, 127, 131-35, 142-46, 244
France, Anatole, 47
Frank, Anne, 166
Free-loan societies (Gmilath Chessod), 44
Friedlander, Israel, 36
Friedman, Rabbi David, 14 *fn.*

Galicia, 22, 24, 26, 27, 31, 40, 62, 91, 102, 106, 126
General Gordon (ship), 118

Index

Germany, 12, 14, 17, 19, 25, 34, 40, 51, 68, 75, 77-83, 85-88, 91, 93-94, 96, 99-107, 111, 113, 126, 130-31, 133, 135, 151-52, 170, 247

Gestapo, 42, 127, 128, 132, 162

Ghetto (Warsaw, Poland), 3-9, 99, 102-107, 113

Giterman, Isaac, 7 *fn.*, 107

Gitler-Barski, Mr., 108-109, 127

Gmilath Chessod, *see* Free-loan societies

Goebbels, Paul, 94

"Gold Train," 169

Goldstein, Bernard, 104, 107, 109-110, 111, 113, 242

Gorell, Lord, 97, 98

Göring, Hermann, 100, 101

Graves, Robert, 54

Greenwald, Mr., 160, 161

Grinberg, Dr. Zalman, 181

Gripsholm (ship), 117

Grosz, Bandi, 155

Guardianship (Refugee Children) Act (England), 98

Guzik, David, 5, 7 *fn.*, 107-108, 109

Haber, Fritz, 78-79, 80

Habimah (Jewish Art Theater), 73

Hadassah, 58, 59

Haganah, *see* Jewish Defense Force

Hamburg-America Line, 83, 84

Harrison, Earl, 170-71, 173

Hebrew Immigrant Aid Society of the United States, 63, 64, 83

Hebrew Sheltering and Immigrant Aid Society, 143-44

Hebrew University (Jerusalem), 29, 30, 247

Heine, 19 *fn.*, 79

Herzl, Theodor, 15, 18, 47, 74, 75, 247

Heschel, Abraham Joshua, 14 *fn.*

Hess, Moses, 247

Heydrich, Reinhard, 99, 100

Hibbat Zion ("Love of Zion"), 47

Himmler, Heinrich, 99, 128, 151, 152, 155, 165, 166, 168

Hirsch, Baron Maurice de, 42, 74, 76, 83

Hitler, Adolf, 10, 13, 39, 75, 77, 79, 81, 84, 90, 100, 101-102, 105, 114, 130, 152, 155, 156, 166

Hoare, Sir Samuel, *see* Templewood, Lord

Hoess, Rudolph, 99, 153-54, 158, 162, 167, 168-69, 238

Holland, 85, 128

Hoover, Herbert, 31, 32, 39, 58

Horowitz, Louis, 231, 236

Hungary, 32, 39, 72, 91, 126, 135, 149, 151, 152-65, 169, 177-79

ICA, *see* Jewish Colonization Association

Institute for Higher Learning (Petrograd), 72

Institute of International Affairs, Royal, 197, 198

Intergovernmental Committee on Refugees, 170

Iraq, 194

Irkutsk, 64

Israel, 8, 13 *fn.*, 40, 47, 54, 56, 68, 75, 95, 108 *fn.*, 118, 119, 122, 161, 172, 173, 181, 188, 209, 219, 221, 222, 231-32, 250

Issacov, Rina, 13 *fn.*

Italy, 130-31, 133, 244

Jacobson, Israel, 176-77

Japan, 115-16

Jarblum, M., 146

Index

Jerusalem, 57
Jerusalem Post, 234, 235, 239
Jewish Art Theater, *see* Habimah
Jewish Colonization Association (ICA), 42-44, 74, 83
Jewish Defense Force (Haganah), 194, 204, 205
Jewish Ethnological and Historical Society, 73
Jewish Health Society, *see* OSE
Jewish National Colonization Corporation, 53
Jordan, Charles, 118, 178-79, 191, 245
Joshua, 14
Judenrat, 145-46

Kahn, Bernhard, 21-22, 49, 64, 76, 86
Kahn, Gaston, 142, 144, 146
Kamenev, Madame, 73
Kaspi, Major, 181
Kastner, Reszoe, 159-61, 163, 165
Katski, Herbert, 134-35
Keats, John, quoted, 131
Kerr, Philip, 249 *fn.*
Khrushchev, Nikita, 164
Kielce pogrom, 110-11
Kimche, David, 206
Kimche, Jon, 56, 200 *fn.*, 206
Knout, David, 134 *fn.*, 145
Kolchak, Admiral, 62-63, 64
Komzet, *see* Committee for the Settlement of Jews on the Land
Krakow, Poland, 149
Kraus, Miklos, 164
Kristall Nacht, 93-94
Küchler, General von, 100
Kuhn, Loeb and Company, 19

Ladino (language), 13 *fn.*
Landsmannschaften, 73
Laski, Harold, 208, 209

Laub, Morris, 216
Laval, Pierre, 132, 140, 144
Lawrence, T. E., 56
League of Nations, 79, 81
Leavitt, Moses A., 175-76, 187, 202, 242
Lebanon, 56
Lehman, Herbert, 172
Lemberg, *see* Lvov, Poland
Lend-Lease, 121, 123
Lenin, Nicolai, 119
"Liberty Train," 118-19
Libya, 187-89
Lincoln, Abraham, 30
Lisbon, Portugal, 136-40
Lithuania, 25, 31, 32, 34, 35, 43, 44, 115, 120, 126
Lloyd George, David, 55, 248
Lodz, Poland, 11, 23
Ludendorff, Erich, General, 21-22, 49
Lunacharski, 73
Lvov (Lemberg), Poland, 23, 24, 30

Mackensen, Ambassador, 130
Madagascar, 100, 101
Magnes, Rabbi Judah, 29-30, 70, 238
Maidenek, 10
Maladie de Famine, 5 *fn.*, 14
Malben, 231-36
Malinovski, Rodion Y., Marshal, 164
Manchuria, 64
Margolis, Laura, 115-17, 212
Marie-Bênoit, Father, 133
Marks, Sir Simon, 78, 92
Marlowe, John, 55 *fn.*, 250
Marshall, Louis, 16, 17, 76
Maurras, 132
Mayer, Saly, 105, 147-51, 156-158, 159, 160, 163, 165
McClelland, Roswell, 156-58

Index

McDonald, James G., 79-81, 82 fn., 83
McNarney, General, 183, 243
Mein Kampf, 90, 93
Meinertzhagen, Colonel R., 248-249
Melchett, Lord, 76
Micah, 14
Middle East Diary (Meinertzhagen), 249 fn.
Mindszenty, Joseph, Cardinal, 177
Minsk, Russia, 11, 23
Monstein, General von, 100
Montagu, Edwin, 53
Montgomery, Lord, 220, 222
Morgenthau, Henry, 15-16
Morocco, 236
Moscow Art Theater, 73
Mosley, Oswald, 241
Mossad le Aliyah Beth, *see* Committee for Illegal Immigration
Murphy, Robert, 135
Mussolini, Benito, 114, 130, 133, 188

Navemar (ship), 137-38
Neustadt, Leo, 7 fn., 107
Nicholas I, 47
Norway, 128, 129
Notes from the Warsaw Ghetto (Ringelblum), 7
Nuremberg Laws, 78, 80, 81

Odessa, 47
Oneg Sabbath (OS), 6-8, 9, 15, 105
Operation Magic Carpet, 230
ORT (Society for the Encouragement of Handicraft), 37, 186
OSE (Jewish Health Society), 37, 42

Pale of Settlement, Jewish, 22-25, 27, 28, 30, 31, 39, 43, 52, 54, 69, 91, 102, 172, 184

Palestine, 15-16, 20, 21, 33, 39, 47, 48, 52-60, 73, 74, 76, 79, 91, 92, 94, 95, 96, 111, 124, 170, 181, 196-200
Palestine Orphan Committee, 58
Pan Crescent (ship), 214, 215, 218
Pan York (ship), 214, 215, 218
Passman, Charles, 121-24, 216, 231, 232
Patton, George, General, 182-83, 189
People's Relief Committee, 17
Persia, 120-22
Pétain, Henri, 131
Petlyura, Simon, 31, 46
Petrograd, 72
Pilsudski, 36
Poland, 3-15, 25, 31-32, 35-36, 39, 41-44, 72, 86, 88, 109-12, 120, 126, 135, 142
Protocols of the Learned Elders of Zion, The, 101

Quakers, 145

Ravensbrück, 166
Red Cross, 65, 120, 148, 158, 164
Redeemers, The (Schwarz), 202 fn.
Reichenau, Walter von, 100, 102
Reitlinger, Gerald, 101, 107, 152, 153, 156, 159 fn., 167
Ribbentrop, Joachim von, 130
Ringelblum, Emmanuel, 6-10, 105, 127, 135, 243
Rockefeller, John D., Jr., 50
Rockefeller Foundation, 145
Romania, 72, 86, 124, 126
Roosevelt, Franklin D., 77, 81, 156, 159, 163
Rosen, Joseph, Dr., 47-50, 82
Rosenberg, Alfred, 100

Index

Rosenberg, James N., 49, 50, 51, 82, 93, 94, 95
Rosenwald, Julius, 30, 50, 52, 238
Rothenberg, Morris, 92
Rothschild, Lord, 53
Russia, 24-29, 35, 36, 44-51, 72-73, 75, 99, 115, 120-23, 126, 164, 179-80
Russian Committee for Polish Liberation, 123

Sachsenhausen, 166, 170
Saint Gallen, Switzerland, 147-51
St. Louis (ship), 84-85, 115
Salvador (ship), 124
Samuel, Sir Herbert (later Viscount), 59, 92
Schacht, Hjalmar, 100
Schiff, Jacob, 19
Schwartz, Joseph, 92, 109, 135, 136 fn., 137-38, 140, 141-42, 147, 149, 150, 151, 158, 159, 160, 161, 170, 177, 186, 226-227, 230
Schwarz, Leo, 202
Sears, Roebuck and Company, 30 fn.
Seat of Pilate (Marlowe), 55 fn., 250 fn.
Secret Roads, The (Kimche), 206 fn.
Sephardim, 13, 114
Seven Fallen Pillars (Kimche), 57 fn., 200 fn.
Shanghai, 114-19
Siberia, 61-63
Siberian War Prisoners Repatriation Fund, 65
Sieff Research Institute, 78
Siegel, Manuel, 115, 117
Silver, Rabbi Hillel, 52, 94
Slansky, 179
Slovakia, 152

Society for the Encouragement of Handicraft, see ORT
Stalin, Joseph, 114, 180
Standard Oil Company, 16
Stars Bear Witness, The (Goldstein), 104 fn.
State Department, U. S., 26, 28, 64, 65, 118, 135, 137, 138, 151, 157, 164, 176, 201
Stroop, Jürgen, 105-107
Struma (ship), 125, 194
Sweden, 129, 162-64
Switzerland, 142, 143, 144, 147-151, 158, 169
Syria, 56

Talmud, 11, 13, 32, 69, 242-43
Tass, 179
Teheran, 121, 122, 123
Tel Aviv, 73, 230
Templewood, Lord, 97
They Found Refuge (Bentwich), 96 fn.
Titus, Emperor, 11
Torah, 69
Toulouse, Archbishop of, 126
TOZ, 37 fn., 41-42
Transmigration Bureau, 88-89, 136
Treasury Department, U. S., 141, 148
Treblinka, 4, 5, 8, 9, 103, 105, 141, 158
Trial and Error (Weizmann), 14 fn.
Trier, Germany, 12
Trillat, Mlle., 143
Tripoli, Libya, 188-89
Troper, Morris, 83, 84-85, 135, 147
Trujillo, General Rafael, 82, 83
Truman, Harry S., 170, 174-75, 176
Turkey, 15-16, 20, 59, 124-25

Index

UGIF, 146
Ukraine, 35, 36, 46, 48, 50, 51, 73, 120
United Jewish Appeal, 95, 224, 238, 239-41
United Nations, 118, 200, 215, 219, 222, 245
United Palestine Appeal, 94
United Polish Appeal of Great Britain, 86
United States, 81, 82, 84, 85, 87, 170-76
UNRRA, 118, 172, 173, 180, 185, 186

Vallat, Xavier, 132
Versailles, France, school of social work at, 246
Vilna, Russia, 11, 23, 31, 69
Vitebsk, Russia, 11, 23
Vladivostok, 64
Vulcan (ship), 21

Wallenberg, Raoul, 161-64, 165
War of Liberation, 219-22, 229
War Refugee Board (U. S.), 156, 157
Warburg, Edward M. M., 51, 223
Warburg, Felix M., 17, 19, 29, 31, 32, 50, 92, 238
Warsaw, Poland, 11, 23, 24 *fn.*,

35, 69, 98, 103, 109; Ghetto in, 3-9, 99, 102-107, 113
Wehrmacht, 106, 120
Weizmann, Chaim, 14 *fn.*, 24 *fn.*, 33, 51-56, 58, 68, 75, 76, 78, 79, 91, 198, 215
Weizmann Institute of Science, 78
Wertheim, Maurice, 16
Weygand, Maxime, 35
White Russia, 50
Willstätter, Richard, 78, 79
Wilson, Woodrow, 21, 56
Winkelmann, Major General, 152
Winterton, Lord, 82 *fn.*, 101
Wise, Rabbi Jonah, 93
Wise, Rabbi Stephen, 92
Wisliceny, Baron von, 152
Witting, Foreign Minister, 128
World War I, 15, 20, 29
World War II, 56, 98, 113
World Zionist Congress, 6

Yemen, 227-31
Yeshivoth, 32, 38, 69-70
YMCA, 145
Yugoslavia, 135

Ziegelboim, Artur, 113
Zionists and Zionism, 18, 30, 39, 47, 51, 54, 55, 56, 57, 72, 74, 75-76, 79, 91, 93, 95